NetActivism:
How Citizens
Use the Internet

NetActivism:
How
Citizens
Use the
Internet

Edward Schwartz

NetActivism: How Citizens Use the Internet
First Edition
by Edward Schwartz

Published by Songline Studios, Inc.
101 Morris Street, Sebastopol, CA 95472

Editors: Stephen Pizzo and Andy Oram

Printing History: September 1996:   First Edition

Songline Guides is a trademark of Songline Studios, Inc.

Many of the designations used by manufacturers and sellers to distinguish their products are claimed as trademarks. Where those designations appear in this book, and Songline Studios, Inc., was aware of a trademark claim, the designations have been printed in caps or initial caps.

Specific copyright notices and restrictions for software included on the CD-ROM accompanying this book are included on that CD-ROM. All of the specification documents and programs described in this book and provided by vendors for inclusion on the CD-ROM are subject to change without notice.

While every precaution has been taken in the preparation of this book, the publishers take no responsibility for errors or omissions, or for damages resulting from the use of information in the book or the CD-ROM.

 This book is printed on acid-free paper with 85% recycled content, 15% post-consumer waste. The publishers are committed to using paper with the highest recycled content available consistent with high quality.

ISBN: 1-56592-160-7

Cover Design: Edie Freedman
Production Services: Thomas E. Dorsaneo

Contents

About the Author vii

Acknowledgments ix

Introduction 1

Chapter 1 — Getting Connected 21

Chapter 2 — Tools 37

Chapter 3 — Trolling for Information 69

Chapter 4 — Advocacy 97

Chapter 5 — Neighborhoods 125

Chapter 6 — Virtual Politics 153

Chapter 7 — We, the People 175

Appendix — Useful Internet Sites 189

Glossary 195

Index 207

About the Author

Ed Schwartz has been a leader in citizen movements for more than 30 years and a major figure in Philadelphia politics for 20 years. Now he maintains a Web site that serves community activists across the country, a mailing list that discusses civic values, and ties to a community network that organizes citizens across the city.

Ed Schwartz was among the first political activists to see and understand the potential of the Internet to return political power to the grassroots.

Acknowledgments

NetActivism grows out of two broad movements:

- The movement to make the Internet accessible and useful to citizens throughout the United States; and
- The neighborhood and community empowerment movement in this country that has been building for the past two decades.

As a participant in both movements, I am indebted to a great many people for their insights and support in the development of this book.

I owe a tremendous debt to my editor, Andy Oram, at O'Reilly & Associates, for his guidance and enthusiastic support through all phases of the project. It was Andy, in fact, who first proposed that I write *NetActivism* in the summer of 1995, based largely on my participation in various Internet mailing lists. It is safe to say that without his gentle prodding and keen editorial guidance, the book never would have made it to production. I owe an equivalent debt to Tim O'Reilly, Stephen Pizzo, and a number of others at O'Reilly for their enthusiastic support as well.

I am indebted to Rosemary L. Bray for first telling me about this system called "The Internet" back in 1993 (long before it became *a la rage*) and for invoking her considerable powers as a writer and an editor to persuade me that it was possible to write an English sentence without a footnote.

As I note in the text, it was Miles Fidelman of the Center for Civic Networking who prodded me to focus my online activities on the Internet and who guided me through the intricate process of establishing and maintaining 'civic-values' and related email lists. Our partnership itself attests to the power of these new technologies in helping people with similar visions and complementary skills find one another.

I owe Chris Higgins, Max Kraus, and the staff of LibertyNet an enormous debt for their strong support in helping us develop Neighborhoods Online and the related web sites and projects that have grown out of it.

The William Penn Foundation, the Pennsylvania Humanities Council, the National Endowment for the Humanities, the Morino Institute, and the Surdna Foundation deserve credit and our thanks for their financial support in developing our first online projects, along with Corestates Financial, the Samuel S. Fels Fund, ARCO Chemical Company, the Barra Foundation, and the Philadelphia Office of Housing and Community Development.

Above all, I owe an enormous debt to Caroline Ferguson of the Computing Resource Center at the University of Pennsylvania, for her ongoing help and support in every aspect of this work. Beyond conducting the training classes that brought more than 100 Philadelphia non-profits online, she assisted in the management of the email lists, in the development of our Web sites, and in the ongoing technical support that was needed to make the projects work. She offered astute and incisive comments on *NetActivism* as well, as it moved through various drafts. If anyone deserves the rank of co-author here, it is she.

So many people have worked with us in building the Philadelphia neighborhoods' movement described in chapters 6 and 7 that I could not possibly thank all of them here. A few people do deserve mention for their contribution to the projects that have found their way onto the Internet.

First, I must thank the community leaders who have helped us build the Neighborhoods Online network in Philadelphia, as part of the Institute's Social Contract Project. Torben Jenk and Rita Lederer of the Kensington South Neighborhood Advisory Committee, John Carpenter and Joanne Petroski of New Kensington CDC, Jim Laws of Glenwood CDC, Steve Culbertson of the Pennsylvania Association of CDCs, Sam Chalfen of the Energy Coordinating Center, Karem Jamal of the Carroll Park Neighborhood Advisory Committee, JoAnne Kelly of PECO Energy, Dana Beckton of Yorktown CDC, Karl Bortnick of the Mayor's Office of Information Services, Phil Singerman of the Benjamin Franklin Technology Center, and Stan Pokras of Non-Profit Technology Resources have all played important roles here.

Second, I must thank my good friends in Philadelphia politics for their ongoing guidance and support, especially State Representative Dwight Evans, Congressman Chaka Fattah, and former Mayor W. Wilson Goode—now a Regional Director of the US Office of Education.

Third, I must express public appreciation to the rest of the staff of the Institute for the Study of Civic Values—JoAnne Schneider, Mike Marsico, Gloria Kingcade, Rafael Feliciano, and Debbie Lawrence—for keeping the organization alive while I work on projects like this one.

My debt to my mentors and partners in political theory is ongoing—Wilson Carey McWilliams, Bill Sullivan, Dennis Bathory, and Dennis McGrath.

And then there are my wife, Jane; my daughter, Ruth; and my in-laws, Leon and Anne Shull, who put up with me through all these machinations, and who continue to remind me that even in the age of cyberspace, the most important things in life remain here on earth.

That's a lesson, I think, that we forget at our peril.

Ed Schwartz
August, 1996

Introduction

During the month of September 1960, 70 million Americans watched a young Senator from Massachusetts debate the Vice President of the United States four times, in what became the centerpiece of the Presidential campaign. Up to that point, Richard Nixon was nominally ahead, but polls in October showed that 75 percent of those who watched the debates thought that Kennedy had won. By November, it was Kennedy—not Nixon—who won the Presidency as well. Sixty-nine million people voted—about the same number that had seen the debates. For the first time, television had shaped the outcome of a national election. Politics would never be the same.

Eight years later, a small group of students seized control of the administration building at Columbia University and proclaimed themselves the advance guard of a youth revolution that was about to bring modern capitalism to its knees. The most telling placards had less to do with politics than with ratings, however. "The whole world is watching!" they proclaimed. A decade of civil rights and student protests had produced a new way to achieve political recognition—do something dramatic and get on the evening news. At first, peaceful demonstrations were enough. When these became passé, taking over buildings became fashionable. By the 1970s, underground cadres of graduate students were blowing up buildings and robbing banks. Even those who had been activists in the 1930s were baffled by all of this. For them, organizing had involved personal contact with workers in factories and neighborhoods. To the Sixties generation, one-on-one base-building was a waste of time.

Why take a tortuous route to generating support, when television made it possible to reach "the whole world" at once?

- ▶ All Power Through the Media
- ▶ Transmitting to Each Other
- ▶ Political Intelligence
- ▶ Electronic Democracy
- ▶ From the Grassroots
- ▶ NetActivism

ALL POWER THROUGH THE MEDIA

Unfortunately, the contributions of television to both politics and citizen action since the 1960's have been mixed, to say the least. It is a medium that exposes millions of people to personalities and events simultaneously, but by its nature makes all of us feel insignificant in relation to what we are observing. At a political level, if you attend a meeting in which 100 people listen to two candidates debate, you represent 1 percent of the participants. There's a pretty good chance that you'll be noticed from the podium. You may even get to ask a question. Compare that experience to watching a televised debate along with 100 million other people from all parts of the country. Now you represent .000001 percent of the participants—invisible to the candidates and unable to respond. It doesn't matter which journalist gets to ask the questions—or even if there's a surrogate town meeting taking place in the studio. You're not there.

Television has confused the process of building support for issues and causes as well. It has become far too easy to confuse media attention with political power. Demonstrations may offer a fast route to publicity, but not necessarily to public approval. Alternatively, groups that undertake efforts to build support in communities and Congressional districts through door-to-door canvassing and block meetings often feel largely irrelevant, given that such activities rarely do make the evening news. Activists can spend as much time trying to get press coverage as in directing the efforts of their supporters toward lobbying the government itself.

The raw data concerning political participation since 1960 spells out the result. Fewer and fewer of us vote. Most of us who do vote are bitter about the choices we face. People with widely varying views on specific issues are united in their feeling that the government at all levels is out of control and there's little we can do about it. This, despite the deluge of information voters are now able to obtain about politics, politicians, and political issues. Nor did this trend start in the 1990s. In 1968, two researchers from the University of Chicago, Sidney Verba and Norman Nie, documented that it didn't matter how much information was available about politics; people participated only when they felt the sense of belonging to a smaller community. "As cities grow in size,' they warned, "and more important, as they lose those characteristics of boundedness that distinguish the independent city from the suburb, participation declines. And it does so most strikingly for communal participation, a kind of particulation particularly well attuned to deal with the variety of specific problems faced by groups of citizens."[1]

Politics by its nature involves collective action. A candidate for public office must persuade a large group of people to pull the same lever on the same day next to his or her name in a voting booth. A citizens' movement must generate enough letters to convince the President and Congress that they really do represent a sizable constituency. The underlying logic of both kinds of campaigns, then, is to reach as many people as possible simultaneously with a message or messages that will yield this result. Years ago, this was possible only at conventions, meetings, rallies, coffee klatches, parades, subway stops—anywhere people might be found in large numbers.

Today, television and even radio offer both candidates and citizen actions the chance to reach a larger audience in a few seconds than the combined attendance at all of these live events combined. Is it any wonder that politicians themselves now focus most of their money and energy on television advertising and that even advocacy organizations have felt compelled to join them? In seeking to reach us as an "audience," however, everyone associated with politics—inside or outside the system—has left us with little to do but applaud or boo in our living rooms in response to what they are saying, without feeling any connection to the process whatsoever.

Consider those non-partisan "get-out-the vote" campaigns that bombard us between September and November, especially in Presidential election years. First come the ads urging us to register. Then October arrives and we get to watch a few televised debates. Just before the election, the newspapers publish their "Voters' Guides," filled

---

[1] Sidney Verba and Norman Nie, *Participation in America* (New York: Random House, 1969) p. 247.

with ancient pictures of the candidates and microscopic summaries of their backgrounds and views on a handful of issues. Then there are the last minute ads urging us to vote. Most of this is scheduled before and after the evening news, late at night, or on Sundays so as not to interfere with the programs we really want to watch. Through the campaign, the appeal is the same—to each of us, acting alone, in isolation from one another. Does this sound like government, "of the people, by the people, and for the people" to you? Not surprisingly, these televised exhortations generally have little impact on the non-voters they are trying to reach.

The phenomenal success of talk radio attests to how much we want to get the attention of the powers that be. But pre-existing broadcast technologies have moved us in precisely the opposite direction.

TRANSMITTING TO EACH OTHER

So now comes telecommunications—heralded as an even more spectacular technological cure for everything that afflicts us, individually and collectively. For the moment, the main selling point for the Information Highway revolves around goods and services that presumably we'll soon be able to get much more easily for ourselves. By the year 2000, we are told, some yet to be fully configured system of conglomerates will see to it that our telephones and cellulars and PCs and Macs and cable boxes are all tied together, ready to pass along whatever products the conglomerates want to market to us. Just imagine—we'll be buying just about everything we need by phone (no more long lines at the supermarkets), and many of us will even be working at home. All this will help us achieve new levels of personal self-sufficiency, even though we will merely be replacing our dependence on the people closest to us with a new dependence on people who run the machines. None of this will be evident to us, however—that is, until a system crashes and we have to reach technical support.

Similar promises are being made in relation to politics. Already, online services and the Internet itself make it possible to gain quick access to information about government and politics that's been difficult—if not nearly impossible—to find up to now. No longer do we have to read about Bill Clinton in the *New York Times*. Now we can read his press releases on the Internet, direct from the White House. Want to see what a piece of legislation says? Go to "Thomas"—the

World Wide Web site for legislation and the *Congressional Record.* Trying to figure out which of nine candidates to support in a primary? Check out their home pages, organized by independent groups devoted to civic participation and education. All of this is possible from our own homes, sitting at our terminals, acting in isolation from another. Again, however, it may seem to empower us, but where's the "us?" If politics by its nature requires collective action, how does any of this bring it about?

The answer, clearly, is that it doesn't. But that's not the end of the story. Telecommunications itself—even as it is available to us right now—is, indeed, a powerful instrument of collective action, if we choose to use it as such. It has the potential to become the *most* powerful tool for political organizing developed in the past fifty years, and one that any citizen can use. It will only fulfill this potential, however, if we choose to use it in this way. Nor can we expect the major online services to point us in this direction. What's in it for them? They want to provide self-help services to us for a fee, or offer yet another outlet for companies to sell us more stuff. Somehow, helping people use telecommunications to organize mass movements isn't high on the list of salable commodities. Nonetheless, studies—and access charges—show that what most people want to do online is communicate with one another and political issues are among the favorite topics of conversation. Even without help from service providers such as America Online, CompuServe, or Netcom, it won't take much to translate these emerging political conversations into new forms of political organizing.

POLITICAL INTELLIGENCE

CONTACT

Institute for the Study of Civic Values

1218 Chestnut St. Room 702 Philadelphia, Pa. 19107

Phone 215-238-1434

e-mail: edcivic@ libertynet.org

The ability to communicate may be a prerequisite to success in politics, but access to information is critical as well. This is one of the most important lessons I've learned over the past 25 years both in and out of government. In 1973, I worked with a group of political theorists and community organizers to create the Institute for the Study of Civic Values in Philadelphia. Our express aim was to help citizens who wanted to fulfill America's historic ideals through active participation in their own neighborhoods and communities. We established a Neighborhood Leadership Academy with courses in "Building Community" and "Justice and the City." The seminars were well-received, and our emphasis on values did encourage people to fight not only for themselves, but for what they believed to be the general welfare of the country. Yet we learned as well that what com-

What can we do as activists online?

We can use email to send complex messages and material to each other individually within a matter of minutes. Fax machines give us this capacity already (and consider how rapidly these have become standard equipment in offices), but email is faster and a lot cheaper, especially if we need to reach people all over the country. Faxing a 10-page memo to three people can take as much as half an hour; sending it via email takes two or three minutes.

We can communicate with thousands of people simultaneously on our own time for only the access charges of our online service providers. I am not talking about live online "chats," which are possible—and easier—over the phone. I'm referring to Usenet groups, where people post public messages sharing information and ideas with one another, or email mailing lists—even more potent in this area—where people use an electronic list server or "listserv" to email messages back and forth to one another, each message being routed instantly to hundreds of people on the same list. Nearly every political organization in America has some sort of newsletter that it sends to its members at great time and expense. Imagine if we could use email to do this. No more stuffing envelopes all day. Moreover, the people who receive the information via an email list can respond immediately to it—to everyone on the list. No pre-existing technology has even permitted this sort of interchange among large groups of people, let alone made it easy and inexpensive to use.

We can use email to establish ongoing discussions within our civic and political organizations, thereby strengthening the relationships among group members and attachment to the group itself. The hardest problem facing any organization is securing attendance at its meetings, especially now when both parents in families are likely to work and need their evenings to spend time with their children. It's rare for a group to get together

munity activists often need most is hard information, both about government agencies and specific programs, as well as on how the political system works.

Obviously it's necessary to understand how a government operates—what it does, how it's structured, and what its decision-making process is. Familiarity with our own elected representatives is important. Their party affiliation will be obvious enough, but where

more than once a month, and even these occasions involve only a small portion of the membership. The result is that boards and committees end up doing most of the work, which is then conveyed to the membership via a newsletter.

A group that established an email list for its members, however, could conduct business every day. There would still have to be real-time meetings, of course. Even ongoing electronic communication is no substitute meeting face to face. Nonetheless, a list would permit those who could not attend regular meetings to offer suggestions online in their absence. It would enable members to see drafts of proposals prior to meetings and offer feedback before formal discussion began. People could even "sign off" on final drafts of proposals and resolutions without having to wait a month for the next meeting. If citizen activists and political organizers had *asked* the telecommunications industry to develop a new technology just for them, they couldn't have found a better one.

These are just three tools available through the Internet that make it possible for what we call "average" citizens—people like you and me—to develop and act upon civic and political issues with devastating effectiveness. At the core of political empowerment is the ability of people to develop a common course of action in dealing with government. Any change in telecommunications affects this process. Radio and television have concentrated power in the hands of elites who can broadcast to us even though we can no longer connect with one another. The new technologies permit millions of us to find one another. When we add that the same technologies permit us quick access to information about government and politics that has been inaccessible to most of us, then we can begin to grasp the profound change these technologies can bring to the democratic process.

do they stand on key issues? How do various interest groups rate them? Who contributes to their campaigns? It's also good to know how well they did in the last election, since the ultimate threat that we as citizens hold is the possibility of defeating them. Who exerts political influence in your community and how do they exert it? Do you know? If not, you need to find out.

Activists also need basic information about the issues of greatest concern to us. Listing problems isn't hard—pollution, crime, poverty, illiteracy. It's the solutions that elude us. Government at all levels spends billions of dollars each year trying to remedy these things, and sometimes there's progress—but often there is not. Why not? What is government trying to do? Is anything working? Are there alternative ways to approach the problem that might be more successful? Obviously, we can't expect politicians to come up with the same answers to these questions, since disagreement over solutions lies at the heart of political debate. We can at least hope to receive clear information about the programs that government sponsors now, however, as a basis for understanding what it might do in the future. Lobbyists tell us that access to this information is as important to their ability to influence legislators—who themselves don't have time to keep track of most of what government does—as the money their clients contribute to campaigns. What's good for the lobbyists has got be made good for the rest of us.

Government information sites

http://www.whitehouse.gov	The White House Web site enables us to download every speech, proclamation, radio address, and news release from the Executive Branch going back to the beginning of the current administration.
http://thomas.loc.gov/home/thomas.html	"Thomas"–the Congressional online legislative service–permits the same sort of access to bills as of 1993, including *Congressional Record* debate surrounding them.
http://www.house.gov	Both the Republican and Democratic leadership in the Senate and the House support their own home pages, offering their perspectives on matters facing the Congress.
http://www.fedworld.gov	Federal departments have their own home pages as well, with online descriptions of their programs and links to other sites relevant to their goals.
http://www.brook.edu/	Most of the major "think-tanks" are now on the Web–the Brookings Institution, the Heritage Foundation, the Hoover Institute, and many others.
http://www.townhall.com/nationalreview/ http://epn.org/prospect.html http://wwww.mojones.com/	Policy journals provide online editions as well. Among them; *The National Review, The American Prospect,* and *Mother Jones.*

Ultimately, we all need to understand the political system itself. How do the major parties operate? What interest groups are most active and effective where we live? Given that most people are not active in politics, on what basis might we organize them? Are there civic groups that could be moved to start pressuring elected officials as a way of achieving their goals for the community? How about churches and synagogues? Are there business associations that maintain ongoing contact with your representatives, advancing their position on matters that the larger community doesn't even know are under consideration? Who *does* exert real power in our communities and states?

When the Institute started putting its civic education program together in the 1970s, it was difficult to even find printed material that offered clear answers to these questions. Now we use the Internet.

The downside to all this information, of course, is that the more there is, the more difficult it becomes to organize in ways that are useful to us. Even a search on the words "elections" and "Congress"

---

http://www.rnc.org/ and
http://www.democrats.org/

The Republican and Democratic National Committees each has its own Web page.

http://www.libertarian.org
http://www.newparty.org
http://www.reformparty.org

Also represented are the Libertarians and the New Party. There are cyber-groups in each party with sites of their own—Cyber-Republicans and Internet Democrats. Ross Perot dazzled the media in 1995 by showing off a "United We Stand" Web site developed for their national convention. Had the reporters realized that every other political party was already on the World Wide Web, they might not have been so impressed. Now Perot's latest venture, the Reform Party, has a Web site as well.

You can now use the Internet to keep track of your own elected officials, at least at the federal level. Within a matter of minutes, you can find out the voting returns in the last several elections, how every major interest group in the country has rated them, and who gave them Political Action Committee (PAC) contributions in the last two elections.

http://www.nra.org

It's possible to keep track of where a representative stands on key issues. The same service that posts how organizations rate Senators and Representatives—Project VoteSmart—also lists voting records. World Wide Web and Gopher sites managed by particular groups—the League of Conservation Voters, the Christian Coalition, the National Rifle Association—provide their own ratings as well.

using Digital's Alpha Vista or Lycos—two of the best retrieval services on the Net—yields hundreds of sites, only a few of which provide returns for the 1994 elections. Just as serious readers often need to develop systems to organize their bookshelves, so activists need to use bookmarks and other Internet tools to keep the Web and Gopher sites of greatest interest to them literally at their fingertips. This isn't hard, however, especially since there are sites like CapNet devoted to Congress, The Right Side of the Web for conservatives, or my own, Neighborhoods Online, for community activists—all aimed at organizing material related to a particular institution, ideology, or issue in a coherent way.

The important point is that the information is now there to be organized and new resources are turning up online every day. And if public officials don't want to make it easily accessible themselves, independent groups like the Institute for the Study of Civic Values can do it for them.

ELECTRONIC DEMOCRACY

Most important, however, are the new mechanisms available to take on the government. Using email simply to discuss politics and browsing through Web sites will make little difference to elected officials unless they hear from us as well. Citizen power begins when thousands of people start bombarding public officials with letters and calls. In the past, putting such campaigns together—especially around national issues—has required enormous time and expense. The Internet almost makes it easy, especially among people and groups that are already networking online. The process has already begun.

CONTACT

http://www.ai.mit.edu/ projects/ppp/pubs/ 95-2-2.html

Consider these examples, assembled by Mark S. Bonchek of Harvard University and presented at the Midwest Political Science Association in April 1995, in a paper entitled, "Grassroots in Cyberspace: Using Computer Networks to Facilitate Political Participation."[2]

- In July of 1989, an organization of Chinese students living in the United States, known as the Independent Federation of Chinese Students and Scholars, undertook a lobbying campaign to persuade Congress to pass legislation protecting them from reprisals by China for their support of the student rebellion in

[2] Mark S. Bonchek, "Grassroots in Cyberspace: Using Computer Networks to Facilitate Political Participation," Working Paper 95-2.2.: Midwest Political Science Association, April 6, 1995, Sections 5.1-5.3.

Tianamen Square. The lobbying committee used email to coordinate student efforts at more than 160 colleges and universities. Drafts of the proposed bills and detailed analyses of their merits were posted and debated on a newsgroup that was read by more than 20,000 Chinese students in the United States at the time. At one point, the students were able to develop and deliver a survey of Chinese student opinion on the bill requested by a Congressional committee with only four days' notice. The students also used email and their newsgroup to conduct an effective media campaign around the final vote, which yielded stories, editorials, and TV coverage in all the major media markets. The bill ultimately passed, but the students would never have been able to mount this effort without the use of telecommunications to coordinate the disparate chapters within their coalition.

- Also in 1989, a group of 20 activists tied together through the Public Electronic Network (PEN) in Santa Monica, California, developed an online proposal for the homeless that became known as SHWASHLOCK (showers, washers, and lockers). They then used the service to mobilize support. Eventually, Bonchek notes, "they overcame neighborhood and city council resistance, obtaining a $150,000 line item in the budget and approval for converting an old bath house to a facility for the homeless." Subsequently, the group used PEN to develop plans for a cooperative job bank for the homeless and for participation by Santa Monica schools in an international effort to teach children about electronic communication."[3] A follow-up survey of the PEN Action Network documented that it was the online process that enabled the group to plan and execute these various efforts.

CONTACT

Jim Warren
jwarren@well.com
415-851-7075

- In 1993, bill AB1624 became law in California, requiring the government to provide comprehensive online access via public networks to information about state statutes and legislation-in-process without charge by the state. The prime mover here was a prominent figure in the computer industry, Jim Warren—founder of *Dr. Dobb's Journal* and various other trade publications—who is widely recognized as a pioneer in online organizing. In the California campaign, Bonchek notes, Warren used electronic mail and an Internet mailing list to mobilize support and to disseminate information on "current status of

[3] **Ibid.**

the bill; legislative and political obstacles; names, addresses, phone numbers, and fax numbers of important legislators; sample letters and phone scripts; and lessons on grassroots lobbying techniques."[4] Here again, these new tools proved instrumental to building the movement that ultimately secured the passage of the bill.

- On July 7, 1994, a message appeared on the Christian Coalition home page on the World Wide Web urging followers to contact Congress and demand an end to federal support for the National Endowment for the Arts. Three days later, the *New York Times* reported that a group of freshman Republican Congressmen were—lo and behold—demanding an end to federal support for the National Endowment for the Arts. Every local activist who responded to that Web site—or to email messages through the Internet—was able to share in a political triumph that could not have been put together any other way.

These early efforts using online communications for organizing and advocacy suggest how effective they can be. Up to now, only well-financed political action committees and lobbying organizations have been able to launch campaigns of this kind, using bulk mail, faxes, and phone banks that cost a great deal of money. With this new technology, you don't need to be in Washington. You can connect with thousands of people within a matter of minutes from anywhere in the country, and every one of them can respond in kind. Major national groups like the Christian Coalition figured all this out some time ago. It's time that activists at the local level got into the action as well.

FROM THE GRASSROOTS

The one group of people that I believe can benefit especially from going online, in fact, are activists at the local level. These are the people George Bush called the "thousand points of light," who get involved in politics to improve conditions within their own neighborhoods and communities and who fight for an America in which every community supports a decent quality of life. They take part in block cleanups, recycle trash, rehabilitate vacant houses, participate in crime watch groups, and volunteer in schools and adult literacy programs. Their aim is not merely to perform community service,

[4] **Ibid.**

although that's part of it. They simply believe that healthy communities are possible only when residents make a personal commitment to contribute to their well-being. Yet contrary to those who think that "volunteerism" can replace federal involvement in this area, they expect government to remain an active partner in the process as well.

This is also a group of people experiencing an especially high level of frustration right now. Grassroots organizations are now the backbone of every effort to address serious problems at the local level, but they lack clout and even recognition in the broader politics of the country. I speak from personal experience on this point, having worked on behalf of such organizations in Philadelphia and elsewhere for the past 25 years, both in and out of government. Often, we are so tied to our own neighborhoods and cities that we find it difficult to connect with one another. The federal programs that subsidize our work—the Community Development Block Grant, VISTA, the Community Services Administration, and Goals 2000, to name a few—are scattered all over the federal bureaucracy. No national political leader has ever tried to consolidate them into an integrated "Partnership With America's Communities"—or some such catchy phrase—that would help the public see grassroots efforts to rebuild neighborhood in a broader context. As a result, even groups using federal funds successfully to fight drug abuse, improve schools, or help welfare recipients find work are rarely heard in Washington or by the country as a whole.

Organizations of the kind I describe don't often espouse elaborate ideologies. Their members probably show up as "moderates" on opinion polls. Nonetheless, they do bring to America a set of concerns that are becoming increasingly important to the country as a whole.

The first is a deep commitment to civic values, by which I mean the ideals set forth in the Declaration of Independence, the Preamble to the Constitution, and the Bill of Rights. These still shape the way most of us think about politics and what we expect from government. Every American grows up learning that we are all created equal, endowed with the inalienable rights to life, liberty, and the pursuit of happiness. The Constitution tells us that government is supposed to "insure domestic tranquillity," "secure the blessings of liberty to ourselves and our posterity," and "promote the general welfare." Most of us would still like to believe in these ideals, but it becomes increasingly difficult when all we hear is that people are just out for themselves and politicians will do anything to get elected. For activists working to solve problems in neighborhoods and communities, however, the old notion that we owe something to one another remains the only viable principle for America, and they would like to see it restored within the country as a whole.

A second concern involves making government accountable again—of, by, and for the people. For most of us, it simply isn't. A closed circle between politicians, consultants, and lobbyists appears to have shut the rest of us out. In 1992, we elected a Democratic President, hoping that Bill Clinton would bring about something called "change." Two years later, we put the Republicans in charge of Congress for the same reason. Within a year, a lot us were fed up with them too. Somehow, politicians seem to have lost the ability to convey how *anything* that government does can improve conditions where we live. Yet that is exactly what grassroots organizations want most—not "more" government or "less" government as ends in themselves, but government that is effective in addressing the most serious problems we face in our families and in our neighborhoods.

The third and perhaps most important concern is for participation itself—both in our own communities and in politics. After two centuries of intense, often bitter, struggle to ensure that everyone over 18 has the right to vote, half the country rarely bothers. In fact, participation of all kinds appears to be declining Whatever specific problems activists seek to solve, this often appears to be the major obstacle. Hardly a civic association or community meeting takes place where someone doesn't make a speech complaining about apathy. Whatever their broader politics may be—liberal or conservative-grassroots leaders will be among the first to say that nothing government does will ever work if people aren't willing to help themselves. The Internet offers special benefit to activists who fit this description.

At the most practical level, it can help local organizations connect quickly and easily with groups all over the country working to solve the same problems. A service called Handsnet has been performing this role for social action groups for many years. More than 5,000 organizations subscribe to Handsnet, including community development corporations, youth service programs, legal service corporations, and human service agencies generally. Handsnet offers timely information on federal programs and legislative developments, the programs of greatest concern to these groups. Even more important, Handsnet is a system of networks. Organizations that post requests for specific information to Handsnet often get dozens of responses from similar groups throughout the country. There are private forums that facilitate contact among specific kinds of organizations—such as agencies dealing with problems of child abuse. Handsnet has not

CONTACT

Handsnet
*http://www.igc.apc.org/
handsnet/*
HNINFO@handsnet.org
408-257-4585

been cheap—$25 per month plus $9.00 an hour for daytime access. Nonetheless, to many groups, this has been a modest price to pay for the contacts Handsnet has helped them make. At this point, however, the Internet permits such organizations to build relationships with groups using virtually every major online service, and often at far lower cost. In the summer of 1995, Handsnet established its own home page on the World Wide Web.

The Internet can also help grassroots leaders organize information about what remains of federal programs in ways that highlight their importance to local communities. One of my own major projects on the World Wide Web is doing just that. It's called Neighborhoods Online, and it includes pages related to neighborhood empowerment, community development, economic development, neighborhood appearance, security, education, and health and human services. Every program and organization related to these concerns is assembled on Neighborhoods Online in their appropriate categories, and within the first few weeks of its existence, hundreds of community activists all over the country started using it. Now the number runs into the thousands, as there are new sites devoted to specific community issues and problems popping up every day. The conventional media relegates this sort of information to its feature pages, or to one-shot "profiles" of specific programs that seem to be working. The Internet allows us to organize such programs around the concerns they address and make them available whenever we need them.

The Internet can be especially useful, finally, to local activists who want to participate in or even coordinate campaigns aimed at influencing national politics. Consider the Web site developed by an organization called Children Now (Figure Intro-1).

CONTACT

Neighborhoods Online
http://libertynet.org/ community/phila/natl.html

CONTACT

Children Now
http://www.dnai.com:80/ ~children/

FIGURE Intro-1:
Home page of Children Now attracted national attention

You likely have never heard of this organization. It's based in California, not Washington. It receives little, if any, coverage in the national media. Groups of this kind are rarely in a position to advertise.

In the fall of 1995, however, Children Now was able to catch the attention of activists throughout the country with this Web site. Here, they were able to provide information on the federal budget, call attention to a national poll, release a "California Lawmaker's Scorecard," and provide a "County Data Book" on young people in California.

Most important, they offered those who visited the site several opportunities to take action (see Figure Intro-2).

This is one organization in one state focusing on one set of issues. By the end of the year, hundreds of groups like this were appearing on the Internet from all parts of the country. Suddenly, grassroots organizations that have had to struggle just to get their names mentioned in their local newspapers were now finding ways to address the nation.

To be sure, major national groups like the AFL-CIO (*http://www. aflcio.org/*) also started using the Internet in 1995 as well, through their own Web pages and online news releases to email lists. To most organizations based in Washington, however, telecommunications is an afterthought. They gaze out at the country from their headquarters and see 100 million people whom they think they have to reach directly in the quickest possible way. Television serves this purpose quite well, so that's where they focus most of their energy. An organization that has learned how to raise enough money through direct mail to use mass media to reach millions of Americans directly isn't about to devote time and energy toward using the Internet to build grassroots networks of activists. In fact, how many national political groups of any kind can you name that support local chapters that actually meet?

It is the purely local organizations—the neighborhood associations, the community development corporations, civic-minded business associations and union locals, what remains of grassroots

FIGURE INTRO-2:
Children Now's page allowed visitors to act, not just look.

Take Action For Our Nation's Children:

- Become a member of the Children Now Team
- Add your name to the Children Now Internet mailing list

- E-mail the FCC about the Children's Television Act!
- Sign the Contract With America's Children
- Read our Federal Action Alerts and contact your representatives
- Californians: Join our "Children Are Watching Now" campaign.

- Make a difference in your community.
- Encourage your business to make a difference for children.

political clubs—that stand most to gain from the telecommunications revolution. Right now they're not connected to each other in any meaningful way. As a result, they're not even a blip on the radar screen of the pollsters and pundits who shape politics in Washington.

Using the Internet, however, they can turn the transmitters around.

NETACTIVISM

If you haven't started using the Internet yet, you probably think of it as an additional burden— another set of "things" you'll have to attend to in an already overcrowded day. Once you get into it, however, you'll see it as an invaluable resource, enabling you to communicate rapidly with thousands of people all over the country and retrieve information that you now have to spend hours trying to get, if you can find it all.

The challenge comes in making effective *use* of the Internet to achieve the goals we set for ourselves. Businesses are now trying to figure out how to market and sell their products through the Net. Teachers are starting to use the Internet in their classes. Newspapers and television stations are adding online editions and services to both broaden and deepen their outreach to the public.

Here, we are going to explore how to make best use of the Internet as citizens—both in our communities and in politics. If you're a member of a non-profit agency or a local group trying to strengthen your neighborhood, you'll learn how going online can help you strengthen your organization and get the information you need to achieve your goals. If you want to influence elected officials or get involved in politics directly, I'll suggest ways this same technology can help you translate community action into votes. And if you're just an ordinary person who would like to feel you have more effect on the forces that shape your life, I'll help you understand how involvement through the Internet strengthens these possibilities.

To do any of this, however, there are a several key questions we have to answer:

- How do we get started using the Internet in politics? Is there anything special about the computers and software we need, or will the standard mass-market operating equipment do the job?

- How do we establish political membership on the Internet to connect us with people all over the country who share our concerns and priorities? How do we join?

- How do we conduct ongoing conversations through the Internet that reinforce our political work without taking so much time that they begin to compete with it? How do we conduct our electronic exchanges, in effect?

- What information about government, politics, and issues can we acquire through the Internet that isn't readily available elsewhere? How can we find it? How can we use it?

- How can we use the Internet to support national movements and causes at the local level?

- Given that we vote where we live and that this is where our greatest political power lies, how can we use the Internet to help us solve problems facing our communities?

- How can advocates and organizers working in low-income neighborhoods secure effective access to the Internet for the residents of these areas, even though most of them can't afford their own computers?

- Is it possible to use the Internet to promote voter education, registration, and turnout in this country? Given that formal party organizations have disappeared from all but a handful of big cities, can we use the Internet to strengthen the role of volunteers in politics?

- What do we need from software developers and service providers to ensure that people like us can continue to use the Internet to promote political activism in the future?

- What does government need to do—and what do we need to do—to make the Internet an instrument of citizen empowerment in the years ahead?

These are the major questions addressed in this book—in ways that ought to benefit anyone who wants to become an activist online, regardless of your particular point of view.

In effect, *NetActivism* is an organizing manual for citizens who want to use the Internet to improve their communities and gain influence in politics. The Internet already connects us with people all over the United States and the world. The challenge lies in learning how to use this technology to help all of us achieve a central goal of every movement since the 1960s—to gain greater effective control over the decisions that affect our lives. We can accomplish a great deal with the online tools available to us now. Even more will be possible in the future. In this book, we will discuss both: how to use what we have and how to obtain what we need.

We begin in the next chapter with a brief discussion of the minimal computer, software, and online service that you need to use telecommunications for community and political organizing. Every new system will meet these standards, since encouraging people to access the Internet has become the central priority of the entire industry. Grassroots organizations often have to work with second- and third-hand donated equipment, however, so it's important to know what will work and what won't.

Chapters 2 and 3 focus on the two Internet tools central to organizing itself—email lists and the World Wide Web. As we have noted, email lists or "listservs" permit thousands of people all over the world to communicate simultaneously with one another. The Web enables us both to present and to retrieve information at a fraction of what it would cost using conventional media. Even though there are other systems operating through the Net—Internet Relay Chat (IRC) for live chats, Usenet groups for bulletin-board style dialogues and diatribes—I have found that 95 percent of my time as an activist is spent using either email or the Web. Here, I describe not merely how they operate, but what each specifically has to offer those of us who pursue social and political change.

Chapter 4 describes how leading organizations and advocates on both ends of the political spectrum are already using the Internet to advance their respective causes. It hasn't taken long for a number of groups to discover what a potent resource the Internet can be in this area.

Chapter 5 outlines how we can make best use of the Internet to revitalize our own communities and neighborhoods. Much of my own work has focused on this set of problems, and I want to discuss how our efforts to build Neighborhoods Online in Philadelphia can be replicated throughout the United States.

Chapter 6 lays out how we can use the Internet to promote voter registration and participation in elections, and expand the influence of local party activists and policy advocates politics as a whole.

The final chapter sets forth what the partnership among Internet activists, government, and citizens needs to be to use the Internet to reclaim politics in the years ahead.

I believe the Internet can help us strengthen democracy in America, irrespective of our views on particular issues. Going online makes it easier for us to communicate, keep track of what's happening with government and politics at all levels, and convey our concerns to the people in power. Of course, the Internet can also drive us farther apart, if all we seek are new ways to meet our needs entirely within our own homes, without regard for one another.

The technology is nothing more than energy moving through wires and machines. What it does for us and to us depends on how we use it.

Chapter *I* Getting Connected

An activist can only be as effective as his or her tools. So, we'll start with just a few comments on equipment, the software, and the online service you need to make effective use of the Internet for organizing and advocacy. Activists get less help in making these decisions than most people, since neither computer companies nor online services are oriented toward politics.

▶ Decisions

▶ What Is the Internet?

▶ How Do I Connect?

▶ Choosing Hardware

▶ A Checklist for Support

▶ Software

▶ Going Online

▶ Setting Priorities

▶ Ready? Not Yet

DECISIONS

How many directors of non-profit groups have waded through the manual of a database program looking for help in creating an organizational mailing list, only to find a long description of how to set up an export company? In the 14 years I've been using computers in my own work, I have yet to see a single mass market piece of software that included applications specifically geared to political or community activism, with the rare exception of membership list templates provided with database programs like Alpha 6.

This situation is complicated further by the changes that both multimedia and telecommunications are making in the ways we now use our computers. Up to 1994, most of us were content if the machine could run a word processor, a spreadsheet, and a list manager to handle mailings. Now we need to be sure that it can support a CD-ROM drive, a modem, and software that accesses the Internet. There isn't much yet on CD-ROM that is genuinely useful in politics—although the demographic data provided by the Census Bureau is invaluable in community planning. Arguably, a modem can operate from any computer, no matter how antiquated its operating system may be. Nonetheless, software packages such as Netscape developed specifically for the Internet have properties of their own, and the overall capacity of the system does make a difference in how well they function. The basic point is that you now need to assess your current equipment and any new purchases that you make with these new applications in mind.

What, then, do you need? Obviously, you need a computer, a modem, and communications software. You need to find an online service that offers easy and affordable access to the Net. Most importantly—and most often neglected—you need to know where you can get help and support in dealing with all this along the way.

This may sound a bit daunting, but it really isn't. There are plenty of ways to get answers to these questions. You just need to know where to look for them. Let's start at the beginning.

WHAT *IS* THE INTERNET?

The easiest way to understand what the Internet is, is to think of a technology you are familiar with: the phone system.

Plain Old Telephone Service (POTS) extends all over the world. When you pick up your phone and dial, the phone company automatically routes your call through the available phone lines until the phone on the other end rings. As long as the phone you are calling is connected to the phone system, you can reach it. You can talk to anyone who is there to answer the phone.

The same goes for the Internet. But instead of a phone, you need a computer at each end. The Internet is hundreds of thousands of computers, all over the world, connected in a way that lets other computer users call them up and access them. If your computer is connected to the Internet, you can reach any other computer currently connected to the Internet. You can view and retrieve any information on any computer that someone has made available to other computers. And, if you choose to set up your computer as an Internet server, other computers also have access to whatever you make publicly available.

HOW DO I CONNECT?

If you don't already have an Internet connection, then you have some jargon to learn. You will most likely be connected to the Net with a SLIP/PPP account through an ISP (Internet Service Provider) You can also gain Net access through a commercial online service such as America Online" (AOL™), CompuServe, or Prodigy. Here is a brief explanation of the primary ways folks connect to the Internet.

Dial-up connections

This refers to connections where you use your computer, a modem, and a phone line to dial another computer that connects you to the Net.

Modem

A modem allows computers to communicate with each other over a phone line. At the time of this writing, modem speed or baud rate ranges from 2400 to 33,600 (33.6) bytes per second. The faster the modem, the more it will cost. Modem prices range from around $50 to more than $400. The faster the modem, the faster it will transmit data. Faster modems do cost more, but can save you money in the long run if you pay hourly for your connect time.

The gated community or multipurpose commercial provider

This category includes enterprises such as Prodigy, CompuServe, and America Online. These services all started out as closed systems; when you dialed in, you connected to their computers and stayed there. With the growth of interest in the Internet, all of these online services are providing access to the Internet to their subscribers.

You can think of these types of services as gated communities: someone has selected the materials for the system, keeping out materials they consider unsuitable or that won't attract a substantial audience. They contain a range of materials such as newspapers, Chat forums, stock prices, etc. They provide a path to the Internet over their toll road. For heavy Internet users this can be an expensive alternative. On the bright side, these commercial services provide more guidance and often easier-to-use tools than many Internet Service Providers. Using one of these services is great for someone who has no previous online experience.

The full-service Internet provider

These are companies that offer one-stop Internet access, known as Internet Service Providers (ISP). They provide all you need to connect to the Net, including an integrated software package that contains communications software, a browser, an email program, and other tools. The Global Network Navigator™ (GNN®) disk included with this book is an example of this type of account (Figure 1-1).

Local or national Internet provider

This type of account is more for the do-it-yourselfer than either of the above. In this bare-bones scenario, the Internet Service Provider only provides connectivity. They usually provide instructions on how to set up your computer and how to obtain the software you need for your account. The ISP will usually send you a disk containing the software or just tell you how to download it. They may provide a little or a lot of help in getting your system configured. Their service may be great, mediocre, or lousy. In other words, you have to do more homework to get one of these accounts up and running. Ask someone you know who uses the system before signing up, or ask the ISP for references.

So why would you bother with this type of provider? The main reason is cost. Most of these ISPs offer a service option that includes *unlimited* time online, for a very reasonable cost. A $20-50 one-time setup fee and $12-20/month is not uncommon. If you are comfortable solving your own computer problems, you may want to explore this option. Within this category, you may have the choice of types of dial-up accounts:

The shell account A *shell account* gives you a text-only interface to the Net. Shell accounts were the way people used the Internet before

FIGURE 1-1
*Global Network Navigator's home page
(http://www.gnn.com/)*

the World Wide Web introduced the point-and-click graphic user interface to the Net. These are text only accounts. They are used these days mostly by those who are still using an old machine and/or a very slow modem, and who plan to use the account primarily for email.

The issue, basically, is whether you need a graphical user interface (GUI, pronounced *gooey*) to access the Internet properly. A GUI puts the user in a "point and click" environment. (Windows, for example, is a GUI.) GUIs bring obvious advantages, but even today some older systems and some kinds of Net connections can't handle the graphics involved. Such limitations do not extend to text-only transmission. Most people who used the Internet prior to 1994 were quite happy with text, using online software called "pine" and "elm" for email and "lynx" to access the World Wide Web. With the enormous success of America Online—based, in part, on its graphics (or art, as AOL calls it)—and the emergence of Mosaic, Netscape, Microsoft Explorer, and various other graphical browsers, GUIs are now the norm.

The problem is that manipulating graphics makes far greater demands on your computer, modem, and software than any text-based system requires. Since political communication mostly involves words—not pictures—why bother with it?

There are at least three reasons.

First, unless you prefer text to graphics yourself, you're more likely to use a system with a graphical interface for the same reason that everybody else does—it makes complex tasks such as sorting mail or downloading files far easier to perform.

Second, all new software for the Internet is graphical, so if you want to take advantage of the mailers that sort your mail into folders before you even look at it, Web browsers that access video and sound as well as pictures and text, or state-of-the-art desktop conferencing services that various Internet providers are now offering, you will need a GUI to do it.

Third, if you plan on building a Web site of your own, graphics are a prerequisite.

In short, while you certainly can access the Internet without a GUI, if you want to use its full potential in politics, you're going to need one. So shell accounts are not the way to go unless your equipment leaves you no other option.

The SLIP/PPP account A SLIP (Serial Line Internet Protocol) or PPP (Point-to-Point Protocol) account is the most common type of dial-up Internet connection. It allows you to receive both text and graphics. Using a suite of communications protocols called TCP/IP (Transmission Control Protocol/Internet Protocol), dialing up with a

SLIP or PPP account essentially makes your computer a "node" on the Net. You can use all the graphical Internet tools, and can upload and download files directly from the Net to your computer.

ISDN line

Increasingly, ISDN is becoming an affordable option. ISDN lines are special phone lines provided by your phone company that are capable of transmitting and receiving data at 128,000 baud, four times the speed of a 28.8 modem. Cost varies from state to state but installation costs a few hundred dollars, with monthly and usage charges. Check with your phone company for pricing and availability.

Direct connection

While dial-up and ISDN connections are fine for a single user, when you start thinking about getting an entire company or organization networked online, you need to start thinking big. You need to start thinking direct. Direct (or dedicated) connection refers to a connection that lets you connect multiple users to the Internet simultaneously. It uses special digital rather than analog phone lines that have more *bandwidth*; this means the line allows more traffic to go over the wires than regular phone lines. Some common bandwidth terms you might hear are T3 and T1 lines. These refer to high capacity lines that shuttle data not at hundreds of thousands of bits per second, but megabits, or millions of bits per second.

Bandwidth

The size of a network and its ability to carry data. The more bandwidth or larger the network, the more data can go through the network at once. If you have a lot of bandwidth, more users in your organization can be online simultaneously.

A direct connection or dedicated line allows you to leave your computer or computer network connected to the Internet all the time. Unlike a dial-up connection where the ISP maintains Internet service for you, such as Web hosting or mail routing, a direct connection requires that a technically savvy person maintain and troubleshoot the system in your organization. Users' email accounts and Web pages can reside on servers in-house rather than at an ISP. While this situation gives you more control over your network and the ability to use the Net to its full potential, it does require more staff and resources, which are additional costs.

Server

A computer that provides a service to another computer.

This system places fewer demands on individual computers. In the long run, if you are planning to have multiple users on the system, a direct connection can save you money by using fewer phone lines and modems. You also won't need to pay a service provider a monthly fee for each new account. However, the initial cost of installing the network and other equipment can be high. Maintaining the high-speed lines will be an ongoing cost you need to plan for. The prices vary according to the speed of the line.

CHOOSING HARDWARE

Given the growing importance of telecommunications, any new system on the market is likely to meet your basic requirements. The problem comes in determining whether a computer you already own or the older model a company wants to donate to your group can do the job. This is where the question of capacity becomes critical.

Of course, since telecommunications services like CompuServe have been around since the early 1980s—and hand-held personal digital assistants have offered fax and email access for some time—it's possible to go online without all the glitz associated with cool sites on the World Wide Web.

Yet if you want to be able to organize fifty or sixty pieces of email a day, transmit information about issues and legislation directly from the World Wide Web to email lists in which you're participating, or construct a Web site of your own, then at minimum you'll need a PC running with windows or a Macintosh. While specific systems will already be out of date by the time a book like this is printed, we can still suggest the questions that you should be asking about any computer—new or old— you want to use for this purpose.

Basic decisions

Here are the first decisions you need to make.

PC, or Macintosh[1] This is a choice that can generate quite a heated argument among people you thought were above that sort of thing. Again, a lot depends on the overall environment in which you're working. If your group already uses PCs, it doesn't make much sense to buy a Macintosh, even though it's possible to transfer data from one system to the next. If you're buying a system for yourself, however, there are persuasive arguments that the way in which the Macintosh handles memory is far better suited to communications software than anything the PC market has to offer.

Desktop or laptop If you don't plan to travel and you don't see yourself lugging a computer between your home and your office, a desktop is fine. They cost less than laptops and they're easier to use. If being on the road is a way of life for you, however, then a laptop may be a necessity.

---

[1] UNIX is another operating system that deserves consideration here. But unless you are running a large complicated server, you'll probably never need to worry about it (though it remains the system used in most sophisticated Internet servers). A newer, less expensive version of UNIX—Linux—has gained strong adherents as well. If you do intend to explore UNIX, you will need someone familiar with the operating system to help you. If there is such a person available to you, however, it's an option worth considering.

Service provider versus server You can establish a Net presence either by using the services of an Internet Service Provider, which will maintain your home page on their Web server, or you can set up your own dedicated Web server. This choice is relevant only to larger organizations with sizable budgets. Any group that hopes to establish its own Web site must maintain 24-hour access to the Net. A growing number of Internet providers are offering this option—including mass-market services like America Online, CompuServe, and Prodigy. Yet it's important to calculate costs. If you intend to undertake round-the-clock activity on the Web—and you can raise the funds—it may well be worth the expense to invest in a server of your own. As I say, this issue is relevant only to larger organizations, but I raise it here for your consideration.

A hardware checklist

Once you've worked out the kind of system you want, the basic questions that anyone purchasing a computer needs to consider become appropriate for you to ask as well. Again, any new system—especially from an established company—will meet your specifics. Computers that you already own or hand-me-downs may not.

As of the spring of 1996, here's a rock bottom minimum that you'll need:

- At least a 486-66mghz PC or a Macintosh LC2
- At least 8 megabytes of ram
- At least 540 megabyte hard drive for a PC; 80-100 megabytes for the MAC
- At least a 14-inch monitor, preferably 15-inch
- A VGA video card for the PC; the MAC LC2 is OK here
- If you can afford it, a 28.8 mhz modem—rock bottom, 14.4
- A sound system for audio files
- At least 3 slots for peripherals on the PC, preferably 5
- At least Windows 3.1 for the PC

New equipment exceeds these specifications by a good margin, and I would use this only to evaluate what you already own or what might be donated. I wouldn't buy anything second-hand, given the ongoing price wars that will embroil the industry for the foreseeable future.

A CHECKLIST FOR SUPPORT

Even people who learn how to assess the most technical features of available machines often fail to evaluate the support that a manufacturer or dealer is prepared to offer once it's purchased. As anyone who's had to struggle with installing—or worse, repairing—a system will tell you, this is a fatal mistake.

So here are the minimum standards that I would suggest. Moreover, even if you can get a low price on hardware, don't buy it without support unless you plan to go into the computer repair business yourself. I'm not exaggerating here.

You need:

- Manuals that are comprehensive, clear, and easy to read.
- Technical support open at least 12 hours a day during the week and part of the weekend—preferably 24 hours a day. An 800 number is important, even if you have to sign a technical support contract to get it. Above all, it should take less than 30 minutes to reach someone on the phone.
- A computer whose chassis is easy to open and close.
- Fast, on-site service available when the system crashes, offered free initially and then provided under an affordable service contract. For novices and non-technical people, I wouldn't buy any system without this guarantee, even if it gets top ratings in consumer magazines for raw performance.

There is another issue that goes beyond the computer itself. Given that you're going to be accessing the Internet, which phone line will you use? The multiline systems found in many offices frequently don't work with modems. If you need a separate phone line, either in your office or your house, can you afford it?

Nothing will spare you more pain later on than taking these issues seriously before you make any decision of what to buy. More than a few of us have had to learn this the hard way.

SOFTWARE

Traditional communications software packages like Procomm and Wincomm merely provide a "front end" to online services where all the real work gets done. You are not able to download email onto your own hard drive, for example, except through complex file transfer procedures. These packages are limited to text, so even if you use a popular mass-market service like CompuServe, you miss out on the graphical interface that makes it enjoyable to follow.

As you probably know, the major commercial providers such as America Online and CompuServe, along with a number of Internet services such as Netcom, produce proprietary access disks of their own, often by the thousands. America Online started the trend with a vengeance. At one point, it was hard not to find a computer magazine without an AOL installation bundled with the cover. Not to be outdone, other online services soon started flooding the high-tech magazine ranks with installation disks as well.

Around 1994, a new generation of software emerged tailored specifically to the Internet. The most important packages have been offered as shareware, consistent with the open architecture of the Net itself. None of it is especially easy to use. Once you have a Net connection you can use it to download a package called TCP Man from a Web site and then install it onto your machine. This is a network

Questions about communications software

As with hardware, it's important to know what to look for in communications software.

Here, rather than a checklist, I offer basic questions you ought to ask:

- If it's Internet software, is it configured for: a) a specific service; b) several services; c) any service, but you have to configure it? If it's configured for a specific service, is that the only one you intend to use? If it accesses several services, is yours among them? If it forces you to customize the software to fit a service, is it easy to do?

- If it promises Internet access, does it include: a) an email system; b) a Web browser; c) Telnet; d) FTP (File Transfer Protocol); e) access to Usenet; f) its own viewer for video files; g) a player for sound transmissions H) IRC? You may use some of these services only rarely, but as long as you're paying for Internet access, you ought to get the whole package.

- Does the software load everything that you need in one step, or do you have to run pieces of the package—the Web browser, email, FTP, etc.—separately? Once loaded, is there a toolbar that includes all the programs, or do you have to move back and forth in windows to operate each one? Is documentation provided on the use of the programs?

CONTACT

TCP Man

http://www.aone.com/Help/tcpManHost.html

platform called SLIP that you need to load before you can use other Internet software like Netscape and Eudora. As long as you want to remain online, TCP Man has to remain resident in memory. Needless to say, this configuration often causes problems if you attempt to run other complicated programs simultaneously.

Nonetheless, the shareware team of TCP Man, Eudora (email), and Netscape was the route into the Internet for a good many people, and it is still a popular configuration today.

At this point, new products offering access to the Internet, such as GNN, (Global Network Navigator, a disk for which is included in the back of this book) are appearing every month. As I was writing this book, the browser war between Netscape and Microsoft Explorer broke out, so there's no telling where any of that will lead. But in July 1996, Bloomberg reported that the number of people using the Netscape browser had reached a staggering 38 million, putting Netscape way out front.

- Does the email package include folders that permit you to sort out mail by topic? Does it include filters that automatically store messages in particular mailboxes by header or other criteria, making it easier for you to find? Does it give you the choice of leaving mail with the service's server, download it to your own computer, or give you the choice? Is it easy to use nicknames to substitute for complex addresses and to assemble distribution lists? Can you attach external files in their own format (Microsoft Word, Word Perfect, etc.) to messages you send? Can it receive external files? Given that email will be central to your work, the answer to all these questions should be yes.

- If the software includes a Web browser—as opposed to one provided by an online service—is it easy to use? Does it access sites quickly? Does it read the most advanced HTML protocols? Does the browser permit you to email information accessed through the Web directly to colleagues and mailing lists? Is there a good bookmarks section that allows you to store and organize Web sites you need to use a lot?

- Can you download and transmit information easily via File Transfer Protocol (FTP)?

At this point, you should accept nothing less than the following from your Internet Service Provider and software: complete access to all Internet systems, integrated Internet tools (email, browser, etc., all on one menu), and one-stop installation.

If you need updated information on how various products handle these tools, reviews in consumer magazines like *PC Computing* or *MACWorld* offer solid information about them, often with "editors' choice" awards in product roundups that usually do provide a reasonable indication of quality.

Questions about Internet online services

The field changes so rapidly that specific recommendations can become obsolete within a matter of weeks. As with the other choices you've got to make, just know what to ask:

- If you're considering the use of a mass-market service like America Online to access the Internet, what are its current costs, resources, and operating procedures? The mainstay of commercial venders is not the Internet but the services they provide to their members alone—newspapers, clubs, shopping malls, etc. Does any of this interest you? If not, is the ease-of-use that mass market services offer worth the price?

- Whatever the service, if it promises Internet access, does this include all aspects of the Internet, or merely use of some of the services (email, Usenet, World Wide Web, Gopher)? Fast access to email and the World Wide Web are bare minimums, but there's no reason to accept anything less than access to everything.

- What does it cost? Do the costs vary between "prime-time" (usually between 7 AM and 6 PM) and "after-hours"? Are there fees for storing email and related files? With AT&T and MCI joining the service provider war, costs should keep dropping. Check magazine reviews for comparative listings.

- Does it offer high speed access—e.g, 28.8 MHz or higher? If it doesn't, forget it, unless you have no other affordable choice where you live.

- Does the service have local access numbers throughout the country, an 800 number, or a local number in only one city

GOING ONLINE

Once equipped with an appropriate computer, a modem, and communications software, you're ready to go online. Which online service should you use, however? A mass-market commercial provider like America Online? A national Internet Service like Netcom? A local community network?

As with Internet software, by the time you read this book it should be easy to find a service that offers full access to the tools of the Internet at an affordable price from local access numbers all over the United States. You should not settle for anything less.

or community? If you travel a great deal, a service with either an 800 number or local numbers in all parts of the country is a necessity.

- Does the service include its own tools (email, browser, FTP), or is it configured to work with Internet software such as Netscape and Eudora? If it uses its own tools, how do they measure up to other Internet software? Does the email system permit you to organize your mail into folders? Is the browser compatible with state-of-the-art protocols? Can you use FTP easily?

- How long will the service permit you to keep email online before either deleting the mail or reporting to email list servers that your mailbox is full? Is this reasonable, given the number of hours a week you intend to use the service?

- Can the service handle its own demand, or are there long waits to access the World Wide Web? This may not seem important now, but you'll quickly tire of waiting five minutes— or more—to reach a Web site, far more quickly than you think.

- Does the service include an 800 number for customer support? Is it open 24 hours a day? On weekends? How long does it take to get through? You may not need tech support all that often, but when you do, it's usually an emergency, so the need for reliable technical support is a serious consideration.

SETTING PRIORITIES

Selecting the right computer, software, and Internet service to handle your online activities can get to be a frustrating process. Each month, a magazine called *Computer Shopper* appears with more than 700 pages of advertisements for complete systems, individual components, software, computer parts such as ram chips and video boards, and supporting services. People with systems will offer their own advice as to what you should buy—and even more frustrating, what to avoid at all costs.

If you start following the trade publications for any period of time—*PC Computing, PC World, Windows, MACWorld*—you'll discover that each month's "editors' choice" desktop becomes yesterday's news the moment a new generation of chips hit the market. This is a field in which you just have to take planned obsolescence for granted.

The important point is to set your own priorities and keep them in mind with every purchase you make. You want to be able to use email for telecommunications, the World Wide Web to access information, and the full range of tools available online to broadcast your own point of view.

The hardware needs to be able to support all these activities without crashing the moment you attempt two or three operations simultaneously.

The software and online service should give you one-step access to all the resources of the Internet at an affordable price.

You need to identify both online and offline sources of support for those horrible moments when things start to go wrong, either with the system or the software or both.

These are your priorities, and if you're clear about them, you should end up with more than enough system to meet your needs, even if something better does come along. If what you have works for you, then it works.

READY? NOT YET

Once you've assembled your system, how will you be using it? How are you likely to be spending your day? How, in effect, will using the Internet change the way that you work as an activist?

First, you'll be checking email regularly—even hourly. Much of the mail will be generated by email discussion groups that you've joined to network with like-minded people around the country.

You'll be following various debates, reading announcements about forthcoming conferences and events, getting alerts on legislation in which you've got an interest. Much of it you'll read and discard. Some of it you'll file into mailboxes you've created for mail dealing with specific topics. You'll feel moved to answer some of it. And you'll need to give special attention to the mail addressed individually to you—as opposed to messages from the lists—since this will relate to projects you're pursuing online.

Second, you'll be checking World Wide Web sites that contain information you need on a day-to-day basis. These may include online news updates, Presidential statements related to particular topics, reports on legislation, and newsletters from federal agencies and national organizations that address issues in which you have an interest. Accessing information online will become as much a part of your routine as thumbing through the daily newspaper.

You'll be using the Internet for research. Someone will quote from a speech in a message and you'll want to read the entire text. You'll need census data or the updated statistics on the economy. You'll want to know how specific federal programs operate. Some of the Web sites you use regularly may help you find this information, but often you'll have to start from scratch. In those cases, you'll be using the various Internet search tools provided through the World Wide Web—entering a word or two that describes what you want ("census," "welfare," "Clinton" or "economy," for example) onto an online form and then sorting through "hits" to find the site with the information that you need.

You'll be posting your own information and alerts to the Internet. At the least, you'll be using mailing lists for this purpose, since they will be reaching the people and groups with whom you most want to communicate. If you become active on a number of lists, you'll often find yourself posting the same message to several of them in order to reach as many people as possible. It really is quite exhilarating to sit at your desk and transmit something to thousands of people within a matter of minutes that would cost hundreds of dollars to mail.

Moreover, at some point you may decide to develop and manage your own Web site. Learning how to write home pages doesn't take much more time than mastering simple desktop publishing programs like Microsoft Publisher, and the payoff in outreach is considerable. The two Web sites that I learned to manage for the Institute for the Study of Civic values—civic-values and Neighborhoods Online—were accessed more than 20,000 times in the fall of 1995, within a few weeks of landing on the Internet. Of course, once you do assume this responsibility, it becomes important to update your site with new information about your own activities and with links to other Web sites you think people ought to see.

Finally, you'll be helping your friends and neighbors who aren't online take advantage of the resources you've uncovered. You'll be printing out and distributing alerts to people who ought to see them. You'll be incorporating data and information obtained through the Internet into proposals and reports. You'll be telling friends and associates who aren't online about what you can do now that you *are* online, and encouraging them to join you. In fact, having to use conventional mail ("snail mail," as Net users call it) and fax machines to reach people will become an increasing source of frustration, since email is so much easier and faster.

All of this does take some time to learn, of course. This book should prove helpful in guiding you through the thicket of online resources to those that are most useful to you. Gradually, however, you'll develop your own approach to using what's available, and your own system for integrating the Internet into the other work you're doing. Before long, you'll be using email, the World Wide Web, and other online systems without even thinking about it. And you'll wonder how you ever got along without them.

Basic Web terminology

Browser	A user tool that displays Web documents and launches other applications
Home Page	The starting point for the set of pages available for a person, company, organization, or school; also, the first page your browser displays when you start it
HTML	HyperText Markup Language: the language in which World Wide Web documents are written
Hypertext	Documents that contain links to other documents; selecting a link automatically displays the second document
Image	A picture or graphic that appears on a Web page
Link	The text or graphic you click on to make a hypertext jump to another page
Search Directory	A Web site that indexes Web pages and allows you to search for terms you specify
Site	The location of a Web server
URL	The address that uniquely identifies a Web resource

Chapter 2 · Tools

There comes a point after you've set up your computer and installed the software needed to access the Internet when there are no more excuses—it's time to go online. Some people are intimidated by this prospect, but there's no need to be. Thousands have maintained accounts with mass market commercial services like CompuServe for more than a decade. Electronic bulletin boards have had a vast audience as well.

▶ The Email Connection

▶ Listservs and Mailing Lists

▶ Open, Moderated, Approved

▶ Joining Lists

THE EMAIL CONNECTION

With all the major online services like America Online now linked to the Net, gaining "user friendly" access is no longer a problem. My own first foray into the Internet was with a commercial service—Delphi, in January of 1994. At the time, Delphi was offering text-based Net access for what amounted to $1.00 an hour for 20 hours a month (after 6 PM and on weekends, at least). The account gave you Gopher to retrieve information; FTP (File Transfer Protocol) for downloading files; IRC (Internet Relay Chat) for live chats—and most important, email.

You may recall that Delphi was the first service aimed at "the rest of us" that permitted subscribers to send and receive email through the Internet. That, in itself, turned out to be worth the price of admission. Of course, it did take a few weeks to learn how to use these tools, but by spring I was accessing the Net every day and urging my friends and colleagues in Philadelphia to join me.

Today, navigating the Internet is no more difficult than learning how to use a word processing program, and it is considerably less demanding than a spreadsheet. Between self-executing installation disks, online help menus, and dozens of books available for additional reference, you should be up and running in no time.

Finding your online identity	When you sign up for a service, you'll likely be asked to choose a name that establishes your online identity. You should give some thought to this. My own online name and address is *edcivic@ libertynet.org*. The name "edcivic" reminds people that I am Ed with the Institute for the Study of Civic Values. The address identifies the service that maintains the account—in this case, LibertyNet. As an activist, you'll be eventually communicating with hundreds of people through the Net. It's important that they remember who you are.

Once you log on, you'll want to look around. Assuming that you're using a comprehensive Internet service, you should check out the specific tools it supports—the World Wide Web, which we'll discuss in some detail in the next chapter; gopher; Usenet groups, the public forums supported by the Internet; Internet Relay Chat (IRC); and File Transfer Protocol (FTP). Again, you may rarely use services like IRC or even Usenet, but you at least should familiarize yourself with them from the start.

As an activist, however, the most important Internet system you need to understand remains email. For all the hoopla surrounding Web sites, it is email that you will be using most. The heart of our work as advocates and organizers is communicating with other people. We are constantly trying to connect with others who share our concerns, both within our own communities and around the country. Yet we all know how difficult it is to get together. Most people running civic and political organizations are happy if they can attract 50 people to their monthly meetings. Planning a regional or national conference takes months. A protest march or major demonstration like the Million Man March or the Children Defense Fund's "Stand for Children" demonstration on June 1, 1996 becomes a major national event. Up to now, however, these have been our only means not only of voicing our concerns to the larger society, but of talking with one another. Otherwise, we have had to rely on organizational newsletters and an occasional fax.

Email is now creating entirely new ways for people to maintain contact with one another. Communicating with individuals is simple enough. You find out a person's online address (as in *edcivic@ libertynet.org*) and post a message to it. The message arrives within a matter of minutes. One-to-one communication on the Internet is a lot less complicated than using a fax machine, and considerably faster.

BASICS OF EMAIL ADDRESSING

Like a letter sent via postal mail, your email message needs an address for the person you're trying to reach, and a return address to show who sent it. A typical address consists of two parts separated by the @ symbol: the user's name and the domain where the user is known:

```
username@domain name
```

The domain name usually identifies the hostname of an organization, which could be a commercial business, a network provider, or an educational or governmental institution.

The address of this book's publisher (Dale Dougherty) is:

```
dale@songline.com
```

"dale" is the username and "songline.com" uniquely identifies the organization Songline Studios on the Internet. A GNN user whose account name was "johndoe" would have the following address:

```
johndoe@gnn.com
```

Most hostnames end in a three-letter identifier. These three letters indicate the type of organization, as shown below:

.edu	education
.gov	government
.mil	military
.net	network resource
.org	other nonprofit organizations
.com	commercial organizations

Other identifiers exist for countries, and are often used outside the United States.

THE THREE PARTS OF A MESSAGE

An email message usually has three parts: the message header, the message body, and the signature. Figure 2-1 shows a sample message.

The message header contains information about the message, such as its sender, the subject of the message, the date it was sent, the addresses of other people sent copies of the message and additional information about the route the message took to get to your computer. The header is similar to the top of a formal memorandum.

FIGURE 2-1
An email message

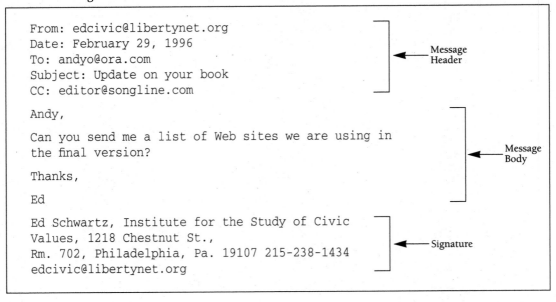

```
From: edcivic@libertynet.org
Date: February 29, 1996                          ┌── Message
To: andyo@ora.com                                └── Header
Subject: Update on your book
CC: editor@songline.com

Andy,

Can you send me a list of Web sites we are using in   ┐── Message
the final version?                                    ┘   Body

Thanks,

Ed

Ed Schwartz, Institute for the Study of Civic
Values, 1218 Chestnut St.,                       ┌── Signature
Rm. 702, Philadelphia, Pa. 19107 215-238-1434    └──
edcivic@libertynet.org
```

The following example shows a message header with five fields:

```
From: edcivic@libertynet.org
Date: February 29, 1996
To: andyo@ora.com
Subject: Update on your book
CC: editor@songline.com
```

When you create a new message, you must supply the To field and, optionally, the Subject field and the CC (for Carbon Copy) field. The mail program will automatically supply the From and Date fields when you send the message. There are often more than five fields in a message header, but our example shows the most useful ones. Your email program should allow you to control which fields are displayed.

The message body contains the text of the message as you typed it. In addition to simple text notes, you can also use email to send large documents, pictures, sounds, or programs as *attachments*. These non-text files can be attached to the body of the message in most email programs. When creating the message, you can use the Attach function to select the file you wish to send. The user who receives the message must have the program required to read or view the file once it is detached from the email message.

BASIC EMAIL FUNCTIONS

An email program allows you to send mail to other users and read mail that arrives in your mailbox. It displays the messages in your mailbox as a list, identifying the sender, subject, date, and other information. You can reply to mail you've received, including the original message as part of your reply. You can also forward mail you've received to another user.

Mail programs also help you manage your mail. After a while, your email will begin to accumulate. You will want to delete old messages, sort them by date or by sender, and save important or related messages in a file.

Any email program will allow you to do the following functions:

- Read a mail message
- Create a new message
- Reply to a message
- Forward a message to another user
- Delete a message

- Save a message to a file
- Sort the message listing

Make sure you understand how to perform these functions in the mail program you use. Create a sample message. You can practice sending a message by sending one to us to let us know what you think of this book. Use the address *netactivism@songline.com*.

LISTSERVS AND MAILING LISTS

As I indicated in the Introduction, the most compelling opportunity created by email is the chance to reach hundreds—even thousands—of people all at once. And they can reach you. All you have to do is join what is called an Internet mailing list (or *listserv*, after one of the first software programs to make this kind of communication possible). It's like joining an organization in the real world, except here you are tied together online and you use email to establish and sustain relationships with other members of the list.

Of all the new tools available to activists online, this is the most powerful. We've always been able to get information in some form through books, newspapers, magazines, and the mass media. If we want to talk to individuals or even small groups we can use the telephone. Yet no other medium can match what happens on an email list where each subscriber exchanges messages with every other subscriber, as if they were all participating in a meeting.

It is on email lists where people share information and ideas and explore common projects. It is around mailing lists that virtual communities form among people who have never met one another. They offer an entirely new way to participate in the civic and political process.

The most important decision, then, that you will make as an activist online is which email list or lists you choose to join. Ironically, for all that's been written about the Internet over the past few years, little has appeared explaining how these lists work. Let me, then, offer you the benefit of my own experience.

I want first to discuss how you go about subscribing to a list and what it means to participate in one. From there, I'll offer a brief explanation on how email lists are created and structured online. With this as background, we'll examine three distinct kinds of lists, in terms of what subscribers share with one another. I will conclude with some general advice on what to consider in determining which lists you join.

Kinds of lists	▪ **Information lists**, where people merely seek and offer specific information to each other on an area of mutual concern
	▪ **Dialogue lists**, where subscribers exchange views on issues and ideas
	▪ **Project lists**, where subscribers use email to collaborate on a specific project on which all active list members are working

PARTICIPATING IN A LIST

How do you join and start participating in an electronic mailing list? Here's how I did it.

Since I had no idea how an Internet mailing list actually worked, I decided that the best way to find out was to subscribe to one. I bought the 1994 Edition of Eric Bran's *Internet Directory* and scoured 105 pages of lists looking for those related to community and neighborhood issues. At the time, only one even came close—a list called Communet, described as follows:

Communet: On community computer networks, including Freenets, city BBS, information kiosks, and downtown information systems, Indian reservation networks, community computer conferencing systems, interactive systems run by newspapers, rural and area networks.[1]

It wasn't exactly about neighborhoods, but it was close enough, and since LibertyNet was being organized as a local community network, Communet seemed like a good place to get information on how other such networks were developing around the country.

As with all email lists, subscribing to Communet involved sending the right message to the right address, which the *Directory* listed as follows:

```
listserv@uvmvm.uvm.edu (Bitnet:listserv@uvmvm.edu)
[body=SUBSCRIBE communet first-name last-name]
```

---

[1] *The Internet Directory,* by Eric Braun (New York: Fouwcett Columbine, 1994), p. 44.

This meant that I was to send the request to *listserv@uvmvm. uvm.edu* and to include only one line in the body of the message itself: *subscribe communet Ed Schwartz*.

That's all there was to it. Within a few minutes of sending this message, I received a response that laid out the basic procedures of what I had just joined:

```
Your subscription to the COMMUNET list (Communet:
Community and Civic Network Discussion List) has been
accepted.

Please save this message for future reference,
especially if you are not familiar with LISTSERV....In
fact, you should create a new mail folder for
subscription confirmation messages like this one, and
for the "welcome messages" from the list owners that
you are will occasionally receive after subscribing to
a new list.

To send a message to all the people currently
subscribed to the list, just send mail to
COMMUNET@UVMVM.UVM.EDU.* This is called "sending mail
to the list", because you send mail to a single
address and LISTSERV makes copies for all the people
who have subscribed. This address
(COMMUNET@UVMVM.UVM.EDU) is also called the "list
address"....

You may leave the list at any time by sending a
"SIGNOFF COMMUNET" command to LISTSERV@UVMVM.BITNET
(or LISTSERV@UVMVM.UVM.EDU)....

Contributions sent to this list are automatically
archived. You can get a list of the available archive
files by sending an "INDEX COMMUNET" command to
LISTSERV@UVMVM.BITNET (or LISTSERV@UVMVM.UVM.EDU). You
can then order these files with a "GET COMMUNET
LOGxxxx" command, or using LISTSERV's database search
facilities....
```

I was now an official subscriber to Communet.

Today, if you sent the message *subscribe Communet FIRST NAME LAST NAME"* to *Listserv* at Communet's current address, (*elk.uvm. edu*), you would get an equivalent response.

It didn't take long to realize that on this sort of mailing list, it was the members who participated, not a specific group of editors and writers. Someone would raise an issue for consideration, offering his or her own views on it. Others would respond—usually within a matter of minutes. By the end of the day, there might be as many as twenty messages, back and forth, all addressing the same topic.

On Communet, moreover, the conversation was intelligent, intense—and voluminous. Here was an eclectic group of systems operators, computer professionals, and civic activists from all over the country struggling to build online services for their own communities and regions. Day after day, they went back and forth over what such systems should offer and how they should be put together. The following exchange was typical:

CONTACT

Putnam Barber

http://www.eskimo.com/ ~pbarber

pbarber@eskimo.com

206-443-5974

```
===========================================================

From: Putnam Barber

Subject: Re: Self-defeating Access Overload?

Analogies with national parks and concrete highways
are suggestive but misleading. There are structural
limits to the carrying and storage capacity of the
net, for sure, but expanding them does not require
paving over neighborhoods or building new (?) Grand
Tetons, just spending money for this instead of for
something else. That goes for archives and servers,
too. There may be synchronicity problems—only so many
people can be in one MUD at a time, or any other sort
of data base. But for most ordinary uses, those sorts
of problems can be tamed (and the high speed of the
machines when compared with the low speed of the users
gives the net a big advantage).

Interestingly, the point of inescapable overload is at
the ends of my fingers—I cannot type fast enough to say
everything I want to say, I cannot read fast enough to
see everything I want to see, I cannot think fast
enough to understand everything I want to understand.
And this is with wonderful tools like gopher and WWW
to help me, and "only" some small percentage of the
world linked up.

It's sad but understandable why people who are
overwhelmed already by dealing with mail that is (a
little) expensive and face-to-face contact — I'm
thinking here mostly of elected officials — are scared
of the increased volumes that might come from these
new facilities. New norms and procedures for
communication will develop, but I think it's going to
be much harder to deal with comprehending and using
the messages than with transporting and storing them.
```

So far the discussions are focused on the building of the net — who is going to pay for it, what is it going to look like, and who is going to make money off it. There are surely nuances in those questions that will matter deeply. Of course, for the people who stand to make money, these questions may be more than nuances!

I think we should be trying to collect and develop good ideas about how to make this all work to make healthier communities and more humane and effective governments. We know quite a lot now about what it looks like and what it is like to use it. What we haven't done is to fit that into the on-going routines of government and community life in practical and transforming ways.

"It" in the previous paragraph is low-cost, high-speed, asynchronous communication which is also linked to publicly available, high-volume digital storage of organized stuff—"data" of every imaginable sort. What everyone who uses it now knows is that this is +different+ from all the facilities and resources which are analogies and predecessors. I've seen too little thought about how it's going to make communities different, improve the workings of governments, change the character of public life. If you think about the nasty effect television has had on presidential campaigning in the years since Eisenhower, you will get an idea of the dimensions of the consequences that are possible. Can't we please do better than that?!

Putnam Barber

Seattle

==

CONTACT

Steve Cisler
sac@apple.com
408-996-1010

From: Steve Cisler

Subject: Re: Commercial Activities To Support Telecommunities?

Some people are going to hustle for business, others will put their energy into government grant writing, and others into getting known in the foundation world. People like Brian Campbell of Vancouver Free-Net are going after the taxpayer. If they can show the value of their system, they believe that the large metro area will support the system through a modest assessment. I don't know if it will be a special tax district (like some libraries have), but we in the U.S. should watch their tactics in Canada and perhaps emulate them.

I've been associated with a couple of bond measure losses for libraries and schools, and a nebulous (to most) concept like a community network is a very hard sell.

Steve Cisler

Apple Library

CONTACT
Stephen Snow
shsnow@charweb.org

==

From: Stephen H Snow — Personal Account

Subject: Re: Commercial Activities to Support Telecommunities?

In North Carolina, there are restrictions on what nonprofits can do to compete with commercial services. I propose a much broader, different scheme.

Everyone knows that having information on community systems adds value to the information, especially with the advent of cheaper modems, many public-access sites, etc.

I suggest something like this: Several sliding-scale fee (or, euphemistically) "support" systems, such as these:

1. Government: Sliding scale based on population served by the information. It could be a single #, such as $10,000 from city, $10,000 from county and smaller fees for contiguous smaller towns; or it could be by department: say $1,000 per year per city department; etc.

2. Nonprofits: A sliding scale based on budget size. The $5 million symphony would pay, say $1,000 per year; the $50,000 hospice would pay $100. Under $50,000 budget — they get in free.

3. Businesses: Restaurant menus, for example. $100-$200 per year to put up a menu and that gives the restaurant the right to change the special every day. it could eventually lead to online reservations...It's

not competition because no one is doing it. Count the restaurants in your city and get a feel for the potential revenue there.

I haven't gone through all the possibilities, just some of the major ones. The point is that this schema mirrors the network itself: many small amounts congealing to create a greater whole. No one gets his pocket picked; everyone kicks in a buck and the result is a system that benefits everyone.

Of *course* you still raise money in traditional ways — coffee mugs, small-time solicitations of members, etc. But you don't have to get into a cat fight with other fund-raisers and you don't charge any one group a lot of money.

Also, then, if one group drops out, it doesn't kill you.

One thing to keep in mind: grants and foundation money are there now, but in 5 years when there are 300+ community networks in North America alone, where will the money come from? There won't be grant money enough to go around. The result will be infighting and politics galore (just look at the lack of cooperation in public television for money as an example).

Why scramble around when with a little creativity, your community can support its own network through local means?

Steve Snow

for Charlotte's Web, a Free-Net initiative in Charlotte, NC

After several days of reading posts like this, I jumped into the fray myself:

From: Ed Schwartz

Subject: Re: Commercial Activities —-

This is as good a place as any to jump into this discussion, I guess. First: grants aren't forever. That's the beginning of wisdom. Foundations and public agencies follow fads...A few will innovate, then leave when the novelty wears off...a few will get into a second round to prove social responsibility after it's

respectable...few will stay forever...They just don't.
And "free" nets—nothing is free, right?—depend
entirely on grants and you'll go under.

Second: commercial activities will pay enough to
subsidize part of Freenets if there's a market through
them worth the fees. Otherwise, why should they spend
scarce marketing dollars on this medium. The key is
developing a broad and universal enough
capacity—technical, primarily—to use and want to use
these services so that individual fees can be
modest...Like phone bills for most people. If this is
to be a wave of the communications future, then we
need to be sure that it will be.

Which suggests that: grant seeking, etc., should
concentrate on training the market so that it can be
broad enough to sustain the nets once the grants
disappear. We can fool around with different price
structures for various institutions, but if the use
isn't broad enough, a handful of users won't be enough
to support this.

Ed Schwartz, Philadelphia

This post generated several responses, and before long I was posting regularly to Communet as well. I was no longer just a subscriber,
I was an active participant in an online conversation. Such conversations have now become an important part of my life.

The way I found Communet—through a printed directory—
makes little sense now, since new lists are being organized every
week. Even magazines devoted to the Internet pay much closer attention to Web sites. Basically, this is one online service that you have
to find online.

Your best bet is to find the most current directory of lists on the
World Wide Web that permits you to search by topic. A Web site
called Liszt is a good example. "Looking for an email discussion
group?," it begins. "Enter any word or phrase to search this directory
of 23,213 listserv, listproc, majordomo and independently managed
mailing lists from 555 sites."

Here's what a search on "Republican" found as of November 1995:

CCR-L Cornell College Republicans -mail the phrase
information CCR-L to *listproc@cornell.edu*

college-repub "Davis College Republicans"
-mail the phrase information college-repub to
listproc@ucdavis.edu

cu-republicans "CU Republicans Newsletter"-mail the phrase information cu-republicans to *listproc@lists.Colorado.EDU*

dukegop College Republicans -mail the phrase info dukegop to *majordomo@acpub.duke.edu*

KFCR-L KFCR-L Kansas Federation of College Republicans-mail the phrase info KFCR-L to *LISTSERV@UKANVM.CC.UKANS.EDU*

PRIMARY Republican Presidential Primary Listserv- mail the phrase info PRIMARY to *LISTSERV@UMRVMB.UMR.EDU*

REPUB-L Discussion of Republican Politics- mail the phrase info REPUB-L to *LISTSERV@VM.MARIST.EDU*

rfaa Republicans for All Americans -mail the phrase info rfaa to *Majordomo@efn.org*

rlc-discuss Republican Liberty Caucus Discussion (includes RLC-NEWS)- mail the phrase info rlc-discuss to *Majordomo@blob.best.net*

rlc-news Republican Liberty Caucus News (moderated)- mail the phrase info rlc-news to *Majordomo@blob.best.net*

A query on "Democrat" produced a similar group:

AUDEMS-L American University College Democrats-mail the phrase info AUDEMS-L to *LISTSERV@AMERICAN.EDU*

ccd "College Democrats across California"-mail the phrase information ccd to *listproc@ucdavis.edu*

CDLIST College Democrats Discussion and Information Group-mail the phrase info CDLIST to *LISTSERV@GWUVM.GWU.EDU*

cornelldems-l Cornell Democrats-mail the phrase information cornelldems-l to *listproc@cornell.edu*

dukedems Duke democrats-mail the phrase info dukedems to *majordomo@acpub.duke.edu*

LEFT-L LEFT-L - Building a Democratic Left Movement- mail the phrase info LEFT-L to *LISTSERV@CMSA.BERKELEY.EDU*

LEFT-ORG LEFT-ORG - Democratic Left Organizations discussions-mail the phrase info LEFT-ORG to *LISTSERV@CMSA.BERKELEY.EDU*

```
LEFTRULE LeftRule - Rules for Lists about the
Democratic Left-mail the phrase info LEFTRULE to
LISTSERV@CMSA.BERKELEY.EDU

libdem-1 "Liberal Democrat list" -mail the phrase info
libdem-1 to Majordomo@felix.dircon.co.uk

pads-announce Progressive Alliance for a Democratic
Society\n-mail the phrase info pads-announce to
majordomo@eskimo.com

pads-1 Progressive Alliance for a Democratic
Society\n- mail the phrase info pads-1 to
majordomo@eskimo.com

pol-sci-tech Discuss democratic politics of science &
tech-mail the phrase info pol-sci-tech to
Majordomo@igc.apc.org

uvm-democrats UVM College Democrats discussion list-
mail the phrase information uvm-democrats to
listproc@moose.uvm.edu

VIACON-L Discussion of Issues Related to Viability of
Democratic-Constitutionalism mail the phrase info
VIACON-L to LISTSERV@CNSIBM.ALBANY.EDU
```

Once you find a list that interests you, Liszt makes it easy to subscribe by including a form that lets you send the message directly from the Web page. By the time this book appears, there ought to be many other similar directories, so check out all of them before making any decisions.

You still need to figure out what you hope to gain from a list, however, before joining any of them. In this respect, it's useful to understand how groups establish email lists and three distinct ways in which they can operate.

OPEN, APPROVED, MODERATED

An email list doesn't appear out of nowhere. An organization or individual has to create it. The process involves contracting with an Internet Service Provider to handle the technical aspects of list maintenance, leaving the substantive work of managing the list to its sponsor.

There are three widely used list-management software packages—listserv, listproc, and majordomo—but the basic principle of each of them is the same. Once the software adds a subscriber to the list address (for example, *communet@elk.uvm.edu*), any message sent to that address will be forwarded to the subscriber within a matter of minutes.

The creator of a list also determines its structure. These take one of three forms:

- **Open** This a list where subscription requests are approved automatically and where participants post messages without anyone screening them in advance.

- **Approved** This is a list where the manager receives all subscription requests for approval. Once approved, list members can post messages without interference, as with an open list. The catch is that the list manager can "unsubscribe" people without their consent and refuse to approve their return if they begin to cause problems.

- **Moderated** This is a list where the manager not only approves subscriptions, but screens every message before the group receives it.

You can tell a great deal about a list from its structure. If it's an open list, it is likely to encourage free-wheeling debate. If it's an approved list, the manager wants to be sure that every subscriber is committed to the same basic goals. A moderated list presumes an even tighter focus for the discussion. As with membership requirements in other kinds of organizations, the structure of a list gives you an idea both of how it operates and what it's trying to accomplish.

The main question, then, is what you hope to gain from participating in an email list. I would group them into three broad categories: informational lists, dialogue lists, and project lists. Moreover, as is the case with all organized groups, there is a direct relationship between what a list demands and the sense of community and solidarity built among its subscribers.

INFORMATIONAL LISTS

As the label suggests, informational lists exist exclusively to provide information to their members about a particular topic. This can come from a single source, as when the list is little more than an online newsletter. Or it can grow out of exchanges among members seeking answers to questions that arise in the course of their work. Usually, the manager establishes the kind of information the list will provide, and the members can take it or leave it.

A good example is inet-news, created by an active Communet subscriber named Sam Sternberg. Its sole purpose is to keep journalists and others abreast of the latest sources for news on the Internet.

Every day, subscribers to inet-news get messages like these:

```
From: "Liz W. Tompkins" <liz@kersur.net>
To: Multiple recipients of list <inet-news@nstn.ca>
Subject: Web SOURCE: NH-PRIMARY Web Page
Item: The NH-PRIMARY Web page functions as a
comprehensive archive of campaign activity related to
the 1996 New Hampshire Presidential Primary.
```

http://unhinfo.unh.edu:70/0/unh/acad/libarts/comm/ nhprimary/nhprim.html

```
Coverage includes: -What's New -Polls
 -Democratic Candidates -Issue statements
 -Libertarian Candidates -Media Coverage
 -Republican Candidates -Campaign events
```

```
From: "Liz W. Tompkins" <liz@kersur.net>
To: Multiple recipients of list <inet-news@nstn.ca>
Subject: Web SOURCE: Presidential PRIMARIES
Item: The Washington Weekly-Presidential Primaries
```

```
Presents unbiased portraits of announced candidates
for President of the U.S. Includes portraits of each
candidate, a biography, voting records, how each
stands on key issues, and a speech by the candidate. A
contact address for each candidate is also included.
```

http://dolphin.gulf.net/Primaries.html

Short. Simple. Direct. And extraordinarily useful.

Remarkably enough, even though inet-news is an open list—anyone can subscribe and post to it—most members consistently respect its basic purpose. The manager gets plenty of help when she needs to control it. Since the participants all agree on what they want, they insist upon compliance themselves. The only exchanges permitted to take place involve inquiries about specific news sources. Whenever extraneous discussion does appear—as when a few reporters started debating coverage of the O.J. Simpson trial—other members of the list are quick to demand that it stop.

All informational lists aren't so tightly structured, however. Some encourage participants to help one another. A good example is cd4urban, which explores problems related to community development. An urban planner named Al Boss who had been active in the

CONTACT

Al Boss
alboss@scn.org

international Community Development Society created the list in 1994, to encourage networking among planners around the country. Over time, it has emerged as a place where a wide range of people seek advice on problems related to cities. The following exchange is typical:

From: Kristen Skivington

We, in Flint, Michigan, are beginning a community benchmarking project similar to that done in Cleveland. We are in the process of identifying similar and model cities/counties for comparison purposes.

I am requesting any input on cities/counties you would recommend and any referrals to additional community benchmarking projects. Some information follows:

Description of Flint/Genesee county: government responsiveness; people and support; economics; education and workforce preparedness (numerous indicators within each factor).

-primarily manufacturing (auto)
-county size of approximately 340,000 people
-city in decline, suburbs doing well
-city minority ratio 50% minority, 50% white; county
 19.7% minority

Benchmarking in five categories: cultural and other amenities.

Thank you,

Kristen Skivington

University of Michigan-Flint

Date: Tue, 14 Nov 1995 00:17:09 -0500 (EST)
Reply-To: *cd4urban@u.washington.edu*
Sender: *CD4URBAN-owner@u.washington.edu*
Precedence: bulk
From: 9 <cyyoakam>
To: Kristen Skivington
Cc: *CD4URBAN@u.washington.edu*
Subject: Re: Help: Community Benchmarking

Hello, Kristen! (from UM-Ann Arbor)

We down state here are developing a quarterly newsletter with the very content/benchmarking you are describing. I am also compiling a nationwide list. Let's share ours.

One group that may interest both of us is the:

Public Sector Quality program of the Association for Quality Control, HQ in Minneapolis.

When I get some info from them, I will share it with you.

Do you have the "grand daddy" of benchmarking? The Oregon State Benchmarking program for their communities and rural areas? Cost about $15 and is well worth it - nearly 300 benchmarks, and rising.

Please keep in touch,

Cy Yoakam:
U-Mich, Ann Arbor and
Urban Quality Communications

Date: Tue, 14 Nov 95 12:51 CST
Reply-To: *cd4urban@u.washington.edu*
Sender: *CD4URBAN-owner@u.washington.edu*
From: *woodstck@wwa.com* (Woodstock Institute)
To: *cd4urban@u.washington.edu*
Subject: Re: Help: Community Benchmarking

We do not do the kind of benchmarking you are looking for, but you might be interested in two studies we do. One is an annual compilation of home mortgage disclosure act data (HMDA) for the city of Chicago, broken down by neighborhood and by lender. We are currently working on the 1994 HMDA data for the city of Chicago. This data is available on CD from the FFIEC and on-line from RTK-NET. We also produced a 20 year analysis of economic indicators from the 1970, 1980, and 1990 population censuses and the economic census data. Indicators include income, population, employment status, housing units, lending, and building permits. As I said, this is for the city of Chicago, but might be of use to you in thinking about data collection and analysis.

+++

+ Woodstock Institute is a nonprofit applied research and +

```
+ technical assistance organization focusing on issues
of +

+ community reinvestment and economic development. +

+ 407 S. Dearborn, Ste 550 Chicago, IL 60605 +

+ (312)427-8070 woodstck@wwa.com +

++++++++++++++++++++++++++++++++++++++++++++++++++++++++
```

Replies like these appeared on the list for days.

Lists like cd4urban perform an invaluable service for their members. Up to now, there has been no way for the average citizen or even public officials to access the kind of expertise available here, except through high-priced consulting firms. Now the voluntary agreement of urban policy practitioners from all over the country to participate in this list has created a resource bank that would be difficult to produce in any other way.

At the same time, however, the commitment made by cd4urban subscribers extends no further that being available to share information. Discussion of ideas and issues is limited to addressing specific questions people ask. Nor is there any expectation that members will undertake projects in common. As a result, like all informational lists, cd4urban exists as a resource for each of its subscribers, without making any attempt to galvanize them around common issues or causes.

DIALOGUE LISTS

Far more demanding in every respect—as is reflected in the volume of correspondence they generate—are what I would call dialogue lists. These are created to promote discussion and debate among participants around issues or topics of mutual concern. The exchanges themselves are often similar to the postings on electronic bulletin boards, but there is an important difference. Bulletin boards are public forums, which people access at their leisure. Subscribers to lists receive every single message via email, whether they want them or not. As a participant in one such list put it, trying to keep pace with the exchanges is often like trying to sip water from a fire hydrant. His experience is typical.

The major list that I manage myself, civic-values, is a good example. We established the list in the summer of 1994 with the help of Miles Fidelman of the Center for Civic Networking, as an outgrowth of several of the exchanges about community that had taken place on

Communet. We recruited our first group of subscribers with this simple announcement:

CONTACT

Fidelman
fidelman@civic.net

```
To Communet Subscribers Devoted to Community and
Democracy
```

```
The Institute for the Study of Civic Values and the
Center for Civic Networking have joined forces to
create a new mailing list called civic-values.
```

```
This list is open to Democratic activists and
theorists wherever they may be. Our aim here is to
promote discussion of citizen efforts to build strong
neighborhoods and
```

```
communities throughout the country and to promote
citizen participation in government generally.
```

```
To subscribe to this list, send a message to
majordomo@civic.net
```

```
containing the single line: subscribe civic-values.
```

```
To receive further information about the list send a
message to majordomo@civic.net containing the single
line: info civic-values.
```

```
Join us.
```

```
Ed Schwartz, Institute for the Study of Civic Values
```

```
Miles R. Fidelman, Center for Civic Networking
```

Within a few days, more than 150 people had responded.

As you might imagine, defining the scope of the list so broadly led to exchanges on just about any issue that a participant wanted to raise. It took repeated exhortations on my part to keep us focused on problems related to civic values, local communities, and the structure of American democracy. Ideological conflicts further complicated the process. Initially, civic-values was conceived as a sounding-board for community activists on the Left. In the fall of 1994, however, a number of conservatives joined, after one of their online newsletters called attention to us.

What emerged were exchanges like these:

CONTACT

Tim Mazur
ethics@infinet.com

```
Date: Wed, 29 Mar 1995 11:23:34 -0800 (PST)
From: TMAZUR
Subject: Re: Affirmative Action
To: civic-values@civic.net
```

```
We are asked:
```

"Are we to be saddled forever by favoring certain groups within our society? Where is the politician with guts enough to propose a deadline for minority favoritism, beyond which point all must operate on a level playing field?"

In response:

Let me get this straight—we have over 500 years of overt racism and discrimination in North America ... yet some people are concerned about not-yet 30 years of affirmative action legislation. We have still over 95% of managers who are white males ... yet now people are concerned that the need for "favoring" is over. We set up affirmative action legislation so that we could realize a more equitable treatment of workers in the face of discrimination ... yet now we hear demands for some sort of artificial "deadline," as if choosing some date in the future had ANYTHING to do with why we created affirmative action in the first place.

Very interesting.

Tim C. Mazur

CONTACT

Scott Guthery
*guthery@austion.sar.
lib.com*

Date: Wed, 29 Mar 95 11:40:33 CST
From: guthery
To: civic-values@civic.net
Subject: Re: Affirmative Action

Tim Mazur postures ...

We set up affirmative action legislation so that we could realize a more equitable treatment of workers in the face of discrimination. It's immaterial what you intended to do, Tim. The only interesting question is what did you actually do.

What you actually did is build a giant bureaucracy that feeds on discrimination and addicted an entire generation of black Americans to special privilege....

Date: Wed, 29 Mar 1995 11:23:34 -0800 (PST)
From: TMAZUR
Subject: Re: Affirmative Action

Scott, I first must admit that, of course, you are entitled to your opinion. But tell me ... what color is the grass in your world? Do birds fly? Do mirrors

reflect? For months now I've known your views to be
extreme, but to think that affirmative action has
created a giant bureaucracy and addicted an entire
generation of black Americans forces me to wonder in
which Star Trek movie might I find your world. What
bureaucracy? A relatively small EEOC which oversees
many laws, not just affirmative action.... I'm not a
black American, but my friends and colleagues who are
reflect 0% of being "addicted to special privilege."
Our conversations sometimes include whether
discrimination in employment maybe has or maybe has
not improved over the past 25 years ... but to suggest
that anyone is addicted to special privilege again
forces me to conclude it's just not the same world I'm
in...

Tim C. Mazur

tmazur

At first, I was perturbed by this turn of events. Yet as the Right
gathered increasing strength in the country, I came to see their participation on the list as a rare opportunity to listen directly to what
they were saying. Besides, at a time when America was becoming increasingly polarized, we at least were maintaining a conversation
across ideological lines. That was an accomplishment in itself.

Even after many of the conservatives decided to leave civic-values
to pursue their causes elsewhere, the conversation proved no less demanding. Consider the exchange that unfolded in response to a simple request for information about voter registration from Ed Packard,
director of the Center for Governmental Studies of Auburn University in Alabama:

From: "Edward Packard"
Date: Sun, 22 Oct 1995 16:11:29 GMT+6
Subject: Capitalizing on New Voter Registrations

As you know, Congress passed the National Voter
Registration Act into law in 1993 and it went into
effect in most states on January 1, 1995.

States that have proceeded with implementation in a
timely manner (as we know, some states such as
California and Virginia balked at implementation at
first) have reported dramatic increases in voter
registration during the past 9.5 months.

As the administrator for the NVRA in Alabama, I'm
proud to report that we have registered approximately
110,000 new voters since the beginning of the year.

(If you are curious, about 35% of these registrants
signed up through agency-based programs; another 35%
signed up through driver's license offices; 20% through
the traditional route of the Board of Registrars
office; and 10% by mail....)

Some people...say that if the NVRA leads to increased
voter turnout, it's good law; if not, it's bad law.
(Of course, other individuals think the NVRA is bad
law on its face because it opens the voter
registration system by making registration more
accessible and easier to complete.)

My questions for the participants of civic-values:

*Do you know of any efforts in your area to capitalize
on the new voter registration programs?

*Are there any new voter mobilization efforts being
designed to turn these new registrants out on election
day?

*Or do groups in your area seem ready to rely on past
mobilization techniques (or do they focus no resources
on mobilization)?

Thanks.

—Ed

This request elicited almost no response, so he tried again, this
time asking a more pointed question:

From: "Edward Packard"

Date: Wed, 25 Oct 1995 17:38:52 GMT+6

Subject: Voting

For some reason, I find it interesting that I received
so few responses from the group...

While the focus of this list is obviously much broader
than elections, I wonder why there were so few
responses to a question about mobilization of citizens
to participate in their own governance.

The building of communities does not take place in a
vacuum. Governance is always there... and in many ways

IMHO

Acronym:

In My Humble Opinion

can affect the way communities are built, as well as how... or if... they will grow and prosper.

Is it cliché to speak of voting? Is voting too low-brow? Or is it something that certain segments of the population take for granted?...

—Ed

That got us going:

From: dhomuth (Don Homuth)
Date: Wed, 25 Oct 1995 16:53:29 -0700
Subject: Re: Voting

Good observation, Ed. I think that in some segments, the answer is "yes." I participate on a couple of other lists dealing directly with some political stuff on a partisan basis...For some strange reason, participants have confused the term "politics" with the term "issues" — as though the two were synonymous.

I think it's apparent that they are not. Unfortunately, there are those who continue to (IMHO) delude themselves into thinking that they are. And so we go through these weird little dances, in which each participant believes s/he is a kind of legislator, whose responsibility is to determine down to the last clause precisely how each "issue" will be defined, and that the definition will therefore define, in some odd way, who is appropriate to be a member of the Party. A kind of ideological "cleansing" then ensues, and folks who are not "liberal" or "progressive" or "conservative" enough are invited to leave the Party. Which act thereby ensures the ideological purity of the remains of what had been a Party, but simultaneously marginalizes it for the future.

That is, however, not the functional responsibility of voters. Their job is to compare from among the list of candidates, those persons whose character and capabilities best represent an opportunity to do some Useful Work, in a direction of which the voter approves....

Political campaigns actually like it when people don't register to vote, or declare their intent not to vote. In the modern campaign, those people can be taken off the direct mail, telephone and polling list. They don't cost money, and their opinions don't count for anything at all. They can be safely ignored.

Fools, the lot of them.

D Homuth

CONTACT

Terrie Rowe
rowe@orednet.org

From: Terrie Rowe
Date: Thu, 26 Oct 1995 09:04:51 -0400 (EDT) Subject: Re: Voting

For me, the effort involved is just too much - too time consuming and who has the time? After all the effort to get people registered, how many actually vote? It seems more productive to try to reach those who will actually vote with the issues.

Terrie

From: Ed Schwartz
Date: Thu, 26 Oct 1995 10:52:18 -0400
Subject: Re: Voter Turnout Drives

The stakes are quite high here, Terrie, especially for people who care about the disadvantaged—as you do.

The evidence is overwhelming that registration and voting is weakest among:

People without much education.

People without much income.

People between 18 and 25.

Is it any wonder that the government at all levels is now pursuing policies that hurt these groups?

They no longer count.

But consider this:

In Michigan, where you live, Spencer Abraham (R) beat Bob Carr (D) for the Senate last year by about 278,000 votes:

1,578,770 to 1,300,960.

The Almanac of American Politics tells us that of the 6,983,000 voting age population in the state, only

6,207,662 are registered, and only 3,080,079 of these
voted in 1994.

 It doesn't take an advanced degree in calculus to
figure out if only a portion of the 775,000
unregistered voters and of the registered voters who
just stayed home showed up—given who they are likely
to be—the results might have been quite different....

Ed Schwartz

From: Terrie Rowe
Date: Thu, 26 Oct 1995 12:39:22 -0400 (EDT)
Subject: Re: Voter Turnout Drives

Yes, and I've been following Sen. Abraham's voting
record, and have called his office.

But where to start? I'm not so sure any more. I used
to think it was with the local party office, but
they've disappeared. I've just gotten mail from the
state Democratic Grass-roots campaign.

A non-partisan effort? In middle class suburbia? Where
no one talks to each other?

How do we start?

Terrie

There followed another week of exchanges exploring political apathy, the state of local party organizations, and voter turnout in states
all over the country. There was no decision to take collective action
on any of this. Eventually, we moved on to other topics. Yet while we
were in the midst of it, this one subject generated at least five to ten
messages every day. There were virtually no "unsubscribes" during
this period, however. The "silent majority" of the list—roughly 350
subscribers—were obviously interested in what we had to say.

Dialogue lists like civic-values do offer a terrific outlet for those of
us who enjoy just talking about politics. Now we can debate issues
and ideologies *ad infinitum* with people all over the world. Unlike
talk radio and television, we decide when to participate, not a mod-
erator, and we don't have to wait for someone to answer the phone.
Given that these are written exchanges, we can save comments that
we find especially interesting and use our own postings to sharpen
our polemical skills in a safe environment. There are even times
when what we send to a list ends up reaching a much broader audience. Comments of mine to Communet have ended up in at least two

books on the Internet over the past year, and the opportunity to write *NetActivism* grew directly out of exchanges on civic-values with Songline Studio's parent company, O'Reilly & Associates.

The problem, however, is if a list exists simply to promote discussion, many of its members aren't likely to be activists. People with extensive political commitments in the real world often don't have time to plow through dozens of email postings every day, even if they bear direct relevance to their work.

Dialogue lists aren't so disciplined. They move from topic to topic at the whim of participants. While the process can help participants sort out what they think, it doesn't necessarily encourage them to act. In fact, for many participants, posting to the list *becomes* the political action in which they're engaged, even if it has no real impact on politics. The hardest job I've had in managing civic-values has been to persuade full-time community and political activists to participate in it. Most of them simply don't have time.

Over time, however, a dialogue list like civic-values can begin to create an online community of its own. There are now dozens of people on the list—all seriously engaged in efforts for social change—who see it as an important support system for their work. Some post regularly. Many do not. Yet that they remain subscribers attests to the values the conversation holds for them. And when, in the spring of 1996, a few people suggested that we all ought to get together, there were spontaneous offers to host regional civic-values gatherings from people in every section of the country. The political relationships established online were becoming personal.

PROJECT LISTS

When a list does begin to encourage participants to work together in the real world, then it becomes what I would call a project list. As an increasing number of organizations are learning how to use email, many of them are establishing lists to encourage ongoing communication among members of their boards and committees. It is also possible for a project to grow out of the process of a list itself—as started to happen on civic-values when participants agreed to host regional get-togethers. Either way, the list moves from being an informational resource and a discussion group to a serious instrument of political action.

The simplest list of this kind is one created to help a limited group of people implement a project in which everyone has a clearly defined role. A good example was a list established by the director of LibertyNet, Chris Higgins, for a committee charged with developing

CONTACT

Christine C. Higgins
http://www.libertynet.org
higgins@libertynet.org

a proposal to the Commerce Department under the National Telecommunications Information Agency (NTIA). The aim of the project was to expand online services in three low-income neighborhoods in Philadelphia now designated an "Empowerment Zone" by the federal government.

The committee included people from the Mayor's Office of Community Services; Philadelphia's public radio station—WHYY-FM; the University of Pennsylvania, various civic groups, and LibertyNet itself.

Given the difficulty of coordinating our schedules, the email list proved instrumental in keeping us in touch with one another. Between actual meetings, not only was Chris Higgins able to circulate draft documents to the group—which she might have done using a fax machine—but she could also get immediate feedback, which would have been a lot harder. As important, it was quite easy to send comments back and forth to one another, which would have been next to impossible through faxes alone. The list, in effect, sustained our collaboration and made our few real-time meetings far more productive. The NTIA did fund this proposal in October of 1995, much to our delight. Almost immediately, LibertyNet established a new list for the group that was charged with implementing the program itself.

It is also possible for a list created to encourage dialogue and discussion among people who share similar goals to start generating projects of its own. The first list that I joined—Communet—is a good example. Everyone on the list is either organizing a community telecommunications network or interested in learning about how it's done. We share information on organizational development, network technologies, and services that we can offer our members. We get into debates over structural issues, like the exchange over financing described earlier. A few people on the list keep track of public policy developments in the area and advise us on the latest schemes to "reform" telecommunications under consideration by the Congress.

Within this context, any contribution related to community networking is appropriate, no matter how long. All other posts are not, no matter how short. Communet is also an open list, but its participants are quite effective in chastising people who stray from its objectives. As a result, the list itself has played a major role in advancing the movement. Two national conferences on community networking convened at the Apple Library in Cupertino—called, appropriately, "The Ties That Bind"—and a third in the spring of 1996 in Taos, New Mexico, built sizable attendance merely through announcements on Communet. Many of us—myself included—showed up as much to meet other people on the list as to participate in any of the workshops on the agenda. This is where the virtual community of the Internet gets real.

These fledgling experiments point the way toward a new generation of email lists aimed at linking like-minded activists within the same community or even from all parts of the country with one another, all focused on helping people work together to achieve common goals. As early as 1992, Jerry Brown used an email list to communicate with staff and volunteers in his unsuccessful bid for the Presidency. The candidate didn't make it, but the campaign was a portent of politics to come. It is reasonable to assume that by the end of this decade, every major national political organization will maintain email lists for their members, and most strong local groups will do the same.

Unfortunately, this transition will not be entirely smooth. Project lists do require a discipline from their members that is difficult to maintain. Information lists are easy enough to manage, since they don't encourage dialogue. A project requires discussion, however, and if this gets out of hand, the busiest people will leave. Figuring out how to use email lists to plot strategy and tactics is an art that activists will have to master, if we hope to make best use of this resource in politics. But the potential payoff will be more than worth the effort.

JOINING LISTS

Given the status of political mailing lists on the Internet today, how should we best approach them? What procedure makes the most sense in figuring out which ones to join? Here are a few basic principles that make the most sense, given where we are.

- Decide what role you want participation in email lists to play in the context of your current work. Are you looking mostly for information lists that can help you in projects you're pursuing already? Are you excited about the prospect of exchanging ideas and debating issues with people around the country, as a way of developing new political relationships? Are you preparing to connect with like-minded activists, so you can coordinate tactics and strategies more effectively? These are the most important questions you need to ask, since the answers will shape every other decision you make about lists.

CONTACT

Liszt Discussion Group Directory
http://www.liszt.com/

- Use an online directory such as Liszt to identify lists in which you might be interested. Read their descriptions carefully. Ask yourself which ones really look like they'll meet your needs.

- Be sure to set up folders in your mailer for each list you select and even for topics or issues which are likely to generate most mail. Email is a lot less overwhelming if you get organized before it starts.

- When you do subscribe to a list, be sure to save the message outlining how to unsubscribe. You may well need it.

- Wait before posting to get a feel for how the list operates. As our discussion suggests, lists have different styles and protocols. Be sure you understand what they are before jumping into the fray.

- When you do post, remember that you are speaking to the entire group—not just to the single person whose comment you may be answering. Ask yourself whether your reply is something that the entire list needs to hear. If not, email to the individual separately.

- Over time, be sure to respect the discipline of the list yourself. If it's an informational list, don't start offering your opinions on the issues of the day. Even if it's a dialogue list, stay focused on the topics the list was created to discuss. If you decide you're not interested, then simply unsubscribe.

- Don't get abusive—or "flame," as it's called on the Internet. Nothing kills a list more quickly than people attacking one another.

- If you find some exchanges on a list to be useful, but not all, don't be afraid simply to ignore messages you don't want and delete them. There's no requirement that you read everything posted to a list, anymore than you have to read every page of an organization's newsletter.

- Remember that as absorbing as a list may become, you've subscribed to get help in your work in the community and politics. There may be great benefit from participating in an ongoing dialogue over issues, but at least be clear what you're getting from it.

- Most of all—watch your online time if you are using a provider that charges by the hour. Participating in lists is useful— and it's often fun—but you don't want it to bankrupt you.

Beyond these considerations relating to your own participation in email lists, you should be giving serious thought to the potential this medium holds for the organizations in which you're currently involved. If you belong to a local group, could an email list strengthen participation among its members? If you're part of a regional or national movement, could the list be used to tie key organizers and supporters together? Can this new way of communicating with one another help all of us overcome the obstacles we face in trying to get people involved, by encouraging them to participate via email, even if they can't attend regular meetings? These questions may seem esoteric now, but groups all over the country are starting to ask them. The answers could well reshape civic and political life as we now know it.

3 Trolling for Information

Listservs and email may represent the most powerful new tools available to activists on the Internet, but the mechanisms for retrieving and transmitting information aren't far behind. Before you can change the government, you need to understand how it operates. It helps to know how a Congressman *does* vote before you start telling him how he *should* vote. This is why companies pay large sums of money to lobbyists. It's not simply to figure out who should receive campaign contributions—as important as that is. They also want advice on which arguments have the best chance of moving the Congress in the "right" direction around particular issues. The beginning of wisdom in politics is the knowledge that information is power.

- ▶ Navigating the World Wide Web
- ▶ Government Programs
- ▶ Monitoring Elected Officials
- ▶ Tracking Issues
- ▶ Activist Bookmarks

NAVIGATING THE WORLD WIDE WEB

The Internet is, as Vice President Al Gore described it, an information highway. The same technology that permits us to exchange email with one another also enables us to retrieve data from anywhere in the world. Using the Internet isn't hard. A number of directories and search engines have emerged over the past two years to help us find information. The word processing language used to post information—HTML—is far easier to learn than conventional word processing programs like WordPerfect, all of which now include utilities that convert their files automatically. There's a reason why home pages on the World Wide Web are proliferating at rate of several thousand a day. They're so simple, even a child can create them.

The question for us, then, is how to make best use of this new resource in politics. To be effective, an activist needs to keep track of government, politicians, interest groups, and issues. The Internet is already a gateway to an impressive body of material in each of these areas, and one that is expanding every day. Newer Internet software makes it easy to organize this information as we most want to review it. Electronic cutting and pasting is becoming a new art form.

To give you an idea of what's possible, then, we need to explore basic questions:

- How is information of any kind made available on the Internet?
- What already exists online that relates to government, politics, and public issues?
- How can activists organize the political information that is becoming increasingly available?

We will consider each of these issues in turn.

FROM GOPHERS TO BROWSERS

When most of us started hearing about the Internet, even the terminology seemed pretty strange. We learned that we could Telnet to services that looked like electronic bulletin boards once we reached them. Then we were urged to use something called Gopher to access another network, which we could search using either Archie or Veronica.

In 1995, everyone started talking about the World Wide Web as the place to access not only written material, but graphics, sound, videos, and pornography—not necessarily in that order. All these new terms gave the impression that the Internet was, indeed, an unfathomable place and that it would take a long time to learn how to use it.

By now, the process is a lot less mysterious. Between software packages like Netscape that make it easy to browse the World Wide Web and the invasion of the Internet by all the major commercial services, finding information on the Net is now almost as easy as using an automatic teller machine. The entire process is built around pointers, menus, and directories. In fact, once you get started, it's hard to stop.

There are a few *basic* points, however, that are useful to understand before you begin:

- First, every piece of data that you seek is found in a file on a computer somewhere, just like the files on your own computer. The Internet is treated with such reverence—or trepidation— today that it is useful to remember that what we're describing here is just a giant computer network.

- Second, the computer that maintains the files you access through the Internet is called a server, since its purpose is to serve information to other computers. The various software that coordinates this process is—logically enough—called server software. When you subscribe to an Internet Service Provider, (ISP), you gain direct access to the server that ISP maintains.

- Third, each file on a Web server has an exact address of its own, designated by what is known as a Uniform Resource Locator or URL. The URL includes the file name, the organization which maintains it, and the directory on the computer where it is found. As an example, the URL of Capweb, an excellent guide to the United States Congress, is as follows: *policy.net/ capweb/congress.html.*

  This tells you that the "congress.html" file is located in the "capweb" directory of a server maintained by, "policy.net." This is the same procedure you use in locating a file on your own computer, now applied to accessing files that live on computers all over the world.

Surfing the Net, then, essentially involves using software developed for the Internet to access files located on Internet servers throughout the world. Gopher was the first major software package used for this purpose. It lets you access simple text files, providing they are encoded on a menu that permits the software to read them. The files themselves, however, are no different from the ASCII text files you might create with a word processing program on your own computer.

The World Wide Web is yet another network of files. The files associated with the Web share a common language—HyperText Markup Language or HTML.

HTML—THE LANGUAGE OF THE WEB

When Web technology was first designed, the goal was to develop a way to describe the elements of a page's structure without specifying how the page should actually be displayed. In other words, the Web page specifies *what* to display, and different browsers decide *how* to display it. For this reason, the same Web page is available to anyone on the Net, whether they're using UNIX, DOS, Windows, Mac, OS/2, or any other operating system. If there is a browser that runs on that system, users of the system can view the page.

I'm not going to launch into a detailed explanation of HTML. If you want to learn HTML, and you should, there are plenty of other books and Web sites[1] dedicated solely to that subject. But suffice it to say that every Web page is a plain text file that contains "tags" or codes. These tags tell the browser how to parse and display the file. The codes represent instructions written in HTML. HTML codes specify heading levels (as in an outline), paragraph styles, inclusion of images and sound, addresses of pages to link to, and anything else the browser needs to know.

You can use any text editor to create or modify HTML documents or use one of the growing number of HTML software programs, such as HotDog *(http://www.sausage.com),* NaviPress *(http://www.intercom.com/NAVIPRES/download.htm),* and FrontPage *(http://www.microsoft.com)* that automate the coding process. Also, most popular word processing programs are integrating HTML into their new releases.

THE WEB PAGE

Each file is called a Web "page" because it appears as a page on the screen. A Web browser is the software program needed to interpret these HTML Web pages, just as Gopher is the program needed to access text files. At this writing, Netscape is the most widely used Web browser, but there are a growing number of competitors as well.

---

[1] The Stroud List, *http://cws.wilmington.net/* is one of the Internet's most popular and respected sites for reviews of, and links to, Windows 95 and Windows 3.x Internet programs of all kinds. Choose HTML Editors from the main menu.

Whichever online service you join to retrieve information from the World Wide Web, it is a browser you are using to access it.

Web browsers are considerably more powerful than Gopher. They can read simple ASCII files, as well as documents prepared using HTML. You can use a browser like Netscape to download files to your own computer. Browsers can even access graphics and sound files. This technology has been available to computer aficionados for some time, but it took Netscape to integrate all these features into a single package that made the World Wide Web accessible to the rest of us.

By the summer of 1995, even political organizations were experimenting with the Web's most powerful features. The Christian Coalition *(http://www.cc.org/)*, for example, started including sound files on its Web site. If you clicked on "Audio highlight," within a few minutes you were not simply reading Ralph Reed's speech, you were listening to it. The Web browser downloaded a file called *reed.wav* in the Christian Coalition directory where it could be played by any popular multimedia sound system.

By the end of the 1995, a new company called Real Audio developed an online player that let you listen to sound files without downloading them to your computer. Now you didn't have to fill up your hard drive with an audio greeting from President Clinton at the Democratic National Committee. You could simply listen and leave it online. You could even catch segments of WABC Radio News and CNN broadcasts while you were surfing the Net. The inevitable integration of all these media was now well underway.

The key to figuring out how the World Wide Web works, however, is understanding the term "hypertext" in HyperText Markup Language.

Hypertext is a software code that links a word or phrase to something else—another section of the same document, another document, or even an entire menu of documents located on another computer. By using HyperText Markup Language, a Web publisher can encode a word or phrase in one Web page—that is, on one Web file—so that when you click on the word, you jump to another Web page. The word is usually both underlined and highlighted in a different color to indicate hypertext. Surfing the Net is, in effect, using hypertext to jump from Web page to Web page—from file to file—in this way.

As an example:

You want to access "Hot Bills in Congress this week"—a specific section of the legislative reference service developed for the World Wide Web by the Congress known as "Thomas"—after Thomas Jefferson.

CONTACT

Thomas
http://thomas.loc.gov/

You don't know how to reach Thomas, but your browser includes an Internet directory called "Yahoo" that has a section on government. There, under the Library of Congress, you find the following entry:

THOMAS: Legislative Information on the Internet - In the spirit of Thomas Jefferson, a service of the U.S. Congress through its Library.

When you click on "THOMAS: Legislative Information on the Internet," you find the Web page shown in Figure 3-1.

Click again on "Hot Legislation," accessing another menu, and you get:

Bill Summary and Status

Digests and legislative history of bills and amendments, searchable by keyword, index term, bill/amendment number, sponsor/cosponsor, or committee/ subcommittee.

Bill Summary and Status for the 104th Congress

Hot Legislation

Major bills receiving floor action in the 104th Congress as selected by legislative analysts in the Congressional Research Service.

Hot bills by topic

Hot bills by popular and/or short title

Hot bills by number/type

Hot bills enacted into law

Hot bills under Congressional consideration this week.

FIGURE 3-1

The Thomas site offers an easy way to keep track of legislation

From this menu, you can retrieve the entire text of every bill before the Congress in the coming week.

Once you've finished examining "Hot Legislation," you can return to your original page by clicking repeatedly on a button labeled "Back" on your Web browser until you retrace your steps.

This is the way in which millions of files are now connected to one another through the Internet—and explains why this particular system is called the World Wide Web.

These, then, are a few basic considerations in using the Internet to retrieve information. It should be obvious by now that the World Wide Web has become the primary information system around which most future development will occur. You can still reach Gophers through the Web, simply by designating "gopher" at the beginning of its address. Moreover, as we have seen, you can also use the Web to access different kinds of media, if you have the software to play the files. It's not surprising , then, that to a great many people, the World Wide Web *is* the Internet—given all the attention that it has received. While this isn't true, Web sites have emerged as the primary vehicle not only for sharing information, but for establishing a presence online. Nothing is likely to replace them in the foreseeable future.

How, then, do we use the Web to retrieve information that can strengthen our hand in dealing with government and politicians? How do we organize and maintain the information that we find? These are questions that we are now in a position to answer.

LOCATING DOCUMENTS ON THE WEB

Perhaps the most astounding feature of the World Wide Web is that each document on the Web has a unique global address that allows it to be retrieved directly. This unique address is called a Uniform Resource Locator (URL). Just as individuals have email addresses that locate a person within a specific domain, documents have addresses that locate them in a specific server domain.

A URL has three parts: the protocol identifier, the domain or hostname of the server, and the document's pathname. This follows the syntax for URLs:

```
protocol://domain name/pathname
```

On the World Wide Web, HTTP is the *protocol* or language that browsers use to talk to servers. All URLs for Web sites begin with *http://*. Most Web browsers will communicate using other Internet server protocols, such as Gopher and FTP. Thus, you might see a URL that starts with *gopher://* or *ftp://*.

The next part of the URL is the *server* name. This might be as simple as the domain name, but usually it is preceded by *www*. This prefix is merely a naming convention that many follow, but it is not a requirement. For instance, either of the following URLs will take you to the default page for the GNN server:

```
http://gnn.com/
```

or

```
http://www.gnn.com/
```

However, if you try a site and find that using the simple domain name does not work, be sure to try prefixing *www* to it. If you have the pathname for a specific document, you can also supply it. Otherwise, you will begin at the default home page and you can navigate to the document using links.

It's often possible to guess at a URL. Almost every URL starts with *http://www*. Commercial site URLs generally end with *.com*, government sites end with *.gov*, and educational sites end with *.edu*. A company named XYZ Company, for example, is likely to have a Web page at *http://www.xyz.com*. Similarly, the URL for the White House is *http://www.whitehouse.gov*, and the URL for Cornell University is *http://www.cornell.edu*.

It's not working!

Sometimes when you type in a URL, you'll receive an error message indicating that the server is not available. If you check the URL for accuracy, wait a few seconds and try it again; it may work. Another solution for a particularly long URL is to delete part of the URL and go to the next directory. For example, say the URL you have is :

```
http://www.pbs.org/tconnex/socialstudies.html.
```

If you receive an error message, try *http://www.pbs.org/tconnex/* or *http://www.pbs.org/*. This will send you to the next directory up (or home page) where you can see the links available. The creators of the pages may have changed the page so that your particular link no longer works. Scrolling down on the home page *gnn.com/edu*, you see the Library of Links, the resource you originally wanted, and can now access by selecting it.

SEARCH ENGINES

What if you don't know the URL for a page you want to visit? Maybe you read about it somewhere and didn't keep the reference. Or perhaps you visited the page and want to return, but forgot to add it to your hotlist. Or maybe you are interested in a particular topic but don't even know if a related page exists. Search engines can help you find what you seek.

Search engines periodically scan the contents of the Web to rebuild their massive indexes of Web pages. Some search titles or headers of documents, others search the documents themselves, and still others search other indexes or directories. When you request specific keywords, the engines search the indexes they have built for those words. Your keyword search is not a live search of the Web, but a search of that engine's index.

Two features will probably influence your choice of a favorite search engine. One is ease of use: it should allow you to customize searches without offering so many options that using it is confusing. Second, a good search engine should be accurate: if properly configured, it will return a reasonable quantity of fairly precise results.

There are several indexes and directories on the Net that are both search engines and collections of resources you can easily browse or search. Some, such as Yahoo, are large collections organized alphabetically by subject. Though new ones are being added regularly, here are some of the most popular:

Yahoo
http://www.yahoo.com

Yahoo features a hierarchically organized subject tree of information resources. It offers limited search options, but is often a useful starting place because of its large database of authoritative sources.

Whole Internet Catalog
http://gnn.com/wic/

The Whole Internet Catalog is a collection of Web pages organized by categories and offers many national political resources.

Internet Sleuth
http://www.intbc.com/sleuth/

The Internet Sleuth is less well known than the Whole Internet Catalog, but it offers a wide variety of specialized searches by category.

WEB ROBOTS

Web robots depend on software, rather than people, that automatically searches the World Wide Web for new material.

Alta Vista
http://altavista.digial.com

Alta Vista is the relative newcomer on the block. It is run by Digital Equipment Corporation and has become so popular that it logs more than 2 million visitors a day. If you want a lot of return hits for a query, Alta Vista is the choice.

Webcrawler
http://webcrawler.com

Webcrawler is lightning-fast and returns a weighty list of links. It analyzes the full text of documents, allowing the searcher to locate keywords which may have been buried deep within a document's text. Webcrawler is a good choice if you are looking for a company or organization's home page, since it returns fewer hits to sort through than Alta Vista.

Lycos
http://lycos.cs.cmu.edu/

Lycos is named after a quick and agile ground spider. It searches document titles, headings, links, and keywords, and returns the first 50 words of each page it indexes for your search. Its search engine is more configurable than Webcrawler.

Excite
http://www.excite.com

Excite currently contains searches of 1.5 million Web pages and two weeks of Usenet news articles and classified ads, as well as links to current news, weather, and more. It presents results with a detailed summary to provide you with an annotated selection.

BEHIND THE HEADLINES

New Web sites are appearing with such frequency at this point that any "current" list is bound to be out of date within a matter of weeks. In the last four months of 1995, for example, every major federal agency except the Department of Labor established its own Web site. Both major parties went online, along with home pages for every "third" party from the Libertarians on the Right to the New Party on the Left. Move over, Ross Perot—you've got lots of company. Conservative lobbies like the Christian Coalition have been using the Internet for some time, but in 1995 they were joined by the AFL-CIO, the National Organization for Women, and a wide range of grassroots groups on the Left. This process accelerated in 1996, as the Presidential campaign unfolded.

The critical question, however, is whether the information now found on the Internet adds anything to what is already available in other forms. Do government agencies explain their activities any better through the World Wide Web than through the daily press? Can we use the Internet to monitor what our own elected representatives are doing? Can we find out more about public issues than we can from *Time, Newsweek*, and various policy journals?

The answer to all these questions is yes. There is a growing body of material about government and politics available on the Internet that is almost impossible to obtain in any other way. Moreover, it's the kind of information activists need most in organizing people around causes and campaigns.

- First, there is now extensive information online related to specific federal programs that we can use in arguing for or against them. Most of this material is simply never covered in the daily press.

- Second, we can now easily find out where elected officials stand on particular issues and how interest groups on all sides of the spectrum evaluate their performance.

- Finally, between the World Wide Web and releases issued via email, we can now get up-to-the minute information about the issues of greatest concern to us—even if they're not being covered in the papers every day.

None of this information has been readily available to us in the past. Now we can retrieve it without difficulty. Just a few examples suggest how much is already at our disposal.

GOVERNMENT PROGRAMS

Everyone knows that government sponsors programs, but how many of them do we really understand? Beneficiaries of "pocketbook" subsidies like Medicare and Medicaid or student loans have a ready-made framework for analysis—namely, how much they personally receive. The military budget generates considerable attention, given that national security is at stake.

But what about government assistance to local communities? If your Congressperson held a town meeting on the federal budget, could you offer an informed opinion on whether any one of these should continue?

- Community Development Block Grant
- Small Business Development Centers
- One-Stop Career Centers
- Extension Division, Department of Agriculture
- School to Work Program
- Byrne Criminal Justice Grants

These are major initiatives, spending billions of dollars every year to achieve important goals—physical revitalization, economic development, youth employment, and neighborhood safety. Yet rarely does the press cover these programs. As a result, during what has become an annual struggle over the federal budget, even many community activists are hard put to explain what difference it will make to people within their own communities.

The Internet is already helping to fill the gap. Here are just a few examples.

GOALS 2000

The Goals 2000 (*http://www.ed.gov/G2K/*) program was established in a bill known as the National Education Act, which passed Congress in the spring of 1994. President Clinton considered the legislation to be among his most important accomplishments, especially given his promise as a candidate in 1992 to make educational reform a national priority.

Almost as soon it was established, however, conservatives made dismantling Goals 2000 one of their own major priorities. As an article in the *Christian American,* an online publication of the Christian Coalition, put it, "the language of Goals 2000...offers tremendous insight into the education establishment's vision for altering the traditional function of schools, thereby restructuring society as we know it....In order to receive funds under Goals 2000 appropriations, local schools must include social services in their grant applications...[the] goal is not just the restructuring of the classroom. In order to produce the kind of student we want, we must have a complete restructuring of society.'"[2]

Sounds pretty ominous, doesn't it—federal bureaucrats injecting dangerous "social programs" into the classroom and driving a wedge between America's children and their families? Coalition supporters soon started making this argument in local school board elections around the country and Congressional Republicans used them in targeting the program for extinction in the budget battle of 1995. Goals 2000 is still operating, however, so the struggle continues.

Given that the media hasn't paid much attention to this program, how might you examine it for yourself? Up to last year, you would have had to write to the Office of Education and wait for brochures

[2] Kimberly Parker, "GOALS 2000 SOCIAL ENGINEERS TARGET SCHOOLS: School-Based Social Programs Undermine Parents", *Christian American,* (Washington: Christian Coalition, 1995)

CONTACT

Goals 2000

http://www.ed.gov/G2k

to arrive in the mail. Now, however, you can visit a Web site created specifically by the Office to support Goals 2000. There, you find the menu shown in Figure 3-2.

One or two more clicks, and the Goals themselves appear:

```
GOALS 2000 SETS INTO LAW THE NATIONAL EDUCATION GOALS

**********************************************************

BY THE YEAR 2000...

• SCHOOL READINESS — All children in America will
start school ready to learn.

• SCHOOL COMPLETION — The high school graduation rate
will increase to at least 90 percent.

• STUDENT ACHIEVEMENT AND CITIZENSHIP — All students
will leave grades 4, 8, and 12 having demonstrated
competency over challenging subject matter including
English, mathematics, science, foreign languages,
civics and government, economics, arts, history, and
geography, and every school in America will ensure
that all students learn to use their minds well so
they may be prepared for responsible citizenship,
further learning, and productive employment in our
nation's modern economy.

• MATHEMATICS AND SCIENCE — United States students
will be first in the world in mathematics and science
achievement.

• ADULT LITERACY AND LIFELONG LEARNING — Every adult
American will be literate and will possess the
knowledge and skills necessary to compete in a global
```

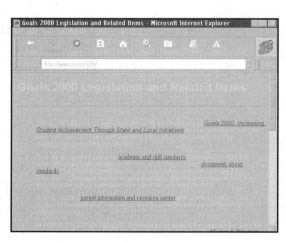

FIGURE 3-2

The Goals 2000 Page is an example of government-run Internet activistism.

economy and exercise the rights and responsibilities of citizenship.

▪ SAFE, DISCIPLINED, AND ALCOHOL- AND DRUG-FREE SCHOOLS — Every school in the United States will be free of drugs, violence, and the unauthorized presence of firearms and alcohol and will offer a disciplined environment conducive to learning.

▪ TEACHER EDUCATION AND PROFESSIONAL DEVELOPMENT — The nation's teaching force will have access to programs for the continued improvement of their professional skills and the opportunity to acquire the knowledge and skills needed to instruct and prepare all American students for the next century.

▪ PARENTAL PARTICIPATION — Every school will promote partnerships that will increase parental involvement and participation in promoting the social, emotional, and academic growth of children.

You can judge for yourself whether you agree or disagree with these goals, and whether you think the Christian Coalition has characterized them fairly. The point here is that at least the Internet makes it possible to find them.

COMMUNITY GRANTS

The Community Development Block Grant (CDBG) provides more than $3 billion annually to cities and smaller communities for housing rehabilitation and related neighborhood improvements. It's operated for more than 20 years, surviving repeated conservative attacks during the Reagan and Bush administrations, and more recently the Congressional Republican sweep in 1992 led by Newt Gingrich.

Ever hear of it? Do you know how your own community uses it? If your local administration won't tell you, just access the HUD Web site (Figure 3-3) and you'll find out for yourself. Not only can you get information on how CDBG functions nationally, you are likely to be able to retrieve the executive summary of the plans that your city submitted to HUD for use of the funds, since these are gradually being added to the site. (*http://www.comcon.org/complans.html*)

Here's a case where the World Wide Web is making the federal government more accessible than many of the local governments that are supposed to be "closer to the people."

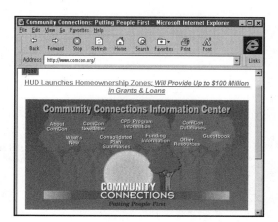

FIGURE 3-3

The CDBG site shows how government can use the Net to distribute information to those who use federal programs.

WELFARE REFORM

The federal debate over welfare reform has tied up Washington and the country for nearly a decade. It has been difficult even for advocates in this area to sort out which proposals make the most sense in helping welfare recipients achieve self-sufficiency.

Some of the most useful information in this area, however, is being generated by the welfare reform programs now being undertaken in each state under the Family Assistance Act. There are a wide range of experiments here, involving workfare, family planning, and new approaches to education and training. Thus, even as President Clinton and the Congress locked horns over what should happen under federal reform, the states were creating their own models—with the Clinton administration's approval. These programs are likely to remain intact no matter what national policy is ultimately put into place.

So where can you get this information?

The answer is the Health and Human Services Web site (*http://www.acf.dhhs.gov/ACFNews/press/index.html*) (Figure 3-4), which provides a full menu of press releases issued in conjunction with each state program the Clinton administration has approved.

The press provides only scant coverage of these various plans— usually in conjunction with stories about the broader welfare reform debate. But now any activist who wants to sort out his or her own position in this area can find more than enough background material within a matter of minutes.

FIGURE 3-4
The HHS Web site servs up press releases the contents of which may otherwise never make to the public in print.

CLOSING THE POWER GAP

I offer these three programs—Goals 2000, the Community Development Block Grant, and welfare reform—only as examples. Detailed descriptions about virtually every program the federal government sponsors is now available online. State and local governments are rapidly joining the Web site parade as well.

Again—this kind of information is power. That's why corporations and large-scale organizations pay such a high price to retrieve it. Knowing how government does operate is essential if you're going to develop serious proposals on how government *should* operate. Up to now, gaining access to material of this kind has been a time-consuming process, available only to organizations with the resources to devote to it.

Now any activist—anywhere—can do it. Just go online and find what you need on the World Wide Web.

MONITORING ELECTED OFFICIALS

The same principle applies to the legislative side of government. Up to now, keeping track of your own elected representatives has required considerable effort. Do you know how they vote? Do you know who influences them? These are the most important questions an activist can ask, but it's not easy to get answers.

Some of this information does appear in the press, but not enough. Even if the newspapers do report on how area Congresspeople vote on specific bills, they rarely monitor legislative behavior over time. They'll allude to pressure from "special interests" around an issue without identifying which ones are involved. Despite widespread concern about the role of money in politics, only occasionally do we read stories analyzing campaign finance reports, even though these are available to the public. Generalities about politics abound, but rarely do we get the details.

At this point, however, a number of services on the Internet have emerged to fill the gap. Between them, you can find out how your representatives voted on recent bills, their ratings from major interest groups, and even the major contributors to their last campaign. The information appears on different Web sites, but you can save them in a single file in your Web browser's bookmarks for quick access. (More on bookmarks later.)

Consider one of my own senators, Arlen Specter from Pennsylvania. As an erstwhile liberal Republican who started his career as a Democrat, Senator Specter is an especially elusive politician, made all the more so by the increased conservatism of his current party. You may recall that he launched a brief Presidential campaign in 1994 to rally "moderate" Republicans, who simply didn't respond.

So where does he really stand? Who supports him? Who opposes him? We can find answers to these questions on the World Wide Web.

As a starting point, a site maintained by Time Warner used to list recent votes, such as these cast by Senator Specter during the last two months of 1995:

```
Senator Arlen Spector Votes: Nov.-Dec., 1995

▪ S19950098 (BALANCED-BUDGET AMENDMENT — Passage)

▪ S19950178 (FISCAL 1996 BUDGET RESOLUTION —
Gramm Tax Cuts)

▪ S19950416 (Welfare-Overhaul-Family-Cap)

▪ S19950419 (WELFARE OVERHAUL - Out of Wedlock Births.)

BILL WHO VOTE

Balanced-Budget-Senate Sen. Specter (R) Yes

 Fiscal-Budget-Gramm Sen. Specter (R) No

 Fiscal-Budget-Adopt Sen. Specter (R) Yes

 welfare family Sen. Specter (R) Yes
```

wedlock births Sen. Specter (R) No

Voting Records Provided By Congressional Quarterly Inc.

Copyright 1995, Time Inc.

Currently, we can turn to Project VoteSmart—an independent, non-profit organization on the Internet—that keeps track of organizational ratings applied to Senators and Congresspeople. Here's how Specter appears:

From Project VoteSmart

Senator Arlen Specter Performance Evaluations by Special Interest Groups *(excerpted)*

How to Interpret These Evaluations

These evaluations are in percentage form. They represent the percentage of time that the incumbent voted with that organization's preferred positions on a number of votes that they identified as key in their issue area. Remember, by definition, these ratings by special interest groups are biased. They do not represent a non-partisan stance...

A final note: The clearest way to read these percentages is, "In [year], the XYZ organization gave Senator/Representative X an 80% rating. That means that on votes they identified as key in their issue area during that time period, he/she voted with the group's preferred position 80% of the time."

Performance Evaluations by Special Interest Groups *(excerpted)*

Issue Area Year Percentage Evaluating Organization

Abortion 1993 0 National Right to Life Committee

Abortion 1994 100 National Abortion Reproductive Rights Action

Business 1994 60 U.S. Chamber of Commerce

Children 1994 67 Children's Defense Fund

Chr.Fam. Issues 1993-1994 50 Christian Coalition

Civil Rts/Lib 1993-1994 50 National Association for the Advancement of Colored People

Civil Rts/Lib 1993-1994 56 American Civil Liberties Union

Conservative 1994 46 American Conservative Union

Consumers 1994 58 Consumer Federation of America

Defense/Foreign 1993-1994 100 American Security Council

Education 1993 68 National Education Association

Environment 1994 54 League of Conservation Voters

Farm 1993-1994 67 American Farm Bureau Federation

Gun Issues 1993-1994 50 National Rifle Association

Labor 1994 38 AFL-CIO

Liberal 1993-1994 47 Public Citizen's Congress Watch

Liberal 1994 55 Americans for Democratic Action

Libertarian 1994 21 The Libertarian Party - Combined Score

Seniors 1994 40 National Council of Senior Citizens

Taxes/Spending 1994 88 Concord Coalition

Veterans 1989-1990 50 Vietnam Veterans of America

Women 1989-1990 86 National Women's Political Caucus

This information is brought to you by Project Vote Smart

If this is more information than you need, VoteSmart also offers a sampling of votes on specific issues. On Goals 2000, for example, Arlen Specter voted yes when it came before the Senate in 1994:

Senator Arlen Specter
Pennsylvania — Republican
Voting Record Sampler
Issue: Education

Goals 2000: Educate America Act

HR 1804:

Vote on the conference report (final passage) of the bill to establish 8 goals for education; establish

voluntary national standards; establish voluntary
opportunity to learn standards; and provide $400
million in aid to schools, among other provisions. The
conference report was adopted 63-22 on March 25, 1994

Senator Arlen Specter Voted YES

This information was still available months later, as an ongoing resource for people and groups concerned about education. VoteSmart
provides sample votes like these on a wide range of issues, covering
all aspects of government and politics.

Even more interesting, however, is a Gopher called Follow the
Money set up by C-Span during the 1994 Congressional campaign to
provide easy access to information about contributions. Since Senator Specter was not a candidate in 1994, his PAC contributions
weren't listed. His colleague in the Senate, however, Richard Santorum, did run in 1994, defeating Harris Wofford in the process.

When I first discovered Follow the Money, I browsed through the
Senator's report. It was predictable, with $500 to $5,000 donations
from various corporate PACs. What stood out, however, were two
clusters of contributions from groups associated with the National
Rifle Association. These were so startling that I even consolidated
them into a little report of my own:

Senator Rick Santorum NRA Contributions

Senate Campaign, 1994 NRA POLITICAL VICTORY FUND NRA
POLITICAL VICTORY FUND NRA POLITICAL VICTORY FUND NRA
POLITICAL VICTORY FUND

10/11/1993	1,000
02/10/1994	3,850
07/20/1994	2,000
09/29/1994	-100
FOR 10/28/1994	1,000
FOR 10/28/1994	48,788
FOR 10/28/1994	6,465
FOR 10/28/1994	13,505
FOR 10/31/1994	6,458
FOR 11/10/1994	2,000
FOR 11/10/1994	1,824
FOR 11/17/1994	403

NRA INSTITUTE FOR LEGISLATION NRA INSTITUTE FOR
LEGISLATION NRA INSTITUTE FOR LEGISLATION NRA
INSTITUTE FOR LEGISLATION

FOR 05/03/1994	44,617
FOR 08/20/1994	20,699
FOR 10/29/1994	74,657
FOR 11/02/1994	1,428
TOTAL	$228,595

None of this came out during the campaign. Perhaps it would not have mattered. There's a sizable NRA membership in Pennsylvania, whose influence in the state over the years is legendary.

Yet when a Senator receives more than $225,000 in cash and in-kind donations from a single organization, the broader public ought to at least know about it. Unfortunately, the press rarely pays attention, unless the source is suspect. Even candidates don't often attack one another at this level, for fear of inciting their own contributors to retaliate. The result is that most of us simply don't know, even if we're deeply concerned about the role of money in the political process. Under the circumstances, the entire system is suspect.

As services like Follow the Money start operating *during* campaigns, however, then watchdog groups and concerned citizens can examine specific contributions for themselves and draw their own conclusions, and the press will likely pay closer attention as well.

Thus, at this point, just two services—VoteSmart, and Follow the Money—are already assembling more hard data about elected officials in one place than has ever been available in the past. Information that used to be the exclusive province of high-paid political consultants is now there for the rest of us. We simply have to learn how to find it.

TRACKING ISSUES

Beyond providing quick access to information about government programs and elected officials, the Internet also provides a unique opportunity to track ongoing political issues. As wire services and newspapers develop online editions, it becomes possible to retrieve stories both before and after they first appear in print. For those who enjoy following a story over time, this is a useful innovation in itself.

For activists, even more significant resources are available. No longer do we have to depend on the daily press to keep abreast of issues that matter to us. We can go straight to the source. Here is how you might proceed:

Identifying an issue

Here is where monitoring the Web sites maintained by various organizations becomes especially important. Most of us don't raise issues, we hear about them from groups that we support. People on the Religious Right no longer have to subscribe to the *Christian American* to learn what it says. They can simply access the journal online. That is how many of them might have learned first about Goals 2000. In fact, this is the way most activists will be receiving alerts about political issues in the future.

Retrieving background material

This used to require combing through obscure policy journals that aren't even found in most libraries. Now, however, Internet search engines make it possible to locate dozens of articles within a matter of seconds. All you do is enter a topic onto an online form. A good example is Digital's Alta Vista, which accesses hundreds of Usenet groups and the entire World Wide Web.

Instructing Alta Vista to search on Goals 2000 in December 1995 retrieved the following:

```
[ALTA VISTA] ] [Help with Query] ] [Advanced Search]

Search the Web or the News Groups

Display results Compact or Detailed [Submit] Documents
1 through 10 of about 50000 matching the query, best
matches first.

No Title

Goals 2000: Educate America TITLE V—NATIONAL SKILL
STANDARDS BOARD SEC. 501. SHORT TITLE. This title may
be cited as the "National Skill Standards Act of
1994". SEC. 502. PURPOSE. It is the purpose of this
title to establish a National Skill Standards...
```

http://www.ttrc.doleta.gov/database/flat-files/S2W/ SKILLSTDBOARD.html

```
No Title

Goals 2000: Educate America TITLE II—NATIONAL
EDUCATION REFORM LEADERSHIP, STANDARDS, AND
ASSESSMENTS PART B—NATIONAL EDUCATION STANDARDS AND
IMPROVEMENT COUNCIL SEC. 211. PURPOSE.
```

It is the purpose of this part to establish a mechanism to—(1) certify...

http://www.ttrc.doleta.gov/database/flat-files/S2W/ IMPROVEMENTCOUNCIL.html

Goals 2000 Legislation and Related Items

Goals 2000 Legislation and Related Items. The Department maintains on-line a growing collection of information about the historic Goals 2000: Educate America Act. This page has pointers to various documents contained on our servers.

http://hkein.ie.cuhk.hk/Overseas/WWWEDGOV/legislation/ GOALS2000/index.html

Goals 2000

Goals 2000. Goals 2000 Harbors Project. GOALS 2000: EDUCATE AMERICA ACT.
http://www.ed.gov/legislation/GOALS2000/

OVERVIEW

The Goals 2000: Educate America Act provides resources to states and communities to develop and implement comprehensive education...

http://kalama.doe.hawaii.edu/hern95/pt031/ goals2000.html -

Louisiana Goals 2000 / LaNIE

Current Reform Activities. Source: Southwest Educational Development Laboratory (SEDL) What are some highlights of education reform? Louisiana passed an omnibus education reform about bill five years ago. "The Children First" legislation, is a...

http://jhanley.doe.state.la.us/G2K&LANIE/ Reform_LA.html -

No Title

Goals 2000: Educate America Act by Erika F. King Note: This file contains the text of an article which appeared in School Law Bulletin, v. XXV, no. 4, Fall 1994, 15-27. Delineation within the text indicating titles and headings are preserved.

http://ncinfo.iog.unc.edu/gopher/pubs/school_law/ articles/

Goals 2000

GOALS 2000 SOCIAL ENGINEERS TARGET SCHOOLS.
School-Based Social Programs Undermine Parents By
Kimberly Parker. Education policy has shifted
dramatically in the last two decades. Debate continues
as the education elite presses schools to assume a
greater...

http://136.177.19.122/slw/politic/g2000.html

Copyright © 1995 Digital Equipment Corporation. All
rights reserved.

These were only seven of the first ten of *50,000* possible "hits." Between them, they included sections of the legislation, a link to the Department of Education, reports on Goals 2000 projects in Hawaii and Louisiana, a law school journal article reviewing the program, and the article in the *Christian American* attacking it. And there was plenty more where that came from.

Tracking the issue in Congress

Here, you can use Thomas to search the *Congressional Record*. As an example, a search on Goals 2000 in December, 1995, turned up 100 responses, led off by this list:

1. CLINTON BUDGET COSTS AMERICAN CHILDREN (House of
Representatives - December 06, 1995)

2. A CALL TO REPEAL GOALS 2000 — H.J.R. 353 (Extension
of Remarks - August 04, 1995)

3. GOALS 2000 (Senate - October 11, 1995)

4. AMENDING GOALS 2000 — HON. WILLIAM F. GOODLING
(Extension of Remarks - February 24, 1995)

5. ELIMINATING NATIONAL EDUCATION STANDARDS AND
IMPROVEMENT COUNCIL FROM THE GOALS 2000: EDUCATE
AMERICA ACT (House - May 15, 1995)

6. AMERICANS SEE THROUGH SCARE TACTICS (House of
Representatives - December 19, 1995)

7. KEEP EDUCATION IN THE BUDGET (House - May 09, 1995)

8. EDUCATION IS A PRIORITY (Senate - October 23, 1995)

9. ON EDUCATION (House of Representatives - December
12, 1995)

10. SECRETARY OF EDUCATION DICK RILEY'S STATE OF
EDUCATION ADDRESS (Senate - February 01, 1995)

11. STATE OF EMERGENCY IN GOVERNMENT (House of
Representatives - June 20, 1995)

12. THE IMPACT OF THE CUTS IN EDUCATION (House of
Representatives - November 29, 1995)

Now you can read what Congressmen and women actually said
about Goals 2000, instead of relying on other peoples' characteriza-
tion of their positions.

Learning when to take action

Activists don't merely analyze—we act. The biggest problem, however, is determining when action is necessary. When do we need to
make sure that our representatives know what we think?

Of course, Internet mailing lists are a good vehicle for sharing this
information, as we have seen. So are Web sites.

Here's what an organization called the Family Research Council
posted to its Web site in relation to Goals 2000 at the height of the
1995 battle over the budget:

CALL LEADERS NOW ON GOALS 2000!

A Few Of HIS Favorite Things...

How's this for an expensive wish list: President Bill
Clinton wants Congress to give him a budget with $7
billion more in education spending, including $750
million for Goals 2000 (funded at $360 million last
year)....

Goals 2000 is not a lot of money in Washington, D.C.
terms, but it gives the federal government a new
measure of power in education. Under this law, the
federal government has the unprecedented authority to
review state curricular standards and assessments. In
addition, Goals 2000 is highly symbolic politically.
If it stays in the budget, then the Clinton agenda to
restructure education is alive and well. On the other
hand, zeroing out funding for Goals 2000 would be a
jump-start toward shutting down the U.S. Education
Department.

A central theme of the balanced budget movement is
that programs the U.S. government has no business
running should not be funded. Goals 2000 ought to be
the first to go....A decision on Goals 2000 spending

> could be made next week at the budget negotiating
> table between Clinton and congressional leaders.
>
> ACTION: Congressional leaders need to know that just
> because Goals 2000 is among Clinton's favorite things
> doesn't mean it's acceptable to you. Contact the
> leadership in both houses (listed below) immediately.
> Tell them you do not want the budget agreement to
> contain funding for Goals 2000. Urge them to support
> the original House position that did not fund Goals
> 2000. Remind these leaders of the significance of Goals
> 2000.

The alert went on to list the phone numbers of the White House switchboard and the entire Congressional leadership, to make it easy for supporters to barrage them with calls. December 1995 was a busy month in Washington, D.C., as you may recall.

What I was able to do in relation to Goals 2000 you can apply to any issue of concern, even those that don't end up making headlines. You can use a search engine like Alta Vista for background information, the *Congressional Record* for legislative history and debate, and a congenial Web site for updates on where it stands in the decision-making process. Nor does it take much time. I retrieved the material on Goals 2000 for this section in less than an hour. Without the Internet, it would have taken days—assuming I could have done it at all.

ACTIVIST BOOKMARKS

The sheer volume of information available through the Internet makes it important to develop an organized system to access it. Web sites usually have complex addresses that are impossible to remember. Much of what we need from a site is often buried behind layers of other links, rather than being displayed prominently on the home page. To undertake a fresh search every time we want to connect to the same site makes no sense. We need to simplify the process.

This is where the "Bookmarks" or "Favorite Places" function on most Web browsers becomes essential. Be sure to find the "Bookmarks" button on the menu quickly, since it will be one of your most important tools. You can use it to store the addresses of entire Web sites you want to revisit, or even specific Web pages within larger sites that you want to use. Especially useful is its ability to store addresses of individual Web pages, without having to navigate entire sites to reach them.

Let's say, for example, that you want to send email to your Congressperson on a regular basis. The House of Representatives home page lists Congressional email addresses, but you don't want to wade through the entire Congress every time you need just one address.

It's not necessary. Each Congressperson has his or her own Web page. Once you reach it, you can use "Bookmarks" on your Web browser to store the address for future reference. When you need it, again, you merely click on the address in the bookmark to get to your Congressperson. Organizing your bookmarks to reach Web pages you use most is an important part of using the Internet to best advantage. In fact, putting together your own bookmark list is as important as figuring out which email lists you ought to join. By assembling a group of the sites you regularly use, you can expedite your day-to-day work on the Internet considerably.

What should an activist's bookmark list include? Here are a few essential items:

- **An anchor site or sites** These are sites whose purpose is to facilitate access to a wide range of Web pages relevant to a specific area of concern The Digital Democrat and GOP Online Web pages are good examples. Created by independent groups, they provide links to national party organizations, party caucuses in Congress, and local party groups throughout the country. In fact, these two sites alone lead to every virtually every other site on the Internet associated with one of the two major parties.

- **Your own representatives** Keeping these names and addresses near the top of the bookmark list reminds you that while talking to other activists is fine, these people are the ones who *need* to hear from you. If they have email addresses, you can send mail to them directly from their Web pages.

- **Daily news site** Pick out one or two of the online news services or online papers with stories of greatest relevance to you and include them here. You'll soon be checking these services in much the same way as you now read the newspaper.

- **Government agencies** Here you include those government agencies most relevant to your own concerns—HUD for housing activists, the Department of Labor for union members, Health and Human Services for people interested in the poor, etc. Internet directories like Yahoo have to list every agency, usually in alphabetical order. You need not be so comprehensive.

- **Presidential press releases and statements** The White House Web site lists Presidential statements by topic—the economy, fiscal policy, crime, etc. You can access these pages directly, without going through the entire online White House tour. Simply access the release topics of greatest interest to you directly.

- **Thomas search engine** Thomas accesses various Congressional Web pages, but the search form to locate specific bills and testimony in the *Congressional Record* is the most useful. It's an obvious must for an activist bookmark list.

- **Public policy sites** While anchor sites often link to public policy groups, think-tanks, and online journals relevant to their concerns, you may want to reach your own favorites directly. This is especially useful if they update their sites regularly with analyses of current events.

- **Internet search engine** As noted earlier, a search engine like Alpha Vista is crucial when you need to access a wide range of information relevant to a specific issue.

An activist bookmark list with links to sites under each of these categories will serve you well. Otherwise, you'll be spending most of your time looking *for* Web pages, instead of looking at them.

The point should be clear: using the Internet, you usually can find out whatever you need to know about a government program, politician, or issue whenever you need to know it. No other information system even comes close to providing this level of support. In fact, the challenge now is not merely retrieving information through the World Wide Web, but learning how to use it in ways that strengthen advocacy online and political action within our communities.

Chapter 4 Advocacy

On February 10, 1996—a Saturday morning—I logged onto the Internet, only to be greeted by a home page from Netscape draped in black. I already knew what the black background represented. Only two days earlier, President Clinton had signed into law the Telecommunications Reform Act of 1995. To those who work to build universal access to the Internet, there was one overriding issue here—the Bill of Rights. Government regulation of what people say to one another—even young people—infringed upon freedom of speech, pure and simple.

▶ Cyberspace Protest

▶ Advocacy and Action

▶ The Christian Coalition

▶ EnviroLink

▶ Children's Defense Fund

▶ Campaigning Via Email

▶ From Advocacy to Empowerment

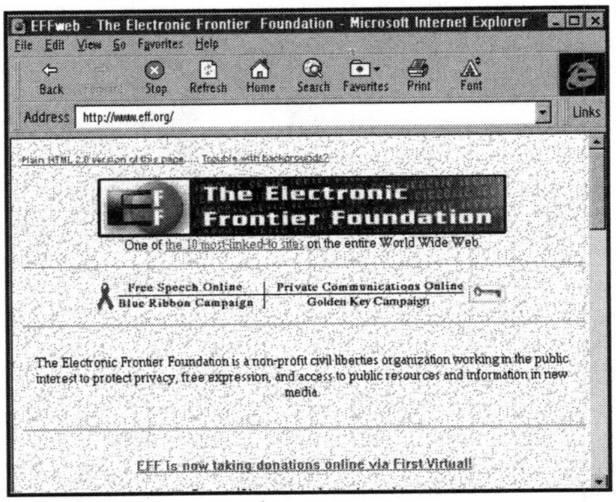

FIGURE 4-1
The Electronic Freedom Foundation has walked point for online civil liberties

CYBERSPACE PROTEST

That managers of online services would be held accountable for what their subscribers did compounded the problem. The only way to insure compliance would involve monitoring chats and exchanges in a way that would turn every conversation into a public forum, equivalent to an operators' eavesdropping on random telephone conversations. As a protest, organizations like the Electronic Frontier Foundation (Figure 4-1) that have led the fight for civil liberties on the Net asked all those who objected to the "Decency" provisions to drape their Web pages in black for forty-eight hours.

CONTACT

Electronic Frontier Foundation
http://www.eff.org/

Text of the CDA

"(d) Whoever —
   "(1) in interstate or foreign communications knowingly -
   "(A) uses an interactive computer service to send to a specific person or persons under 18 years of age, or
   "(B) uses any interactive computer service to display in a manner available to a person under 18 years of age, any comment, request suggestion, proposal, image, or other communication that, in context, depicts or describes, in terms patently offensive as measured by contemporary community standards, sexual or excretory activities or organs, regardless of whether the user of such service placed the call or initiated the communication; or
   "(2) knowingly permits any telecommunications facility under such person's control to be used for an activity prohibited by paragraph (1) with the intent that it be used for such activity, shall be fined under title 18, United States Code, or imprisoned not more than two years, or both."

That Netscape was among those that responded was of enormous significance. Studies indicate that 70 percent of all people accessing the Internet in the United States use the Netscape browser. While most of these people do not access the company's home page automatically, a sizable portion of them do. Thousands of people would be exposed to the message over a four or five day period.

Moreover, Netscape went beyond simply displaying the black background. Those who clicked on "black," to find out "why pages all over the Internet have gone black" reached the Yahoo search page.

Yahoo was among the first comprehensive directories of Web sites and remains an important resource in this area. Again, thousands of people use it every day. Now they were being offered not only information on the Coalition to Stop Net Censorship, but access to "instructions on how you can participate" in the campaign:

```
WHAT YOU CAN DO NOW

1. For 48 hours after Clinton signs the net censorship
language in the Telecomm bill into law, TURN YOUR
WORLD WIDE WEB PAGES BLACK with white lettering. To
know when the bill is signed, check these sources:

Newsgroups: alt.society.civil-disob
 Email:vtw-announce@vtw.org (watch for mail on this
list)
 WWW:http://www.vtw.org/
 Finger:vtw@panix.com

To explain to people who may be confused by the color
change, temporarily add the following link to your
page:

<a href="http://www.vtw.org/speech/">My World Wide Web
Pages are black for 48 hours to protest second-class
treatment from the US Government for free speech. Read
about it at this WWW page.</a>....
```

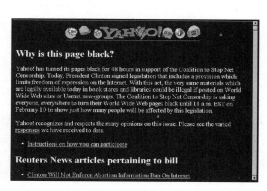

FIGURE 4-2
Yahoo's CDA protest page

Please try and wait though until Clinton signs the bill, for maximum effect....

Also, urge your Internet Provider and any Internet WWW pages you frequent to turn their pages black. Send us interesting sites that comply to *vtw@vtw.org*....

2. Don't forget to send Clinton a message, contact him at:

Email:*president@whitehouse.gov*
 Telephone:202-456-1111
 Fax:202-456-2461

Sample communiqué:

You're about to sign a bill into law that imposes a terrible set of speech restrictions on the Internet that belong in the broadcast medium, not the interactive one.

I'm turning my World Wide Web pages BLACK for 48 hours after you sign the bill as a symbol of protest to show how many people will be affected by this bill....

3. Make a commitment become involved! There will be several court cases coming up to challenge the Internet censorship legislation, as well as an election that will put every single member of the House, and 1/3rd of the Senate (most of whom voted for this legislation) onto the ballot.

Don't let them get away with this. Make this a campaign issue, and keep an eye out for legal defense funds for those challenging these laws in court."

The coalition was now using all the systems of the Internet—the Web, email, and newsgroups—not simply to facilitate communication or to provide information, but to mobilize people to take political action. Using other links provided on the page, you could locate a list of organizations ranging from the Libertarian Party to People for the American Way to the Gay and Lesbian Task Force that were supporting the campaign, another list of more than 300 Web sites that were participating in the online protest, and even a page that permitted you to enter personal reactions

I did my part. I converted the Institute for the Study of Civic Values Web site to black, with links to sites offering instructions on how to participate further. The other Web site we manage, Neighborhoods Online, went black as well. I posted a notice supporting the campaign to the three email lists that I manage—civic-values, penn-neighbor, and neighbors-online. I emailed a note to Senator Arlen Specter urging him to support efforts to repeal the offensive provisions of the Telecommunications Act. The whole process took less than an hour. It cost nothing more than the online connection charges. Yet even these limited efforts reached hundreds of community activists all over the country, along with one of my own representatives in Washington.

Around the same time, Rick Smolen and a team of writers and editors were receiving enormous attention for an online journal called *24 hours in cyberspace*, showing how people all over the world had started to use the Internet to connect with one another. Ironically, the 48-hour blackout protest against Net censorship was simultaneously demonstrating how people all over the country were starting to use the Internet to organize protests against Washington.

ADVOCACY AND ACTION

Advocacy aims at action. We argue. We disseminate information. The goal, however, is to persuade people to act together on behalf of a cause. We start to succeed when people join us. To build support, then, advocates have to include in whatever they convey to the public a coherent plan of action.

At this time, not only groups like the Electronic Frontier Foundation with a mission related to the Internet but other organizations as well are learning how to use the Internet for political advocacy. Nor is this opportunity open only to well-financed groups representing the middle and upper middle class, although these are certainly represented here. Most impressive, however, are the online advocates who are emerging from different parts of the country, representing a wide range of political perspectives.

The systems we have examined operating through the Internet make it considerably easier for *any* movement to broadcast its overall program and goals, publicize where elected officials stand, advise supporters on strategy and tactics, and build solidarity among all participants in the efforts.

As is always the case, some groups are using the Internet for advocacy more effectively than others by keeping in mind what any successful campaign requires. I offer three examples here—the Christian Coalition, EnviroLink, and the Children's' Defense Fund. The ideologies are different, but their use of the Internet is quite similar.

Elements of an action plan

- **A mission statement** that outlines the basic philosophy and ultimate goal and how it relates to broad purposes of the country
- **A direct appeal to groups** in whose name the campaign is being fought
- **A set of laws or administrative actions** that a governmental body must take to move toward the goal
- **A scorecard** indicating where public officials stand on the issue
- **Specific action** that citizens and organizations need to take to persuade officials to support the goal
- **A rough timetable** that spells out how long the campaign is likely take
- **A reporting system** to let supporters know how the campaign is going
- **A communications system** to permit campaign leaders, organizers, and participants to remain in touch with one another

THE CHRISTIAN COALITION

Though based in Washington, the Christian Coalition demonstrates how a group of political outsiders can use technology to propel themselves in a formidable position in American politics. However we may view the Coalition's philosophy and program, its organizing prowess is beyond dispute. From its founding in 1989 as a brainchild of TV evangelist Pat Robertson, it has built a national following of 1.7 million members with more than 1,700 chapters in all 50 states.[1] The Coalition was already a major force in the Republican Party during the 1992 campaign, with effective control of a number of state delegations to the national convention. In the 1994 Congressional elections, it distributed more than 30 million "nonpartisan voting guides" listing candidate views on taxes, a balanced budget amendment, crime, term limits, abortion and education,[2] to supporters throughout the country.

[1] Dan Balz and Ronald Brownstein, "Ralph Reed's Christian Soldiers," *The Washington Post Magazine,* January 28, 1996, p. P. 11.

[2] Ralph Reed, *Politically Incorrect* (Dallas: Word Publishing, 1994) p. 200.

Analysis of Congressional races in states like Washington, Ohio, and North Carolina showed that the Coalition played a critical role in defeating Democratic incumbents in a number of districts. By 1996, it was simply assumed that the Christian Coalition would control as many as one-third of the delegates to the Republican National Convention later in the year. Not bad for an organization that was less than 10 years old.

The man largely responsible for this success—Ralph Reed—makes it clear that new communications technologies have played a strong role in the process. "Indeed," he observes in *Politically Incorrect,* "people of faith are enthusiastically embracing the emerging technologies of computers and interactive television that will make up the information superhighway of the future."

As an example, Reed describes how the Coalition was able to defeat a provision of the Elementary and Secondary Education Act that would have required state certification for every teacher in the country, thus placing thousands of private school instructors at risk. Texas Congressman Richard Armey introduced an amendment to strike this provision and alerted various conservative organizations to what was happening. In response, the Coalition used a nationwide fax network—in Reed's words—"blitzing grassroots activists with action alerts and lighting up telephone trees nationwide." Ultimately, the Armey amendment passed by a vote of 424-1. "A combination of legislative savvy, voter anger, and technologies like fax machines, microcomputers, and talk radio," Reed concludes, "is making it possible for the average person to affect government as never before.[3]

Today, the Christian Coalition has added a Web site to its arsenal that in itself includes everything its supporters need for grassroots organizing (Figure 4-3).

If a Coalition member wants to clarify the organization's mission, the Speeches and Position Papers page provides speeches by Coalition leaders that outline their basic philosophy and concerns. The Web site also lists the specific bills of greatest importance to the Coalition, during any given period. The *Christian American*, in turn, features various articles on the strategy and tactics needed to build support throughout the country. There's a page listing places and dates for Coalition seminars on organizing and advocacy taking place around the country, with a phone number to call to sign up. All of the essential ingredients are there.

[3] Ibid., pp. 157-159.

FIGURE 4-3

Conservative groups like the Christian Coalition quickly saw the potential and set up Web sites

CONTACT

Christian Coalition
http://www.cc.org/

Especially effective is the Coalition's Congressional scorecard (Figure 4-4), which lays out where every member of Congress stands on its major issues of concern.[4]

Scorecards like this serve a number of purposes:

- First, they acquaint their members and voters generally with the specific issues the organization believes to be important.
- Second, they help supporters identify allies and adversaries.
- Third, they make clear to elected officials that their votes on key bills will be given as much publicity as the organization can afford.

The Christian Coalition has figured out how to use the Internet to significantly extend its outreach in this area.

Here is what can happen now when a Republican moderate like Senator Arlen Specter holds a town meeting in a conservative area of Pennsylvania. If only one member of the Christian Coalition has

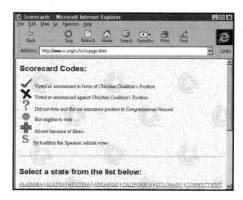

FIGURE 4-4

The Christian Coalition Congressional Score Card

[4] This feature of the Christian Coalition's organization has recently been challenged by the Federal Election Commission as a violation of their non-profit tax status. Non-profits are not supposed to publicly support or oppose individual political candidates. Does a scorecard indicate support or opposition? As the book goes to press, no one knows the outcome of the challenge.

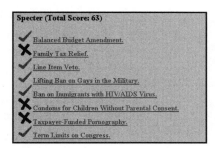

FIGURE 4-5

*Senator Spector gets graded
by the Christain Coalition*

access to the Internet, he or she can retrieve the scorecard shown in Figure 4-5 from the Coalition's Web site and distribute copies to every member of the group.

While the Senator's overall score of 63 is respectable, even the way in which the Coalition characterizes the issues where he voted "wrong"—"family tax relief," "condoms for children without parental consent," and "taxpayer-funded pornography"—would cause him great difficulty at such a meeting. Of course, the Web site does offer an explanation of each vote.

"Family tax relief" refers to a budget amendment introduced by Senator Phil Gramm that would have provided a tax credit of $500 per child and eliminated the marriage penalty in the tax code. It failed by a vote of 69 to 31, but the Christian Coalition supported it.

"Condoms for children without parental consent" refers to an amendment by Jesse Helms that would have prohibited the use of federal funds for the distribution of condoms and other contraceptive devices without the written consent of the parents. This one failed by a vote of 59-34.

"Taxpayer-funded pornography" refers to another Jesse Helms amendment that would have required the National Endowment for the Arts to give grants only to non-profit organizations—not individuals—so as to (in the Coalition's words) "reduce the NEA's ability to continue funding pornographic 'art' projects." The Coalition supported this amendment; this one was rejected by a vote of 65-30.

The scorecard itself does not provide this detail, of course, so Senator Spector would be forced to volunteer these explanations himself, in response to questions like, "How could you possibly support taxpayer-funded pornography?" Candidates for public office aren't the only ones capable of negative advertising.

The Christian Coalition's scorecard makes a basic point about the Coalition's Web site and others like it. The aim is not primarily to "advertise" to neutral observers, but to supply ammunition that supporters can use as advocates within their own communities. These are electronic brochures, equivalent to the printed material the Coalition distributes through the mail. The difference is that the Internet is cheaper, it can be updated regularly, and it can be accessed at any time. This makes it a far more flexible and potent tool than anything available in print. As the Net becomes widely accessible, it will be Web sites and email networks "blitzing grassroots activists with alerts," just as fax machines and telephone trees are being used by the Christian Coalition today.

Moreover, the Coalition itself uses the Internet not merely to inform their followers and others about issues and legislation, but to offer hard-nosed training in organizing and political action. They devote an entire section of their Web site to publicizing seminars in grassroots organizing like these, which took place around the country in 1995:

```
Citizen Action Seminar

Church Liaisons & Civic Concerns Ministries

        What the Church Liaison Does

        Starting a Civic Concerns Ministry as a
        Church Liaison

        Voter Registration Drives

        Petition Drives

        Chapter Support and Finding Volunteers

        Neighborhood Coordinators

        What is a Neighborhood Coordinator?

        How You Can Become a Neighborhood Coordinator

        Winning with the Neighborhood Organization

        The Responsibilities of Neighborhood Coordinators

        Voter Identification

        Voter Identification and its Importance

        Following the Lincoln Plan

        Helpful Hints for Phone Volunteers

        Registering Voters

        Christian Coalition Voter Identification Script

        All Politics is Local

                Knowing Your Political Environment
```

Politics

The Federal Government

State Government

Local Government

What and Who Do You Know?

Issues

The Age of Information

Basic Lobbying

Much Ado About Something

Become Part of a Team

Contacting Elected Officials

Calling Your Elected Officials

Writing Your Elected Officials

Meeting With Your Elected Officials

The Power of Numbers

How Bills Become Law

Federal Process

Statewide Process

Local Process

Those who might be wondering how a so-called "fringe" group like the Christian Coalition could build so strong a political base in so short a period of time would do well to examine the curriculum of this seminar. The Coalition conducted about ten of these workshops every month, in communities all over the country. No doubt thousands of people participated in them. The results speak for themselves.

In short, what we find here is a superb use of the World Wide Web to put the basic principles of political advocacy into practice. Those who access the site learn first-hand the Coalition's basic mission and the issues it takes most seriously. Supporters can use its legislative scorecards to evaluate their own representatives in Congress. Activists can sign up for a grassroots seminar in community organizing. During the 1996 Presidential primaries, you could even download the Coalition's Voters' Guide from the site. Advocacy doesn't get any better than this.

ENVIROLINK

Some may argue that while the Christian Coalition has brought new people into the political process, it is hardly a mom-and-pop operation. Pat Robertson spent years promoting his syndicated television series and satellite broadcast network before entering politics. Ralph Reed inherited both this media infrastructure and its army of volunteers in putting the Christian Coalition together. He may deserve credit for having built a potent grassroots lobby from this foundation, but he had considerable resources at his disposal, far beyond what most organizations are in a position to raise. Is this what using the Internet for advocacy requires?

Hardly.

A good example is EnviroLink—a Web site devoted to environmental issues. Its home page (Figure 4-6) is rather unassuming.

As you move to the Environmental Library, however, you begin to realize how comprehensive the overall site really is: Among its most impressive features, moreover, is a menu with the clear mission of promoting environmental activism:

```
Environmental Activism:

What You Can Do to Protect the Planet

This is a listing of resources and information that
may be of use to activists. We have broken the
information down into some of the major categories of
activism. The EnviroLink Network produces some of
these, but the majority are just gleaned from the
Internet. If you know of any resources that we should
include, please send us a note.

Since environmental issues are usually complicated,
EnviroLink devotes an entire menu to sites offering
background on each of them. Its list of topics, now
organized under the broad categories of earth, air,
```

CONTACT

Josh Knauer
Executive Director
The EnviroLink Network
http://www.envirolink.org

personal home page:
http://www.envirolink.org/
homepp/josh

FIGURE 4-6

EnviroLink provides a comprehensive gateway to environmental acitivism on the Net

fire, and water, covers the environmental waterfront, so to speak:

- Agriculture (sustainable and organic farming)
- Air Pollution
- Animal Rights Issues
- Biodiversity
- Bioregionalism (issues affecting specific bioregions)
- Corporate Accountability
- Dams, Dikes, Reservoirs, etc.
- Endangered Species
- Energy Issues (focus on alternatives)
- Fish Issues
- Forest Issues
- Green Design
- Hazardous Wastes and Toxics
- Human Rights
- Indigenous Peoples' Issues
- Light Pollution
- Mining Issues
- Nuclear Issues (energy source, proliferation, waste)
- Oceanic Issues
- Outdoor/Wilderness Recreation
- Ozone Issues
- Pesticide Issues
- Politics
- Population Issues
- Recycling
- Sustainable Communities
- Sustainable Development
- Transportation Issues (alternatives, etc.)
- Waste Issues

- Water Pollution

- Wildlife

- Wise Use Movement

How might a citizen group approach a menu like this?

Consider, as an example, the information accessed under "Hazardous Wastes and Toxics":

```
Agency for Toxic Substances and Disease Registry - US
Government COPA's PCB Info Remediation, Health
Effects, Superfund case studies, dioxin and more
Cumulative Index Risk: Health, Safety & Environment -
Quarterly Journal HazDat Database, the Agency for
Toxic Substances and Disease Registry's Hazardous
Substance Release/Health Effects Database
International Congress on Hazardous Waste National
Toxicology Program - US Government Pesticide
Information Service (PESTIS), a searchable database of
pesticide information PVC, la historia mas toxica
jamas contada, the toxic effects of PVC, in Spanish
only Right-to-Know Network (RTK-NET) ToxFAQ,
Frequently Asked Questions about toxic and hazardous
waste Toxic Chemical Profiles Verde Valley Toxic Pond
Toxic Mining Practices in Montana & Wyoming World Wide
Film Expeditions
```

A community organization with concerns about an area landfill, a trash incineration plant, or emissions from a nearby industrial park could use this menu to determine its rights under the law (Right-to-Know Network), federal policy surrounding hazardous waste (Agency for Toxic Substances and Disease Registry), and even profiles of specific toxic chemicals. In the past, many local groups concerned about these problems had to speak in general terms because they lacked the kind of detailed resource materials EnviroLink now makes instantly available.

The "Environmental Activism" page, in turn, offers information and advice on how to take direct action:

```
Action Alerts!
```

- The Environmental Action News, your resource for up-to-date environmental actions going on around the globe

- The 2 Minute Activist— Spend just 2 minutes every day to save the earth

- Starting from Scratch: How to Start and Maintain a Group

- A Campus Blueprint for the development of a "greener" campus environment

- Community Organizing

- Planning an Action

- Things to Think About

- All About Media

- Arrests

- Rainforest Action Groups

Types of Activism

- Direct Action

- All About FOIA (The Freedom of Information Act)

- Influencing the Government

- Track what bills are active in the US Congress on the Thomas Web Site

- Visit the U.S. House of Representatives

- Go to the U.S. Senate Gopher

- Project Vote Smart

- The League of Conservation Voters

- Letter Writing

- Lifestyle Changes- Things That You Can Do On A Personal Level

- Petitions

- The World Peace Petition

Legal Resources

- Federal, State and Local Laws On-Line

- I Just Got Arrested, Now What?

- Grand Juries

- Legal Defense/Support Organizations

This page accesses sites that would be useful to any activist, along with material of special interest to environmentalists. You can subscribe to an email list devoted to recycling from the site. You can get advice on how to lobby Congress and then get the addresses—email or otherwise—of your own Congressperson and Senators. You can read an Environmental Legislative Scorecard prepared by the League of Conservation Voters, a Washington-based group that keeps track of environmental legislation. In fact, EnviroLink provides menus with access to more than 350 environmental organizations and 25 federal agencies charged with regulatory responsibility in this area. For updates, you can search the archives of the Environmental News Service from the site. In fact, within a matter of minutes, you can find almost anything you need related to advancing an environmental issue or cause of concern to you.

Who, then, is responsible for all this? A major national group like the Sierra Club? The Environmental Protection Agency? A company like Waste Management, with a financial stake in cleaning up the environment?

None of the above.

As the home page explained, EnviroLink was started by a student:

> EnviroLink is the largest on-line environmental information resource on the planet, reaching well over 1.5 million people in over 130 countries every month. All services provided by EnviroLink are FREE to the user and are available 24 hours a day to anyone who wishes to use them.

> The EnviroLink Network was created in 1991 by Josh Knauer, while he was a freshman at Carnegie Mellon University. Since that time, EnviroLink has grown from a simple mailing list of 20 student activists to become one of the world's largest environmental information clearinghouses.

> At EnviroLink we're committed to promoting a sustainable society by connecting individuals and organizations through new communications technologies. We recognize that our technologies are just tools, and that the solutions to our ecological challenges lie within our communities and their connection to the Earth itself.

EnviroLink is still in Pittsburgh, where it began. It's still supported and maintained largely by volunteers. In the 1960s, students and community activists tried to show what they could accomplish through demonstrations and direct action on behalf of social change. Today, it's possible to pursue the same basic objectives through the Internet.

CHILDREN'S DEFENSE FUND

Among the most serious concerns surrounding the Internet is that of access on issues involving the poor. Given that online access requires expensive equipment and considerable skill, aren't we creating a new "information gap" between the haves and have nots that will exacerbate the wide inequality between rich and poor that already exists in America?

At a personal level, the risk is quite real, and how we extend access to telecommunications to everyone ought to be a major concern for our communities and society as a whole. I'll say more about this in the next chapter.

Yet at a political level, the Internet has the potential to help the poor. It's cheap. It's easy. It reaches millions of people. What other medium offers as much to groups without resources? It doesn't matter how rich or poor we may be—on the World Wide Web or an email list we are all the same. We will have to help low-income individuals go online, but their organizational advocates are being handed a powerful new weapon.

CONTACT
Children's Defense Fund
*http://www.tmn.com/cdf/
index.html*

One group that has already figured out how to use it is the Children's' Defense Fund, based in Washington, D.C. Founded in 1973 by Marian Wright Edelman, the Defense Fund has been among the few organizations since 1994 to gain public attention for its defense of poor children in the face of the Republican Congressional "revolution." Whether in response to welfare reform or threatened cuts in Medicaid or attacks against programs like Headstart, Ms. Edelman manages to appear on the evening news and public affairs programs like Nightline with considerable regularity.

And the Children's' Defense Fund is now a force on the Internet as well. Its Web site (Figure 4-7) speaks directly to its overall mission.

You can access basic statistics from the CDF site on how much it costs to raise a child, along with descriptions of ongoing campaigns to advance the interests of children generally—and poor children in particular—throughout the United States.

The main strength of the Children's Defense Fund site, however, lies in its strong advocacy around immediate issues of importance to

FIGURE 4-7
*The Childrens Defense Fund
Site. It's about the kids.*

the poor. As of February 1996, for example, CDF was urging people
to write to President Clinton:

Give President Clinton a Wake-Up Call

Tell Him Not to Abandon Our Children

Children are under attack. Congress wants to cut
funding and shred the federal safety net for children.
President Clinton can and must stop this attack on
children by refusing to

sign these immoral and unjust proposals when they get
to his desk.

E-MAIL PRESIDENT CLINTON NOW!

 TELL HIM:

 DON'T ABANDON AMERICA'S CHILDREN!

Do Not Sign Any Welfare or Medicaid "Reform" Bill That
Makes More Children Poor, Sick, Hungry, or At Risk of
Neglect or Abuse.

It was also speaking out against the latest plan endorsed by governors to "reform" Medicaid:

Governors' Medicaid Plan Threatens Children

The National Governors' Association (NGA) plan to
dismantle and slash crucial federal health, nutrition,
and income safety nets would leave millions of
children "poorer, hungrier, sicker, and at greater
risk of abuse and neglect," according to CDF President
Marian Wright Edelman.

"I am deeply saddened by and oppose strongly the proposals by the nation's governors," Edelman said on February 6. "CDF urges the Congress and the President to reject these flawed anti-child proposals. No proposal that leaves children worse rather than better off should become the law of the land."

The plan adopted by the governors is a threat to children because:

It would eliminate guaranteed health coverage for poor children 13 through 18 years old with working parents...

It would eliminate current guarantees that children will receive coverage of all medically necessary health care...

 It would eliminate guaranteed health coverage for children who are disabled according to federal SSI definitions...

It would eliminate existing federal guarantees of coverage for children and parents receiving AFDC...

It would deny access to federal courts to overturn illegal state denials of coverage....

It would allow states to contribute much less to Medicaid, forcing further cutbacks....

It would let states use federal Medicaid dollars to pay for current state responsibilities....

Needless to say, this is the sort of critique you wouldn't find in most newspapers.

Finally, CDF was using its Web site to promote its Stand for Children March, which took place on June 1, 1996:

On June 1, parents and grandparents, aunts and uncles, teachers and preachers, and others who care about children will come together in Washington, D.C., to Stand for Children.

Endorsed by more than 400 national, state, local, and grassroots organizations, Stand for Children will bring together at the Lincoln Memorial Americans of every race, religion, income, age, and faith.

"We will affirm our responsibility for all children as families, as communities, and as a national community," said CDF President Marian Wright Edelman

on February 1, announcing plans for the national day
of commitment to children. "Together, we will commit
ourselves to taking positive personal and collective
action to see that no child is left behind."

Be here in Washington on June 1 to:

Stand together and speak truth to power for children
with our presence, voices, votes, and hearts.

Stand for something more than ourselves, more
important than money, and more lasting than things.
Stand with those who can't stand alone or for
themselves: the young, the weak, the disabled.

Stand and be counted for children in good times and
bad. We will draw a line in the political sand that no
office-holder of any party or ideology will dare cross,
declaring that we are a people who place good policy
over good politics, moral principle over political
power, collective opportunity over personal
opportunism, basic morality over money, and
spirituality over materialism.

In short, the CDF Web site retains the singular focus on advocacy
that shapes the entire organization. In just a few pages it covers all
the bases: its mission; specific issues of concern; a political target—in
this case, President Clinton—and specific actions people can take to
support its goals. The fundamental objectives remain the same, but
the issues change over time. The Children's Defense Fund has
learned how to update its Web site quickly so as to keep pace with
the twists and turns of the political process.

CDF also makes good use of email to keep its supporters abreast
of ongoing developments in Washington. Regularly, it posts a legislative report to a number of lists where subscribers are likely to be
sympathetic. These, too, are always to the point:

CHILDREN'S DEFENSE FUND

Friday, January 12, 1996

Legislative Update

**BUDGET TALKS ON HOLD - BOTH SIDES AGREE TO BALANCE,
BUT WHOSE PRIORITIES?**

On Tuesday evening of this week, budget negotiations
between the Congressional Republican leadership and
the White House were put on hold until possibly next
Wednesday. [That same evening, the President vetoed

the welfare bill (HR4).] The latest stumbling block in these negotiations is not who does or doesn't support a balanced budget — both the President's and the Republicans' balanced budget plans are certified by the Congressional Budget Office (CBO) to produce a balance in 7 years — but whether to drastically cut safety net programs for the neediest Americans in order to pay for tax cuts for the rich.

A COMPARISON OF THE LATEST BALANCED BUDGET PLANS

MEDICAID

MEDICAID MEDICAID MEDICAID MEDICAID MEDICAID MEDICAID

| President/Democrats | -$52 billion (maintains entitlement) |
| Republicans | -$85 billion (eliminates entitlement) |

WELFARE/EITC

WELFARE/EITC WELFARE/EITC WELFARE/EITC WELFARE/EITC

| President/Democrats | -$43 billion (maintains AFDC entitlement) |
| Republicans | -$75 billion (eliminates AFDC entitlement) |

CORPORATE WELFARE

| President/Democrats | -$60 billion |
| Republicans | -$26 billion |

TAX CUTS

TAX CUTS TAX CUTS TAX CUTS TAX

| President/Democrats | +$87 billion |
| Republicans | +$203 billion |

WHAT'S NEXT

If a resolution is not reached soon, the Republican leadership has indicated that it may try to force the President's hand by bringing a new balanced budget plan up for a vote in both the House and the Senate. Their hope is to get enough conservative Democrats to support the legislation in order to ensure enough votes to override a potential presidential veto. It's also possible that the Republican leadership may bring up a new welfare bill (possibly the original Senate-passed version of HR4) for a vote in both bodies.

With this in mind, two groups of Members are particularly important at this time: (1) the House Coalition, or "Blue Dog" Democrats, whom Republicans hope to negotiate with on the budget and welfare, and whose budget and welfare bills now include the cash assistance and Medicaid guarantees (a list is attached); and (2) the 35 Senate Democrats and two Republicans who voted FOR the Senate welfare bill, but AGAINST the final conference version of the bill (they, too, are listed below).

Members of both groups need to hear that you appreciate their support of the federal welfare safety net for children, and that poor children need them to stand tough on protecting this important guarantee for children. Nothing that hurts at least 1 million children (as the Office of Management and Budget has said the Senate bill will do) can be morally or politically right. If anyone on either list of Members is from YOUR STATE, please call them.

CDF issues a Legislative Update like this at least once a week. I always forward it to the civic-values list, as do managers of a number of other lists devoted to social change. As a result, thousands of people who likely had never even heard of the Children's Defense Fund are now responding to its appeals. Most important, they like it. A number of civic-values subscribers acknowledge that their primary interest in the list lies in the periodic alerts and updates they receive. It's like having an advocacy news service piped directly into their homes. Moreover, this news service so cheap that even an anti-poverty organization like the Children's Defense Fund can afford to use it.

CAMPAIGNING VIA EMAIL

Is it necessary to create a Web site to conduct a serious campaign around an issue on the Internet?

Not really. A home page is important in helping an organization establish a presence on the Net—a specific place where people can find out about a group's mission and program. Effective advocacy, however, involves broad outreach to people who may know nothing at all about the group and are never likely to find it on the Web. The Children's Defense Fund may use its Web site to publicize its positions on issues and its current lobbying efforts, but it achieves far greater outreach by transmitting its legislative alerts to various email lists than by simply posting them to the home page and hoping lots of people will see them. That's an online version of preaching to the choir.

In fact, one of the most effective campaigns conducted via the Internet in 1995 involved an organization that doesn't even have a Web site—OMB Watch. OMB Watch is a watchdog agency based in Washington that keeps track of federal regulatory agencies. Even now, few people have even heard of it. Yet thousands of people on the Internet are now familiar with OMB Watch as a result of its relentless campaign to prevent Congress from passing what became known as the Istook amendment—after its sponsor, Rep. Ernest Istook of Oklahoma—or, as opponents eventually called it, the "Silence America Act." OMB Watch material on this amendment did end up on various Web sites, including my own. But email was how we received it.

The basic aim of the Istook amendment—which was attached to various Congressional budget resolutions throughout the fall of 1995—was to prevent any organization that received federal funds from engaging in advocacy on behalf of their members or clients. "Advocacy," as defined in the bill, went way beyond legislative lobbying to include, "carrying on propaganda," "participating in any judicial litigation or agency proceeding (including as an amicus curiae) in which agents or instrumentalities of federal, state, or local governments are parties," and "any attempt to influence any legislation or agency action through an attempt to affect the opinions of the general public or any segment thereof." Thus, if a social service agency that received federal grants to run a homeless shelter were to produce public service advertisements calling for increased public funding for the homeless, it could lose its funding, even if the ads made no reference to specific bills. Non-profits were to be given a choice of providing direct service to the needy or speaking out on behalf of the needy, but they couldn't do both.

As important as this legislation was to social service agencies and community groups, it received only sporadic attention in the press. Istook introduced it in August, while most people were on vacation. There were so many wars being waged around the "Contract with America"—including fights over appropriations bills, welfare reform, the Crime Bill, Goals 2000, Americorps, even funding for Congress itself—the Istook amendment was just another battle. As non-profit organizations did find out about it—from the American Cancer Society down to soup kitchens operating in inner-city neighborhoods all over the country —they came to see it as a fundamental infringement of their First Amendment rights, aimed at preventing them from informing the larger public about the plight of the people they served.

The first responses fit a familiar pattern. A coalition of Washington-based organizations, including groups such as the American Association of Retired Persons and the Red Cross, alerted their affiliates around the country, urging them to write to their representatives in Congress immediately.

OMB Watch then decided to take a technological leap forward by using the Internet to build national opposition to the bill as quickly as possible. It scheduled dozens of community workshops in September, designed to alert community-based organizations and nonprofits about the amendment and what they could do about it. To sponsor local meetings around an issue was not unusual, especially in response to a crisis. This time, however, each workshop concluded with an overhead projector demonstration of email and an appeal to start using it to receive information on the campaign and generate pressure on Congress.

From that point forward, every listserv related to non-profit organizations, civil liberties, and social change started circulating OMB memoranda like this one:

```
STATE AND LOCAL SIGN-ONS (11/14/95 Update): The
following state and local organizations have signed on
to the following statement opposing the Istook
Nonprofit Gag Bill. Please check the state by state
list to be sure that your organization (if it is state
or local) and/or your affiliates are signed on.

To add your organization (or yourself as an
individual) to the list, please call the contact
person for your state at the phone number provided.

SERVING THE PUBLIC GOOD

A Position Statement on Advocacy By Nonprofit
Organizations

The nonprofit sector plays a key role in our society
today. In partnership with government, nonprofit
organizations are engaged in service delivery,
research, educating the public, and much more — in
general, they work to build a better world, at home
```

and abroad. People across the country use nonprofit organizations to learn more about key issues of the day, and to link up with other citizens to create a more powerful voice. Nonprofit organizations themselves also speak to policy makers and the public on behalf of the people they serve. Advocacy by the nonprofit sector has led to significant improvements in people's lives at the local, state, and federal level.

Because nonprofit organizations do not stand to profit by lobbying and can provide enormous insight on public policy issues, Congress has encouraged them to lobby. However, it has placed detailed restrictions on nonprofit organizations on the amount of money that can be used for these purposes.

Nonprofits also are barred from using any federal funds for lobbying and partisan politics. Nonprofit organizations faithfully comply with all these restrictions and support enforcement of penalties if the rules are ever violated. However, some in Congress are proposing to go beyond current restrictions to silence the advocacy voice of the nonprofit sector. They would, for example, expand the lobbying restrictions to include all advocacy activities, bar certain organizations that engage in advocacy from receiving any federal grants, and prohibit federal employees from making workplace contributions to nonprofits that engage in advocacy. Such efforts will have a chilling impact on the democratic process as well as the rights of individuals and organizations to participate in public policy debates.

The organizations listed below oppose any effort to restrict the advocacy voice of the nonprofit sector. Curtailing the historical responsibility to speak to the public and to policy makers on behalf of the people whom nonprofit organizations serve would be a severe blow to our democratic freedoms.

(A long list of organizations followed.)

Istook amendment alerts became a regular feature of the civic-values list throughout the fall, and we included a special section on the amendment on the Institute home page. Here was a case where the list and the Web site complemented one another. Whenever people wanted the full text of the amendment, we referred them to the Web site. It was through civic-values and other lists, however, that they received updates and alerts on the campaign itself. A wide range of email lists joined the campaign on this basis. Eventually, the campaign succeeded. By December, even a number of Republicans had turned against the amendment and prevented it from reaching the floor.

The Istook campaign demonstrates how activists combine the resources of the Internet with conventional mailings and community meetings to mobilize broad-based campaigns. We can use Web sites to explain the issues, provide information on where Representatives and Senators stand, and publicize upcoming events. We can post updates and alerts to email lists where participants are likely to get involved. Nor do you need dozens of people to do all this—just one or two can mobilize thousands. There's a reason why this technology is making so many politicians nervous, and it isn't pornography. It's advocacy.

FROM ADVOCACY TO EMPOWERMENT

The Internet obviously makes available a terrific new set of tools for advocacy that grassroots organizations and active citizens can start using in their work right now. The Christian Coalition, EnviroLink, the Children's Defense Fund, and OMB Watch are just four of hundreds of organizations that have started using the World Wide Web and email to mobilize their supporters. The process will only accelerate in the years ahead.

Whether these new tools end up giving citizens real political power, however, depends on both how and *where* we deploy them. Elected officials represent districts. People live in communities. Empowerment begins when people start organizing within their own communities to influence representatives in these districts. That's why OMB Watch started to build its campaign against the Istook amendment though local workshops. This is where grassroots political power lies.

Unfortunately, many of the groups most associated with the Internet have been slow to learn this basic political lesson. As an example, even before the passage of the Telecommunications Reform Bill, the Electronic Frontier Foundation (EFF) called upon supporters to flood "key members of Congress" with calls, faxes, and letters on December 12th, 1995, protesting its offensive provisions. It worked. For several weeks thereafter, EFF reported through its Web site that more than 20,000 people had bombarded so-called "key members" on the designated day.

What difference did it make, however? Unless they're planning to run for higher office, legislators couldn't care less about people who don't live in their districts. In fact, a flood of email and faxes from here, there, and everywhere merely makes it harder for them to sort out how their own constituents feel. The Telecommunications Act passed by an overwhelming margin later that month and the President signed it, thus producing the 48-hour Web site blackout in February. So much for December 12.

Compare this approach to the way in which the Christian Coalition operates—both online and off. They may be using telecommunications to connect supporters with one another, but their primary goal is to strengthen chapters within specific legislative districts. Everything the Coalition offers online, from issue papers to legislative scorecards to training curricula, is pointed in this direction. As a result, when the Christian Coalition talks, Congress listens. Ralph Reed even takes partial credit for the passage of the Community Decency Act.

The same political opportunity is available to any group that wants to use the Internet in this way, but organizing within communities and districts must become their primary objective. Groups like the League of Conservation Voters, EnviroLink, or the Children's Defense Fund know this. They already reach thousands of organizations and individual members throughout the country with regular mail and faxes. As they have come to understand the power of the Internet, they wish that they could reach everyone using its tools, but most of their supporters still aren't online. They need help—not in lobbying Representatives and Senators in Washington, but in mobilizing the people who elect them.

What is needed, then, is a long-range organizing strategy aimed explicitly at extending the use of the Internet for political empowerment. Community groups need to encourage their members to go online. Internet activists need to share their technical expertise and skills with organizers working at the grassroots level. These groups should be supporting one together. Such an alliance could transform not only the Internet, but modern politics itself.

5 Neighborhoods

We vote where we live. Political empowerment begins with this insight. Years ago, Congressman Tip O'Neill from Massachusetts, then Speaker of the House, made the observation that "all politics is local." Even though this line is now a political cliché, most of us continue to ignore it. We talk about politicians as if they were an alien army beholden to sinister forces beyond our control. Of course, powerful lobbies in this country do work to hard to dominate Congress and state legislatures in this way. Whether or not they succeed, however, remains in our hands.

▶ Isolation, Ignorance, Impotence

▶ Organizing Neighborhoods

▶ Neighborhoods Online

▶ Neighborhood Web Sites

▶ Online Recruitment and Training

▶ Neighborhood Online Networking

▶ Neighborhood Online Advocacy

▶ From Neighborhoods Online to Empowerment

ISOLATION, IGNORANCE, IMPOTENCE

Elected officials still need our votes to win their campaigns. In fact, politicians at every level live in terror that someday a group will figure out how to organize in their districts and defeat them. Whatever they do to appear invincible—television ads, direct mail, mass rallies—is aimed at avoiding defeat. As long as their *we*, their constituents, see them as being beyond reach, no one will challenge them.

Why, then, do we let them get away with it? Dealing with government does require a certain amount of initiative and information, but so does finding a job or buying a home or raising a family. If we manage to meet these personal challenges, why are we so bewildered when it comes to dealing with government? When asked by pundits and pollsters, many of us express three basic feelings in relation to politics: isolation, ignorance, and impotence. These are serious obstacles to participation—but that's all they are: obstacles. Each one of them can be overcome.

Isolation reflects a breakdown of relationships on our blocks and in the neighborhoods where we live. Even people who are active around particular issues like the environment often don't know their next door neighbors. Is this your situation as well? Have the people on your street or in your apartment building ever met to address a problem? Is there an organization in your area trying to organize people around common concerns? If none of this is happening, you are effectively isolated from the people with whom you might share genuine political power—your own neighbors. Together, we could add up to a significant force within several legislative districts, but not if we remain isolated from one another.

Ignorance in this case relates to a lack of knowledge of how government operates. Recall how many federal programs mentioned in the chapter on obtaining information are rarely even mentioned in the press. Now apply this to your own priorities for government. Here are the major concerns voters have expressed about this country over the past twenty-five years:

- Economic dislocation
- Crime
- Substandard education
- Poverty and welfare
- The environment

Which of these most concerns you? Do you know what government at any level is doing about it? If you're unhappy with existing programs, are you aware of possible alternatives? If not, you're not likely to participate. You'll feel that you don't know enough to offer an intelligent opinion—either to a representative or to other people in your community who share the same concerns.

Isolation and ignorance lead to impotence—the sense that nothing you do could possibly make a difference. If we never meet with people in our neighborhoods and we have no idea how to solve major problems, then on what basis can we participate? Millions of Americans express such feelings about politics now. A lot of us have stopped voting. It's not that the non-voters think government is unimportant. They've concluded that *they're* unimportant, at least far as influencing elected officials is concerned.

These are serious problems, as the anemic level of political participation in America makes quite clear. Yet we can overcome all of them and going online can make a difference in the effort. To be sure, using the Internet in and of itself will not cause these obstacles simply to disappear. Yet the systems we've been examining here—email, listservs, the World Wide Web—do give us new weapons in the struggle. Email and listservs help us combat isolation. The World Wide Web gives us access to useful information. Together, they represent a powerful new set of tools for political advocacy. We have seen how major organizations like the Christian Coalition and the Children's Defense Fund already use these resources to mobilize support for national issues and campaigns. Now at the local level we can also use them to strengthen relationships among participants within our own organizations and to give us a platform we've never had before. Want to bring government back to the people? Here's a new weapon in the fight.

DOWNTOWN MINNEAPOLIS RESIDENTS ASSOCIATION

Consider the Web site of the Downtown Minneapolis Residents Association, shown in Figure 5-1.

There are thousands of civic groups like this all over the United States. This one has been formed to represent residents and businesses in a rapidly growing area of downtown Minneapolis. As the Web site explains, the group is open to "any person of voting age who is a resident property owner, tenant, or non-resident property owner of residential property in the area of one of the three neighborhoods of Downtown West, Downtown East, or North Loop, as defined by the City of Minneapolis."

FIGURE 5-1
Minneapolis boosterism

At this site, we also learn how DMRA operates. Board meetings—open to the public—take place every month. There's an annual meeting in December. Most importantly, the organization makes it clear that helping residents influence the major decisions that affect them in the neighborhood is their overriding goal:

First, DMRA provides a forum where residents can voice their opinions and concerns. Residents voice their opinions and concerns by attending community meetings, serving on committees, writing for The DOWNTOWNER or running for a position on the Board of Directors. Residents can also be heard by simply contacting a DMRA Board member or a DMRA staff person.

Second, DMRA organizes residents so that they can effectively act on their interests and concerns. It organizes residents by conducting community meetings and forming committees. The community meetings and committees formulate strategies that are implemented into a plan of action to address issues that affect downtown residents.

Third, through the Board of Directors, DMRA formulates a general direction that the Minneapolis downtown area should move in order to facilitate residents' interests and concerns. The DMRA Board of Directors is comprised entirely of downtown residents like yourself.

Fourth, community leaders, politicians, agencies, and other organizations often need to receive feedback about plans and ideas they have for the downtown area. These people and organizations can find out the

opinions and thoughts of the community by contacting
DMRA. DMRA maintains a pulse on resident opinion by
conducting community meetings, surveys, direct
contact, and publications. These are the primary roles
DMRA plays. They are not exhaustive. It performs other
functions and plays other roles in the downtown
community.

In short, DMRA exists to combat the sense of isolation, ignorance,
and impotence that prevents people from participating in the community and politics. In the past, they would have had to rely entirely
on mailings and meetings to reach area residents, as all civic groups
have done. As their Web site demonstrates, now they are learning
how to use the Internet as well.

The DMRA Web site itself combats isolation by giving everyone in
the neighborhood an online center they can call their own. By including a script on the home page that records the number of times
the site has been accessed or "hit," the group conveys to residents
that they are not alone. Within its first three months, the site had
been accessed 518 times. When we consider that most civic groups
in America average between 50 and 100 people for their monthly
meetings, this was a promising start.

The Web site also gives DMRA an inexpensive means of providing
residents information about upcoming events. Here an online
newsletter (Figure 5-2) announces a meeting relating to a Neighborhood Revitalization Program developed with the city.

The lead article in the newsletter goes on to explain the organization's proposed Neighborhood Safety Program:

First, DMRA will work with Community Crime Prevention
(CCP)/SAFE to develop a "block leader" or "block club"

FIGURE 5-2
DMRA's online newsletter

model for the downtown area. This model will help
residents organize and communicate between themselves.
It will allow residents to become more involved in the
overall organizing process. Also, the `block club"
model will encourage leadership roles for residents in
the downtown neighborhood who wish to assume a more
active role.

Second, DMRA will establish a fax line so that it can
easily inform other agencies about
resident-safety/crime concerns. Conversely, other
agencies will be able to fax announcements and
concerns to DMRA so that DMRA can alert residents by
fliers, the DMRA newsletter, or by phone.

Third, DMRA will encourage cooperation and alliances
with downtown security personnel through bulletins
and/or meetings.

Also on the site at the time were announcements about a forthcoming series of meetings on the impact of "adult entertainment" on
the neighborhood, plans to establish a neighborhood grocery store,
and specific projects envisaged under the Neighborhood Revitalization Program itself. Residents can access profiles of other Minneapolis neighborhoods from the DMRA home page, including several with
civic associations that are now developing Web sites of their own.
This is the sort of information that citizens can't find in the daily
press—at least not organized in this way. Yet the DRMA Web site
makes it instantly available

Most important, perhaps, DRMA uses its home page to help residents connect with their elected representatives at all levels of government. Every official is listed—from councilperson to
President—with an address, phone number, and fax. The state Representative and state Senator have email addresses, which makes it
possible to connect with them online. Civic and political participation has always been strong in Minneapolis. Here, the Internet is being used to make it even stronger.

It becomes clear from examining the various neighborhood profiles on the Minneapolis Freenet that eventually every community organization will have a Web site of its own. There is already a
city-wide email list for neighborhood activists, involving more than
100 subscribers. By the summer of 1996, the city of Minneapolis will
be online as well, providing its own information on city services that
neighborhood organizations and residents can use. Minutes of city
council are already online—and the DMRA Web site accesses them.

As Julie Idelkope, a policy aide to mayor Sharon Sayles Belton, puts it, "politicians in Minneapolis ignore the neighborhoods at their peril." Using the Internet, there is now an even greater opportunity to bring them closer together.

ORGANIZING NEIGHBORHOODS

It is my strong conviction that groups like the Downtown Minneapolis Residents' Association offer the best chance to help ordinary citizens gain significant power within the political process. Of all organizations, these hold the greatest potential to overcome the sense of isolation, ignorance, and impotence that discourages people from getting involved. Want to change the politics of your community? Organize the neighborhoods. I speak not merely as analyst here, but as an activist. This is what I've been doing for the past twenty years.

When I organized the Institute for the Study of Civic Values in Philadelphia in 1973, it was with the explicit aim of helping citizens fulfill the historic ideals of the country, as expressed in the Declaration of Independence, the Constitution, and the Bill of Rights. For me, this was a logical outgrowth of a decade of involvement in the student movement of the 1960s. In 1967, I had helped build a major movement for "student power" on the nation's campuses as president of the United States National Student Association. At that time, we sought to apply basic principles of American democracy to the governance of higher education. We insisted that colleges and universities should be preparing young people for responsible and effective citizenship. Now it was time to advance the same philosophy in the communities and neighborhoods where people lived.

Those who joined me in setting up the Institute were equally committed to this agenda. They included a number of labor and community activists in Philadelphia, along with some of the leading political and social theorists in the United States—Wilson Carey McWilliams, author of *The Idea in Fraternity in America;* John Schaar, well known for his articles on democratic values for *The New York Review of Books* and *The New American Review*; and George Bonham, founder and editor of *Change in Higher Education*. Whatever our differences, we all agreed that there need to be new programs in political education that applied the country's civic values to the problems of America, as we experienced them within our own communities.

On this basis, the major program we established was called, simply, "The Neighborhood Project." We began by offering innovative seminars on "Building Community" and "Self-Help Community Development," all aimed at helping ordinary citizens learn how to organizing their neighborhoods around principles like democracy and justice. Soon, we were producing Nader-styled research papers on the city's community development program and the mortgage lending practices of local banks. In 1976, we helped form a city-wide coalition called the Philadelphia Council of Neighborhood Organizations, involving more than 150 groups representing thousands of people. Over the next decade, we built a network of neighborhood credit unions, community development corporations, and neighborhood job banks that virtually redefined what community and economic development meant in Philadelphia. No longer were neighborhoods merely places where people lived. They were a cause.

In the process, we turned Philadelphia politics upside down. When we started, the mayor was Frank Rizzo—our "tough" police commissioner in the 1960s who had become a national symbol of resistance to social change. By 1980, a new reform mayor, Bill Green, appointed a veteran neighborhood activist, W. Wilson Goode, to serve as the city's managing director. This was the highest appointed post in city government.

Soon we were working with Goode to develop a series of neighborhood meetings on his annual budget that involved thousands of people from all parts of the city. In 1983, W. Wilson Goode was elected Philadelphia's first African-American mayor. That same year, I won election as a councilman-at-large on Wilson Goode's ticket, campaigning on what I called "the neighborhood agenda." From that point forward, no one has been able to win an election in Philadelphia without making the neighborhoods a centerpiece of his or her campaign.

I believe this is what people who are deeply frustrated about politics and government in other cities and communities around the country need to do as well. As Congresspeople discover when they return to their districts, national issues are often just abstractions unless they reflect real problems we're experiencing where we live.

Think about your own neighborhood or community as an example. What's wrong with it? What needs to happen to make it right? What can you do yourself—and what could the people of the neighborhood accomplish, if you all got together? What help, then, do you need from government? Answering questions like these and then taking action is the key to reclaiming politics and making it work—for you, for your community, and for the country. I know this is harder to do than I've just made it sound, but it's possible. I've done it.

Fortunately, I'm not the only one in this country who has come to this conclusion. The movement we built in Philadelphia in the 1970s and '80s has been gathering momentum all over the United States. It's been happening in Minneapolis—as their Web site suggests—but also in Boston and Atlanta and Seattle and Dallas and in hundreds of smaller communities like Boulder, Colorado. It's the best kept secret in American politics. Only now are major newspapers and magazines like the *New York Times, US News and World Report,* the *Dallas Morning News,* and *USA Today* starting to pay attention. But what the media now calls the "citizens' movement" has been building for some time.

The question, then, is how can more of us get involved in organizing our own neighborhoods and communities in the years ahead, as a way of holding government accountable? What obstacles do we face? How might we overcome them?

The obstacles are considerable. They reflect many of the same problems that face us as individuals when we try to act alone. Community groups remain isolated from another. Unlike churches, unions, or chapters of a single national group like the NAACP, no structure ties them together. Empowering such groups involves building coalitions, as we had done with the Philadelphia Council of Neighborhood Organizations in the 1970s. This wasn't easy then and it still isn't. PCNO itself, as an example, no longer exists.

If it's not easy to get good information about government programs generally, it's especially difficult to find out about programs that operate within neighborhoods, since these don't get media coverage unless someone either attacks them or rips them off. As an example, even though I started my career in local government as a city councilman, I also spent more than four years directing Philadelphia's Office of Housing and Community Development, which administers our federal Community Development Block Grant. I mentioned this program in Chapter 4, in explaining the kind of information now available through the World Wide Web.

HUD spends more than $4 billion of what ABC Nightly News calls "your money" on housing rehabilitation, business development, and social services through CDBG, in communities all over the country. Every city has to go through an elaborate process of planning and public hearings in developing the "Consolidated Plans" that now appear on the HUD Web site. Is all this news to you? That's my point. Even when newspapers cover federal housing programs, they're rarely explained in this way. And as I noted earlier, this is just one among several federal programs operating in neighborhoods that remain largely invisible to the general public.

Most seriously, even though thousands of local civic groups and even various national neighborhood coalitions have emerged over the past 25 years, they appear to suffer a collective case of political impotence during political campaigns. Ever hear of National Peoples' Action or the National Association of Neighborhoods or the Industrial Areas Foundation? Between them, they represent at least 3,000 neighborhood associations all over the United States. They're not afraid to lobby for legislation that affects neighborhoods and communities, like the Home Mortgage Disclosure Act regulating banks. Yet unlike the Christian Coalition, or the environmentalists, or the Children's Defense Fund, when politicians start running for office, they disappear. If even the national coalitions don't get involved at this level, what are local groups supposed to do?

These are significant problems. In fact, I left city government in 1992 to return to the Institute for the Study of Civic Values full-time to grapple with them again. It was clear that the neighborhoods movement itself had to be revived and redefined. Manufacturing jobs had been dwindling for years and now even unskilled jobs in the service sector were disappearing as well. Economists were warning us that everyone would need a college degree to make it in the future, but we had more than 300,000 people in Philadelphia alone without high school diplomas. The homeless were lying all over the streets. Citizens were becoming painfully aware of these harsh new realities, but politicians still weren't dealing with them. How could we turn this around?

That's when I started hearing about the Internet. There wasn't much happening online related to politics and virtually nothing dealing with neighborhoods, but the more I learned about it, the more I started to see the potential.

The Internet could make it possible for local groups within a city and throughout the country to connect with one another in ways that had never been possible before.

With Congress and federal departments and even state and local governments starting to go online, the Internet could give us quick access to information about programs and legislation that we could use ourselves and share with other people.

Most important, the Internet offered even grassroots groups a new platform to convey our own views—first to one another, and then to the politicians themselves.

At some point, I no longer had to be persuaded. In 1995, the Institute for the Study of Civic Values launched "Neighborhoods Online."

NEIGHBORHOODS ONLINE

Neighborhoods Online is an Internet service developed by the Institute for the Study of Civic Values to support neighborhood activism both in Philadelphia and throughout the United States.

Neighborhoods Online: what we're doing	First, we're building a Web site, with the aim of making it easy for groups and concerned citizens to access information about programs, issues, and political developments that are relevant to neighborhood empowerment. Second, within Philadelphia we're pursuing a systematic strategy to help civic organizations and human service agencies access the Internet and learn how to use email and the World Wide Web in their work. Third, we're developing email lists for Philadelphia (*neigonline@libertynet.org*) and the Commonwealth of Pennsylvania (*penn-neighbor@civic.net*) with the aim of creating networks of neighborhood activists who are especially interested in broad-based community organizing and political empowerment.

Above all, however, Neighborhoods Online represents the kind of partnership between community organizers and Internet activists that we must establish if this technology is ever going to emerge as an instrument of political empowerment.

Our Philadelphia partner is LibertyNet, a regional community network serving the nine-county Delaware Valley region. I learned about LibertyNet around the time that I was getting interested in the Internet myself. Its sponsors included the Benjamin Franklin Partnership, a Pennsylvania Economic Development Agency; the University of Pennsylvania; WHYY—Philadelphia's major public radio station; the Free Library of Philadelphia; and the Philadelphia school district. Especially since there was no one in the planning group with a full understanding of the grassroots organizations that I most wanted to bring online, I thought there might be a basis for collaboration.

So in the spring of 1994, I started exploring with LibertyNet's director, Chris Higgins, how we might work together. Gradually, the basic elements of the project took shape—the Web site, the recruitment and training strategy, and a system of local networks. That summer, the William Penn Foundation—a local foundation with a long-standing commitment to neighborhood empowerment—provided a start-up grant of $50,000. We unveiled Neighborhoods Online in February of 1995 to a packed audience of community activists who now wanted to access the Internet as well.

Our other partner—especially for several of the email lists we manage—is the Center for Civic Networking. CCN was formed in 1993 by Miles Fidelman and Richard Civille—two veterans of cyberspace—with the express purpose of showing people like me how to use the Internet to promote citizen participation and sustainable community development.

It was Miles, in fact, who persuaded me (via email, of course) to start using the Internet itself, as opposed to specific services like Delphi and America Online. We were exchanging posts on Communet via Delphi—the listserv I joined when I first got an Internet account—when he started challenging me in a number of private notes to take a more serious look at what I might do online. That spring, he helped us set up the main Institute mailing list—civic-values. CCN even threw in an ISCV Gopher for good measure. We've been working together ever since.

Today, Neighborhoods Online is among the leading Internet resource centers promoting neighborhood activism throughout the United States. We've been in operation for less than a year, and already hundreds of people are connecting with us every day. They include organizers, staff members of non-profit organizations, elected officials, journalists, college faculty and students, and just average citizens looking for new ways to solve neighborhood problems. Not only do they access our Web site, many are participating in our email lists as well.

Indeed, while each of the services offered by Neighborhoods Online stands on its own, they also reinforce one another. Together, they represent a comprehensive support system for neighborhood activism which we believe will grow in scope and significance in the months and years ahead.

CONTACT

Miles Fidelman
Center for Civic
Networking
mfidelman@civicnet.org
Richard Civille
Center for Civic
Networking
rciville@civicnet.org

NEIGHBORHOOD WEB SITES

The Web site involves ongoing collaboration between the Institute and LibertyNet. Initially, I provided the content; LibertyNet produced the Web pages. Then a programmer at LibertyNet—Nate Gasser—showed me how easy it was to learn HTML. Now I provide both the content and the pages, but I still need Nate to supply scripts for more complex operations.

There are, in fact, two distinct Web pages associated with Neighborhoods Online.

The basic site at *http://libertynet.org/community/phila* focuses primarily on Philadelphia (Figure 5-3).

We maintain a separate menu (Figure 5-4) for neighborhood activists around the country at *http://libertynet.org/community/phila/natl.html.*

The local menu accesses Web pages created by civic groups, human service agencies, and state and city agencies that operate within Philadelphia. It does include federal agencies and national organizations related to neighborhood empowerment, but our primary emphasis is on local programs and groups. We've even developed separate menus for each of our twelve Neighborhood Planning Districts, comparable to neighborhood menus are being developed in Minneapolis, Boulder, Colorado, and on a number of other local community networks.

We added Neighborhoods Online: National to the site in August of 1995. Here, we access only the federal agencies and national organizations, without the Philadelphia programs and groups, as a service to neighborhood activists throughout the country. As a result, Neighborhoods Online: National has developed a life of its own. You can find it on Web pages managed by HUD, the National Civic League,

FIGURE 5-3

Neighborhoods Online, Philiadelphia

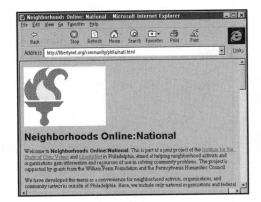

FIGURE 5-4
*Neighborhoods Online,
national page*

National Public Radio, the Community Development Society, and local community networks from Fairbanks, Alaska to Tempe, Arizona. We're now being accessed more than 1,000 times a week. Clearly, we're meeting a need.

What makes these menus unique is not simply the information we provide-which is largely retrieved from other sites—but the way in which we organize them. The people who live in a neighborhood want it to be clean, safe, economically viable, and a decent place to raise their children. As a result, the primary concerns of community organizations have been housing and community development, neighborhood safety, economic opportunity and security, and education. We divide Neighborhoods Online into Web pages that reflect these concerns, while providing a specific menu devoted neighborhood empowerment itself (Figure 5-5).

What programs and services do we include?

The Philadelphia Web page devoted to "neighborhood appearance and environment" (Figure 5-6) is a good example.

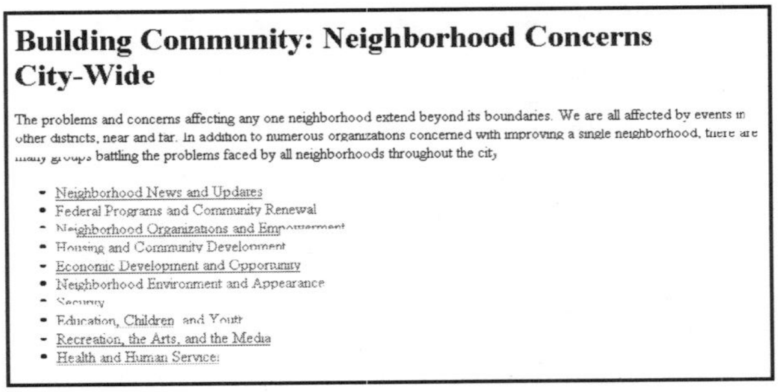

FIGURE 5-5
*Neighborhoods
Online list
of programs
and services*

Building Community: Neighborhood Concerns City-Wide

The problems and concerns affecting any one neighborhood extend beyond its boundaries. We are all affected by events in other districts, near and far. In addition to numerous organizations concerned with improving a single neighborhood, there are many groups battling the problems faced by all neighborhoods throughout the city.

- Neighborhood News and Updates
- Federal Programs and Community Renewal
- Neighborhood Organizations and Empowerment
- Housing and Community Development
- Economic Development and Opportunity
- Neighborhood Environment and Appearance
- Security
- Education, Children and Youth
- Recreation, the Arts, and the Media
- Health and Human Service

FIGURE **5-6**
*Neighborhoods getting
down to specifics*

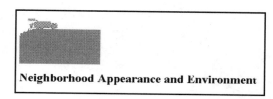

Neighborhood Appearance and Environment

Philadelphia Organizations:

City and State Government Organizations:

- Streets Dept.

- Licenses and Inspections

- Water Dept.

- Pa. Dept. of Environmental Resources

- Philadelphia Anti-Graffiti Network (Gopher description)

Federal Agencies and Resources:

- White House Releases on the Environment

- The Environmental Protection Agency

- Environmental Protection Agency Mission

- EPA Citizens' Guide to Environmental Protection

- Environmental Protection Agency: Regional Offices

- Community Based Environmental Protection

- EPA: Protecting and Restoring America's Water Resources

- EPA Press Releases (searchable)

National Organizations:

- EnviroLink

- League of Conservation Voters

- Communities and the Environment, Alliance for National Renewal

- National Graffiti Information Network

- Pro-Paint Anti-Graffiti Systems

- Environmental Health: Toxic Substances and Public Health

Note that the menu accesses both government agencies and non-profit organizations related to the environment. Most local community networks, including LibertyNet, assign these to distinct locations such as "The Government Center" or "The Community Center." Our premise here, however, is that a neighborhood activist trying to deal with toxic wastes shouldn't have to wander back and forth between Web menus to find solutions. They should be able to reach all the relevant online resources from one place. That's what we offer here.

We also access only those sections of a Web site that would be of use to a neighborhood activist. This becomes especially important in relation to federal agencies, which by their nature meet a variety of needs. The EPA Citizens' Guide to Environmental Protection is a terrific resource for community activists, but it isn't even mentioned on the EPA home page. You can access it directly from Neighborhoods Online.

We try to include at least one source of current news on each menu. Here, it's the White House Releases on the Environment, which is found somewhere in the White House Web site under "Press Releases by Topic." Similarly, you can access the HUD Daily Focus Message from the Community Development menu, the Goals 2000 Weekly Updates from the Education menu, and Nando Political News from the Empowerment menu— all of which are buried in the Web pages of their respective hosts. Here, again, you can access them directly. We've even developed a separate News and Update menu that incorporates all these sites for people who want fast access to current news related to neighborhoods covering a variety of subjects.

Finally, we've built two Neighborhood Empowerment menus— one for Philadelphia and one for the country as a whole—which access information related to planning, organizational development, and politics. These both include the Census Bureau's online service that enables users to retrieve demographic information by tract, zip code, or county. We incorporate Web sites with information about fund-raising and non-profit management on the Empowerment menus, along with news about issues that affect community organizations directly, like the Istook amendment.

Moreover, the Empowerment Menu in Philadelphia contains an added feature—one related to directly political accountability (Figure 5-7). Here, we access not only the names and addresses of our representatives in Congress, but their interest group ratings and their PAC contributions as reported, respectively, by VoteSmart and C-Span's Follow the Money Web site.

There's not a single local community network in the United States that lists its elected officials in this way, but why shouldn't we? It's not

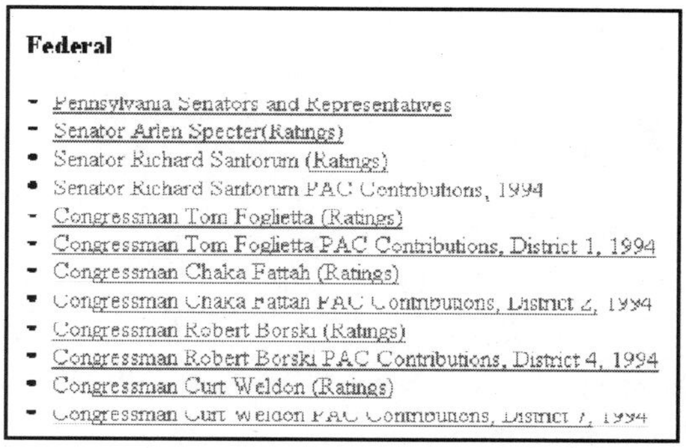

FIGURE 5-7

NOL also uses its site to provide outside links to services like Project VoteSmart so citizens can check up on their own elected representatives.

Federal
- Pennsylvania Senators and Representatives
- Senator Arlen Specter(Ratings)
• Senator Richard Santorum (Ratings)
• Senator Richard Santorum PAC Contributions, 1994
- Congressman Tom Foglietta (Ratings)
- Congressman Tom Foglietta PAC Contributions, District 1, 1994
• Congressman Chaka Fattah (Ratings)
• Congressman Chaka Fattah PAC Contributions, District 2, 1994
• Congressman Robert Borski (Ratings)
• Congressman Robert Borski PAC Contributions, District 4, 1994
• Congressman Curt Weldon (Ratings)
- Congressman Curt Weldon PAC Contributions, District 7, 1994

technically difficult. Just link to their specific addresses in VoteSmart and C-Span, and let these services do the rest. It's an ingenious way to let our elected representatives know we're watching them.

The whole point of Neighborhoods Online, in fact, is to connect both community organizations and active citizens with resources that can help us address the serious problems facing us in our neighborhoods. Nor are we bound by the rigid distinctions between government programs and voluntary associations that have acquired such significance in national politics. At the local level, we need everything we can get. If it's helpful and it's online, we include it. The National Civic League is even sponsoring a project it calls the Alliance for National Renewal, aimed at strengthening partnerships between community groups and government all over the United States. You can access it directly from Neighborhoods Online. You can also reach Neighborhoods Online from the National Civic League. Gradually, cyberspace is bringing us together.

ONLINE RECRUITMENT AND TRAINING

The Institute is also working with LibertyNet to help non-profit groups in Philadelphia gain access to the Internet. After all, why design an elaborate Web site like Neighborhoods Online if people can't use it? Unfortunately, as one organizer put it in a post to Communet, "Non-profits operate on two sets of priorities: critical and urgent. Going online rarely gets beyond urgent."

This was certainly true in 1995, when we launched Neighborhoods Online. Most groups were enthusiastic about the service, but unable to take advantage of it. It is less true now, but there are still significant obstacles we have to overcome.

- An organization's staff and board has to be convinced that the Internet can benefit them.
- The organization needs to be able secure an Internet account without a lot of hassle and at reasonable cost.
- The organization's staff needs to be trained and given technical support in using the Internet.
- The organization needs to see a way to reach its members through the Internet, even if this can't happen right away.

Fortunately, over the course of the first year of the project, the Institute and LibertyNet found ways to address these problems. Moreover, as the Minneapolis Web site suggests, similar projects are developing in other cities as well.

The main selling point for the Internet has been Neighborhoods Online itself. We were careful to wait until there were enough organizations and agencies on the Web site before even unveiling it to the non-profit community. Now we can display the wide range of federal agencies, national organizations, and even local groups that have emerged on the Net since we started. Every city department in Philadelphia had its own Web site by the summer of 1996, which was of special interest to local groups, providing quick access to information about programs and services that is not easy to obtain.

In the beginning, the Internet was a hard sell. Now, all it takes is a few minutes to demonstrate what's available through Neighborhoods Online, and non-profit directors want to sign up. In the first year, we enrolled 75 groups. By the time this book appears, the number will more than double.

Thanks to the Philadelphia-based William Penn Foundation and other local support, LibertyNet was been able to offer one free account to each non-profit organization—at least for the first year. Even after this period, subscriptions are less than $20 for 20 hours a month. Organizations are not only given the opportunity to develop their own Web pages, they are expected to do so, since the whole idea is to build LibertyNet into the premiere Internet resource center for the entire Delaware Valley. This does take time, but the cost is less than $100 and LibertyNet offers HTML training workshops such as the one I first attended, so gradually groups are taking advantage of the offer.

The Institute and LibertyNet collaborate in providing training and support to groups that subscribe through Neighborhoods Online.

CONTACT

Caroline Ferguson
University of Pennsylvania
caroline@pobox.upenn.edu

Much of the Institute's training occurs at the Computing Resource Center (CRC) at Penn in one of the best labs in the city. There, a gifted trainer—Caroline Ferguson—works directly with us to offer workshops in email, the Web, and Neighborhoods Online itself. Following the introductory workshop, LibertyNet staff members—in this case, Americorps volunteers—are available to give hands-on support to non-profits experiencing difficulty in installing the Internet software (Eudora and Netscape) or in maintaining their accounts.

Our most ambitious project, however, is a long-range effort to help organizations connect with their own members through LibertyNet and Neighborhoods Online. The individual neighborhood menus that we are gradually taking shape are part of the effort, since they feature announcements about programs and services that ordinary citizens use, like home improvement loans or low-income fuel assistance grants in the winter.

Again, however, what good does it do to provide information if no one has access to it? Here, a partnership with the Free Library of Philadelphia provides the solution. Thanks to a $1.2 million grant from the William Penn Foundation, each branch library is now receiving 12 computers linked to the Internet, LibertyNet, and Neighborhoods Online. These will all be in place by the end of 1997—with staff trained to show people how to use them.

LibertyNet has been aggressive in its efforts to extend Internet access to Delaware Valley residents as well. In 1995, for example, it was one of a handful of organizations nationally to win a coveted National Telecommunications Information and Assistance (NTIA) grant from the Commerce Department to provide broad Internet access to residents of three low-income neighborhoods in Philadelphia designated as a federal Empowerment Zone.

The Bridge Project, as it is called, is offering Internet access not only through libraries, but community centers and even a "truck with a tale" provided by the Free Library to run Internet demonstrations at neighborhood events. The Institute's own role in the project has been to develop and maintain an Empowerment Zone Online menu as part of Neighborhoods Online, with links to agencies and organizations that can assist both organizations and individuals in meeting the substantive goals set for the Empowerment Zone itself. Here again, we all work together as a partnership in these efforts— even using an email list ourselves to share ideas and information as the project unfolds.

In effect, then, helping community organizations learn how to use the Internet has turned into an organizing project in itself in

Philadelphia, managed largely by LibertyNet and the Institute, but now involving a number of other groups. From a modest beginning, we've reached the point where virtually every community development corporation, neighborhood advisory committee, adult literacy program, job training agency, and human service provider is either already online or trying to figure out how to get there.

Eventually, we even intend to help block captains gain access to the Internet. There are 6,000 block associations in Philadelphia that constitute the backbone of clean-up, recycling, and town watch programs in neighborhoods throughout the city. We believe that being able to communicate with these groups via the World Wide Web and email—and to help them connect with one another— would provide an enormous boost to civic participation in Philadelphia generally. The police department has been supplying CB radios to town watch groups for years on this basis. In this case, we believe that we can work with the libraries to build the network. Sound far-fetched? Remember when no one had fax machines? As far as we're concerned, it's just a matter of time.

NEIGHBORHOOD ONLINE NETWORKING

Our ultimate goal, in fact, is not merely to help individual neighborhood groups secure Internet accounts, but to help them start functioning as part of a network. Even the Neighborhoods Online Web site is more an electronic resource center than an instrument of empowerment in itself. I still believe that the greatest tool for political organizing on the Net is the email list, where people can share information with one another and develop strategies for change. On this basis, we now manage four separate lists related to neighborhood activism—each with its own subscribers, but all moving in the same direction. Over time, it is likely that these will prove to be the major vehicles for change.

We've created two lists related to Pennsylvania—neighbors-online, for groups in Philadelphia; and penn-neighbor, for activists throughout the state. Our specific aim here is to strengthen relationships among neighborhood organizations that may know about one another, but don't work together. The groups working on housing rehabilitation, anti-drug campaigns, and educational reform are often quite different, even within the same neighborhood. We include them all in neighbors-online and penn-neighbor. Now we're at least describing our programs to one another and sharing announcements of upcoming events. Most importantly, when legislation that affects all of us comes down the pike—like proposals to throw people off welfare even when there are no jobs—we're in a much stronger position to give it our undivided response.

We support two national lists as well—civic-values—which I described in Chapter 3—and a list called buildcom, that focuses directly on community organizing.

As I've already indicated, civic-values functions as a dialogue list for people who enjoy discussing issues and ideas. It's not narrowly focused on neighborhoods, but we do explore how problems such as corporate downsizing and programs such as welfare reform affect us in our own communities. Indeed, if any of our lists do end up producing a neighborhood agenda for America, it will be civic-values, given the number of participants who already have proposed ambitious projects of this kind.

Buildcom is the Institute's first project list, with a somewhat different—but related—objective. Over the past three years, we have been experimenting with a new approach to community planning, whereby we use principles in the Preamble to the Constitution like "secure the blessings of liberty to ourselves and posterity" and "promote the general welfare to help civic groups and government develop explicit social contracts for neighborhood improvement.

We've had considerable success with this process in Philadelphia, where we've tested it in a number of different neighborhoods. We've even developed a discussion guide describing the process—which we now call "Building Community in the American Tradition"—for use by groups around the country as part of the National Endowment for the Humanities "National Conversation on What It Means to Be an American."

Now, however, we're helping activists in other cities learn how to use our process via an email list —buildcom— thanks to a grant from the Surdna Foundation. Gradually, we are demonstrating that you can even use the Internet to help people learn how to organize. The implications for political education in the years ahead are enormous, especially since "community organizing" is not likely to be a course you will ever take in school.

Moreover, in terms of organizing itself, it is important to note that while each of our lists has an identity and a purpose of its own, they all reinforce one another. The Web site provides visibility. The email lists encourage us to work together. Together, they constitute an online system for neighborhood empowerment that will simply grow stronger as more groups start using the Internet in the years ahead.

NEIGHBORHOOD ONLINE ADVOCACY

In the previous chapter concerning advocacy, I made the point that while both email lists and Web sites gave us powerful new tools to mobilize people and put pressure on the President and Congress, we run the risk of diffusing our efforts so widely that they lose their political effectiveness.

We can avoid many of these problems, however, by focusing our energies on the legislators who represent us directly. Within Pennsylvania, at least, that's what Neighborhoods Online is helping us do.

Something that occurred even as I was writing this chapter indicates how the process has started to work already. I took a break to check my email. There, I discovered a Web page reproduced as a post from another email list in Pennsylvania list that monitors social welfare legislation:

FedCuts-Pennsylvania Home Page

Sponsored by the Federal Budget Cuts Task Force of the PA House

Democratic Policy Committee and the House Intergovernmental Affairs

Welcome to the Federal Budget Cuts Page. This purpose of this page is to explain and provide detailed information on the significant impact of the proposed Republican budget cuts on the Commonwealth of Pennsylvania and the residents of our state.

The following information is available:

- **Proposed Budget Cuts: National Numbers**

- **Proposed Budget Cuts: Pennsylvania Impact**

- **Proposed Budget Cuts: County by County**

- **Proposed Budget Cuts: Philadelphia Region**

- **Proposed Budget Cuts: Pittsburgh Region**

What you can do now to fight the cuts:

Testimony from public hearings on the impact of the federal budget cuts that have been held around the state will be posted soon in the following links.

- **Impact of Federal Budget Cuts: Philadelphia : Coming Soon**

- **Impact of Federal Budget Cuts: Pittsburgh: Coming Soon**

- **Impact of Federal Budget Cuts: Erie: Coming Soon**

- **Impact of Federal Budget Cuts: Southwestern Pennsylvania: Coming Soon**

To keep you fully informed here is additional information on this topic.

- **Are they Cuts or Reductions in Spending?**

- **Let Washington Know: Email to Congress**

- **Other Organizations Interested in Budget Cuts**

Below are some home page locations for a variety of State Representatives.

- **Italo Cappabianca's Home Page**

- **State Representative Larry Curry's Home Page**

- **State Representative Lisa Boscola's Home Page**

Comments or Problems

Again, thanks for visiting the Federal Budget Cuts/PA Home Page. We hope to hear from you again soon.

For information on this home page, please send e-mail to *italo@moose.erie.net*, phone us at +1 717-787-4358.

Almost immediately, I took the following steps:

First, I found the Web site itself and linked it to the Empowerment menu on Neighborhoods Online.

Then I forwarded the email message both to penn-neighbor and neighbors-online, alerting 150 more organizations who share the same Senators and governor and even some of the Congresspeople that this information was now available.

At the same time, I posted the actual data on the cutbacks as separate email messages to our lists, transmitting it directly from the Web sites.

Finally, I sent a note to State Representative Italo Cappabiannca from Allegheny County—the sponsor of the Web site—thanking him for the information and offering him the opportunity to send us future releases of this kind.

The whole process took fifteen minutes.

The next morning, I received the following note from Representative Cappabiannca:

Thank you for sending out the posts, I was trying to
get you to

email about the health cuts page that I have linked to
my home page.

Either…*http://moose.erie.net/~italo*

or *http://www.libertynet.org/~pahouse/healthcut*

I've never met Representative Italo Cappabiannca before. Pennsyl-vania's a big state. I'm in Philadelphia; he represents Allegheny County. Even though we're both active in politics, it's not likely that we'll meet.

Arlen Specter and Rick Santorum need to hear from both of us, however, especially around the federal budget. Now, thanks to the Internet, they will. This is where online organizing within the same cities and states really begins to pay off.

FROM NEIGHBORHOODS
ONLINE TO EMPOWERMENT

Participating in the affairs of our own neighborhoods empowers us at two levels.

First, we can take direct action to deal with situations we can han-dle by ourselves. We can sponsor block cleanups and recycle trash. We can join a town watch and look out for one another's homes. We can solicit volunteers to help kids with their homework. Some of us can even learn how to run GED classes for adults who don't have high school diplomas. These are simple steps we can take in our own behalf, once we start working together.

We can also pressure elected representatives to deal with problems that require their assistance. We might be able to clean a block by ourselves, but somebody's got to pick up the trash. We can watch out for one another's homes, but we still need the police and the courts to catch and prosecute criminals. We can help children do their home-work, but we need good schools to assign it. We can encourage high school drop-outs in the neighborhood to get their GEDs, but we need a State Department of Education to award them. Even much of what we now characterize as "voluntarism" in America still depends upon an active partnership between government and citizens to make it work.

Neighborhoods Online is not the only project aimed at helping people use the Internet to empower their communities. The

Downtown Minneapolis Residents' Association didn't need Neighborhoods Online to get started, nor did any of the other civic associations in Minneapolis. They link to it on their Web site, but their primary work is their own.

The City of Boulder, Colorado, has developed an entire neighborhood handbook (see Figure 5-8) for local neighborhood associations that it makes available through the Net. The Boulder Community Network boasts one of the best neighborhood support systems in the country.

The National Telecommunications Information and Assistance Agency that funded LibertyNet is supporting hundreds of similar efforts around the country, many of which are aimed specifically at empowering communities and neighborhoods of the disadvantaged (Figure 5-9).

In short, communities and neighborhoods all over the United States are discovering that the Internet represents a powerful vehicle for change. It is clear that even if every individual in America will not be able to go online, every organization in America is likely to try, since the potential for empowerment is too great to ignore.

What, then, can you do to join the bandwagon? How should you proceed?

Here are a few suggestions.

If you're not already involved in a neighborhood organization, you should find out whether one exists and simply join it. If such a group does not exist, you might at least consider trying to organize your block.

If the group that you join does want to use the Internet, use what you've read here to guide you.

The organization obviously needs an Internet Service Provider that will work with it. In this case, "work with it," means:

- Providing full Internet access at an affordable rate
- Helping the group set up its own Web site
- Working with the group to create an email list for its members

Who might serve this role?

CONTACT

City of Boulder, Colorado
*http://bcn.boulder.co.us/
government/boulder_city/
neighborhood handbook/
hndbkhom.html*

FIGURE 5-8
*The City of Boulder
Colorado's community
network handbook*

Welcome to the Boulder Neighborhood Handbook

Click introductory remarks by the author, Molly Dersonville, Neighborhood Liaison
- SECTION I - NEIGHBORHOOD ORGANIZATIONS
- SECTION II - CITY DEPARTMENTS
  SECTION III - BOARDS AND COMMISSIONS
- SECTION IV - GENERAL INFORMATION
- NEIGHBORHOOD HANDBOOK REGISTRATION

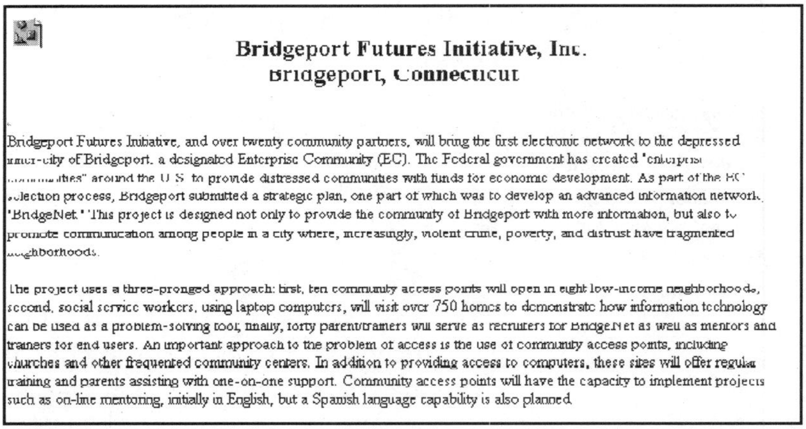

Bridgeport Futures Initiative, Inc.
Bridgeport, Connecticut

Bridgeport Futures Initiative, and over twenty community partners, will bring the first electronic network to the depressed inner-city of Bridgeport, a designated Enterprise Community (EC). The Federal government has created "enterprise communities" around the U.S. to provide distressed communities with funds for economic development. As part of the EC selection process, Bridgeport submitted a strategic plan, one part of which was to develop an advanced information network, "BridgeNet." This project is designed not only to provide the community of Bridgeport with more information, but also to promote communication among people in a city where, increasingly, violent crime, poverty, and distrust have fragmented neighborhoods.

The project uses a three-pronged approach: first, ten community access points will open in eight low-income neighborhoods, second, social service workers, using laptop computers, will visit over 750 homes to demonstrate how information technology can be used as a problem-solving tool, finally, forty parent/trainers will serve as recruiters for BridgeNet as well as mentors and trainers for end users. An important approach to the problem of access is the use of community access points, including churches and other frequented community centers. In addition to providing access to computers, these sites will offer regular training and parents assisting with one-on-one support. Community access points will have the capacity to implement projects such as on-line mentoring, initially in English, but a Spanish language capability is also planned.

FIGURE 5-9
Bridgeport Futures site

CONTACT

Doug Schuler
Seattle Community
Network Association,
Computer Professionals
for Social Responsibility

http://www.scn.org/ip/
commnet/hom.html

douglas@scn.org

The ideal partner would be a local community network like LibertyNet or the Boulder Community Network. These networks are being created exclusively to serve their own communities and that's what motivates the people who run them. They are well covered in Doug Schuler's book, *New Community Networks: Wired for Change*, published in 1996 by Addison-Welsley.

The people running community networks need you as much as you need them. They depend upon people who are prepared to learn and then take responsibility for themselves—as we at the Institute for the Study of Civic Values have done in Philadelphia. At the same time, community networks also bring with them people with the technical expertise in using the Internet that civic associations need. This is precisely the relationship that the Institute has established with LibertyNet. If your group replicates it, you'll be in good shape.

If there's not a community network to serve as an Internet provider, you should check out a local university or college or even the public library system. The Seattle public library, as an example, has been helping Seattle residents access the Net for years, and this is a growing trend among libraries in generally.

Obviously, training and technical support will be important to the organization as well. It will need help in developing a Web site and in establishing the email list for its members. Ultimately, someone in the group will have to take responsibility for maintaining and managing your online systems, and make sure that they're kept up to date.

Most importantly, the group will have to find ways to help their members gain Internet access as well. Obviously, everyone doesn't have to sign up with the same Internet Service Provider— unless there's a good reason to do so (better access rates, technical support, etc.)—since the Internet connects us all. Alternatively, no group can reasonably expect everyone to secure online accounts right away. Yet if an organization's leaders are convinced that by using email and the Web they can strengthen relationships within the community and expand their power in dealing with government, then they should be doing everything they can to help local residents take advantage of this opportunity as well.

A group should be clear, of course, that even with the support of an Internet Service Provider or a local community network, a project like Neighborhoods Online is a major undertaking. I devote at least an hour a day to email generated by our various lists; several hours a month to maintaining and updating the Web site; and a sizable amount of time in helping groups and active individuals go online. Our training sessions alone involve at least 10 hours a week, between the time it takes to recruit participants and conduct the actual sessions. A organization that wants to move in this direction needs to make sure that there are people in the group prepared to take these responsibilities seriously

Nonetheless, I have no doubt that thousands of community organizations will be building their own email lists and Web sites over the next several years, as an integral part of their programs. The benefits are becoming obvious to everyone, with or without the assistance of this book.

Moreover, the timing is exactly right. The "citizens' movement"—as many in the press are now calling it— is not some new invention of the 1990s. It is, in fact, an attempt to recover an ethic that we nearly lost—namely, that we all ought to help one another and participate in community affairs. Once again, this spirit is bringing all segments of this society back to civic and political life. As of March 1996, for example, there were Million Man March organizing committees in more than 350 communities around the country, according to the *New York Times*, involving thousands of African-American men in self-help projects and voter registration drives. Americans are no longer rallying around leaders. We are rallying around ourselves.

Now—through the Internet—we can start talking to one another.

6 Virtual Politics

It is clear that people all over the country are now prepared to fight for improvements in their own communities and neighborhoods and to lobby for and against legislation at the national level. I assume that you are one of these people if you're reading this book. But there is a curious twist to the attitude of a number of activist groups—especially those involved at the neighborhood level. They want to influence government, but avoid politics. Politicians are just a bunch of crooks, they say, so we ought to avoid them at all costs.

▶ Power and Politics

▶ Our Underused Political Resource: Votes

▶ The Grassroots Game of Politics

▶ Downloading for Democracy

▶ Issues Advocates

▶ Voter Activists

▶ Broadcasting to the Politicians

▶ From Volunteers to Voters—Making the Connection

POWER AND POLITICS

As someone who has worked both as a community activist and as—dare I say it—a politician over the course of my career, I have serious problems with this attitude. I think it's a mistake for anyone to take this position, given the importance of government and politics in our lives. For citizen groups, it's a disaster.

First, anyone who thinks you can divorce politics from government is just fooling himself. If you're in a group that's mobilizing people to pressure the mayor and the city council on behalf of a project, you're involved in politics, whatever you choose to call it. A little truth in advocacy would be appropriate here.

Second, contempt for politicians leads to defeat. Elected officials run for office. Politics is a good part of what they do. Why, then, should a group that ignores politics expect to be taken seriously by them? At best, you're irrelevant. At worst—if you'll pardon the expression—you're a pain. Either way, you won't get anywhere.

Third, avoiding politics protects the powerful from the powerless. The only thing that pleases a politician more than the support of friends is the non-involvement of his enemies. Activists who say "politics sucks!" are simply going along with the program.

There's only one way to get rid of "evil" politicians: replace them with good ones. That's hard work, but not impossible. And over the long haul, there's only one sure way to change politics itself: shift the structure of power from money and media to people working at the grassroots level. That's even harder work, but still not impossible.

Either way, you've got to get involved. Staying out of it just leaves the rest of them in charge.

OUR UNDERUSED POLITICAL RESOURCE: VOTES

Where do you begin? Well, as a starting point, it helps to recognize that you have access to a powerful political resource—more powerful even than money: votes. As an activist, you expect politicians to be accountable to you, your organization, and your community. Politicians expect you to vote for them in return.

Moreover, if you can produce votes on election day, you don't need to be a big bucks contributor. All the money in the world doesn't matter to a politician if he still can't get the votes. Ask Steve Forbes and Phil Gramm. They'll tell you.

So even if your organization itself is non-partisan, if politicians think your group has real influence with the voters, their door will always be open to you.

I speak from personal experience. In 1976—after two years of functioning merely as a community activist—I became a committeeperson in the Democratic Party organization in Philadelphia, representing the 13th Ward, 1st Division. This is an elected position, but no one else wanted the job, so I ran unopposed. The division itself covers four square blocks of an economically and racially diverse section of northwest Philadelphia known as Germantown. I had been head of our neighborhood civic association—the Southwest Germantown Association— but now I wanted to see whether by getting involved in party politics, I could help the community even more. It was the next step in building the neighborhoods movement described in the previous chapter.

Soon, my top priority became getting the highest possible voter registration and turnout that I could. That's what would give my division and Southwest Germantown clout with City Hall. So I started to use my experience as an activist to political advantage. I organized block cleanups. We set up town watch throughout the division. I saw to it that the city removed abandoned cars in record time. These services were available to everyone, but since I was doing the work, I was getting the credit for "delivering" them. And I was going door-to-door with postcards, registering people to vote.

There were 278 Democrats in the 13th Ward, 1st Division when I became a committeeman in the spring of 1976. By the fall, there were 380. We got an 86 percent turnout. More people voted for Jimmy Carter in November than had been registered in May.

It was then that I joined forces with another committeeperson in the neighborhood to help a parents' group fight for new basketball and tennis courts in a nearby park. Loretta Witt had carried her division by as much as I did, and between us we could deliver 500 votes. Suddenly, our district councilperson, Joseph E. Coleman, was anxious to hear what we had to say. The Fern Hill Park playground was finished in less than a year.

In 1979, Joe Coleman faced an unexpectedly tough opponent in the Democratic primary. It happened, however, that my polling place was located directly opposite the playground in Fern Hill Park. As people came to the polls, I pointed to the basketball and tennis courts and warned that if we voted against Coleman, no politician would do anything for us again. I carried my division for him by more than 100 votes. Joe Coleman won that primary by only 18 votes.

Over the next two years, Southwest Germantown received significant funding for a community development corporation to rehabilitate abandoned housing. The Fern Hill Park playground expanded and capital improvements began in another neighborhood recreation center as well. An industrial strip adjacent to the neighborhood became a city enterprise zone.

In 1982, Joe Coleman was chosen by his colleagues to become the first African-American president of the city council. In 1983, his support proved critical to my own election as a councilman-at-large on a "neighborhood agenda."

I know that a lot went into making all of these things happen beyond raw politics. But being able to deliver votes when they were needed as a committeeperson in the 13th Ward, 1st Division was critical as well.

It's a lesson I've never forgotten.

This is what you've got to learn how to do as well—to turn all the good work you're doing for a cause or a community into votes for the people who support you. That's what the Christian Coalition and the National Rifle Association and the AFL-CIO are doing and it's why they have power. If you're not doing this, and you're feeling frustrated and powerless, that's why.

In 1994, George Nethercutt upset Thomas Foley—then Speaker of the House—in Washington's 5th Congressional District by 4,000 votes. Nethercutt got no more votes than the Republican who tried to beat Foley in 1992—110,000. But Foley's vote dropped from 135,000 to 106,000 between the two elections. There weren't more Republicans, just fewer Democrats—in Foley's race and in Congressional districts all over the country. The conservative activists worked their heads off, and the liberals stayed home. How many voters did you bring to the polls in 1994?

There is only one question a grassroots organization needs to ask about every election if it wants to influence politicians—how many voters can get we to the polls? It doesn't take a miracle. It takes work.

THE GRASSROOTS GAME OF POLITICS

What does it take to expand voter participation in our neighborhoods, as a way of asserting our power in politics? How can we use the Internet to help us in the process?

The political establishments in both parties are not addressing these particular questions with any seriousness these days, so we have the field largely to ourselves. Even in the spring of 1996, as I write, most pollsters are already trying to figure out who is "likely to vote" in November so that proper media can be developed to appeal to them. The unregistered and unlikely voters will be dismissed as irrelevant long before the formal campaigns begin. The only groups taken seriously here are demographic groups—women, African-Americans, fundamentalist Christians, angry white men, etc.—not real organizations with constituencies, programs, and demands. There won't even be much work for volunteers, unless they want to raise money.

The role of the Internet in the process will be negligible as well, for all the hoopla surrounding it. To be sure, most candidates for major offices will have Web sites—which the press and political junkies will use to retrieve position papers and speeches and keep track of the campaign schedule. Groups like the League of Women Voters will be posting their non-partisan "know the candidates" guides to the World Wide Web in various parts of the country, for those who like to study such material before making up their minds. In fact, an organization called The California Voter Foundation has developed an especially useful model in this area (Figure 6-1).

All of this is merely an extension of politics as broadcasting, however—via the media, via the mail, and now via the Internet. The politicians speak; the voters listen. Even if an online voter guide can help us overcome our ignorance of candidates and issues, we remain isolated from one another and without influence in the process. We

FIGURE 6-1

The California Voter Foundation has used its Web site to increase public participation in the political process

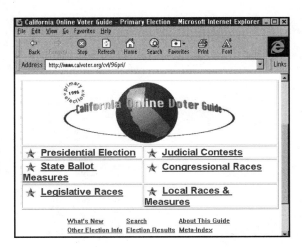

go to the polls, cast our vote, and wait for the returns. That's all we can do.

And many of us will simply stay home. In 1992, according to the *Almanac of American Politics*, only 104 million people voted in the Presidential elections out of 185 million people eligible for this privilege. That's 56 percent. If you're reading this after the 1996 election, check out whether the turnout was any better. I'm not placing any bets on it.

Getting voters to the polls is not about political broadcasting—it's about political organizing, especially where we live. It's got to be personal—one voter at a time. That's what I learned as a committeeperson all those years. Everything else—direct mail, phone banks, campaign advertising—falls on deaf ears. You can add exhortations via the Internet to the list as well. Why should people who hate politics on television try to find it on the World Wide Web? They won't, and every politician knows it. That's why most of them don't take the Net seriously. But using the Internet as a resource system for political organizing is another matter. Now the aim is not to reach the people least interested in politics, but the most committed—activists who will to go door-to-door with fliers and registration cards and information about the campaigns. These are the people who can mobilize the larger population if given proper support. But they won't be given much support at all—at least not by the candidates for major offices. That's not the way the game is played right now.

So if you're a party activist at the local level, an advocate for a particular cause, or a neighborhood leader, you have the grassroots game of politics to yourself. You should play it to win. You've always been willing to use your own network of personal contacts and volunteers to do the work in the streets. Now, there are Web sites and email lists disseminating material through the Internet that can help you. If you had to rely on conventional sources for resources like this—organizational mailings, political journals, newspapers—you'd never find it. Now you can locate it online, print it out, and distribute it. We ought to call it "downloading for democracy."

The process has already begun.

DOWNLOADING FOR DEMOCRACY

You should think about what's available in terms of three kind of activists—party activists, issues activists, and what I would call "voter" activists—those concerned with voter registration and turnout as ends in themselves. There are already significant projects in each area as I'm writing this book, and by the time it appears there will be more. Pick and choose what you need.

PARTY ACTIVISTS—DIGITAL DEMOCRATS

The words "voter registration" or "voter education" are not found on the Web sites maintained by either the Democratic or Republican National Committees—at least as of April 1996.

Both parties give us a full menu of platforms, procedures, speeches, "talking points" on current issues, and links to other Web sites maintained by legislators and leaders. It's preaching to the choir, but they do a reasonable job of it.

The Democratic National Committee provides an online form for people who want to volunteer for one of the following activities:

- Raising money
- Putting up a lawn sign
- Working as a precinct captain
- Writing letters to the editor
- Participating in a "talk radio" campaign

The Republicans include an online survey to get feedback on how they're doing in Washington, with questions like these:

```
To combat violent crime which approach do you favor:

Blame society, ban guns and pour more money into
social engineering programs like "midnight
basketball".

Punish lawbreakers with stiff mandatory sentences,
build more prisons and eliminate parole for violent
criminals.

No opinion.
```

You can even buy a GOP golf shirt from their Web site (Figure 6-2).

What's missing is any serious emphasis on grassroots voter education. That you have to work out for yourself.

Within the Democratic Party, however, there is at least one organization unabashedly promoting the Internet as a resource for local organizing. It's called Digital Democrats, created by a software developer named Charles Gallie from San Francisco and a freelance reporter, Jim Bui from North Carolina, who had not even met when they started to put the project together.

GOP Golf Shirt (30k)

Short-sleeved, 100% combed cotten interlock shirt by Outer Banks is the winning ticket! Comfy and durable, with features that include a knitted polo collar and welt cuffs, 2-button placket, 2" side vents and 2 1/2" locg tail. In five colors

```
RE1000WH        white
RE1000HG        hunter green
RE1000CO        coral
RE1000NA        navv
RE1000WI        wine
S -- XL         $32.00
XXL             $35.00
```

FIGURE 6-2

A little fundraising maybe?

Their mission statement makes it clear that they intend to use the Internet to rebuild grassroots involvement within the Democratic Party:

> We, a small group of Democratic Party activists, announce the formation of a grassroots virtual organization to rebuild and revitalize the Democratic Party from the ground up....
>
> Our objectives are:
>
> ...Build a nationwide volunteer, cyber army of several hundred thousand computerized volunteers supplemented by thousands of non-computerized volunteers working for local Democratic candidates, Democratic clubs, and Democratic Party organizations.
>
> ....Build a database of the households in America for use in voter registration and GOTV(Get Out the Vote)....
>
> ....Tie all of our volunteers together using the Internet and software provided by our organization and others, to collect and manage all of this information.
>
> ...Develop the largest most comprehensive GOTV effort ever mounted using all the new technology including fax machines, bar code readers, a network of computers scattered across the country, Fax-In, Fax-Back, voicemail, and 800 numbers.

At this point, they're a model for what any group of this kind—partisan or non-partisan—can do.

They maintain a Web site, shown in Figure 6-3.

FIGURE 6-3

Home page of the Digital Democrats

They publish an online newsletter:

Dear Democrat,

Our new online newsletter in the first three weeks has exceeded our expectations. With no advertising budget, no institutional funding, and no public announcement, the "Internet Democrat" has acquired 2,500 subscribers and is attracting about 100 subscribers every day.

Our goal—to bypass the cynical mainstream media filter, to empower citizens at the grassroots and present an alternative to the rabid right-wing—is well on its way to becoming reality. Imagine a revitalized Democratic Party, with thousands of new volunteers eager to help, well-informed and mobilized at a moment's notice, ready to win legislative victories and get out our vote in crucial precincts all across the country...

They even encourage you to download a shareware software package called Precinct Worker (Figure 6-4), which includes a simple database program for voter registration drives (complete with every member of Congress), a file summarizing the accomplishments of the Clinton administration, and a database covering the key votes of the 103rd Congress.

Even the Christian Coalition doesn't offer this much.

Digital Democrats does include links to the conventional Web sites within the Democratic Party—the Democratic National Committee, the Democratic Senate Leadership Council, and various state Democratic committees. But in using the Internet to promote grassroots involvement in their party, they are miles ahead of all the rest.

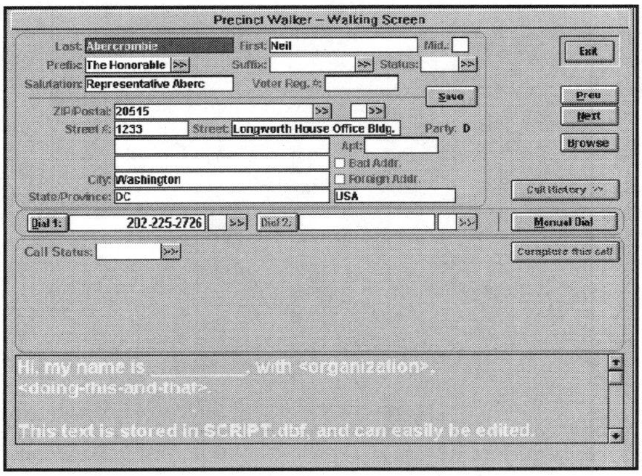

FIGURE 6-4

Web sites can be used to provide organizing tools. Precinct Worker, is free to anyone who wants to download it

ISSUES ADVOCATES

A number of issues organizations are now using the Internet to mobilize grassroots efforts around campaigns as well—including some that we examined in Chapter 5.

The Christian Coalition is the trend-setter here, of course. Its Voter Guides now appear online. All you have to do is download a special piece of software called an Adobe Acrobat Reader from the Coalition site itself, and it reproduces a crisp copy of the one-page guide for redistribution as you see fit (see Figure 6-5).

Ralph Reed is no longer alone, however. The League of Conservation Voters (LCV) is now urging its followers to use its scorecards in Congressional campaigns by retrieving them from the Internet.

FIGURE 6-5

A complete Voter's Guide was downloadable from the Christian Coalition Site

George Nethercutt may have presented himself as a political outsider against Tom Foley in 1994, but now he runs on a record of his own. Figure 6-6 shows what the League of Conservation Voters thought of it.

See how easily it reproduces. What we described as merely an online legislative monitoring system in Chapter 5 becomes a piece of campaign literature. All grassroots organizers need to do is add a few choice comments of their own, print it out, and a flier is ready for the masses.

The women's movement has joined the cyberspace fray as well. On November 2, 1995, the American Association of University Women announced that it, too, would conduct a voter education campaign—backed by 110 organizations—designed to reach "millions of women who did not vote in the last election."

In launching the campaign, AAUW further announced that it would distribute what it called Get the Facts bulletins through an email and fax network that had already enrolled more than 5,000 subscribers. As Anne Bryant, AAUW's executive director, put it, "We expect every woman who receives a Get the Facts alert to pass it on or post it up. From the laundromat to the factory to the boardroom, women will share these alerts with their co-workers, friends, and others in their community....Women don't trust politicians any more than men do. But women trust each other."

Get the Facts bulletins are short, specific, and tailored to local concerns. An electronic mailing on education and job training circulated in February 1996 offered the following assessment of Congressional action on the budget:

> The education bill passed by the House cuts $3.7 billion from education and more than $2 billion from job training.
>
> These cuts hurt students by:
>
> threatening girls' and boys' safety in 14,000 school districts by cutting funds for school safety officers and drug abuse, sexual harassment, and violence prevention programs; jeopardizing women's and girls'

FIGURE 6-6

George Nethercutt unseated the Speaker of the House, Tom Foley

LEAGUE OF CONSERVATION VOTERS
1995 National Environmental Scorecard

Rep. George Nethercutt (R)
Washington
1995 LCV Score: 0%

access to training in nontraditional fields such as
math and science which is key to high-skill and
high-wage jobs; and denying 1.1 million students
crucial help in math, reading, and writing.

Those who received the alert were advised to "post it in public
places such as supermarkets and child care centers," and to "meet
with your Senators and Representatives when they are in the districts. Ask them how they voted on education and training issues."
Bulletins like these are now reaching thousands of groups around the
country at a fraction of what it would cost to mail them.

I have no doubt that by the time you read this book, every national organization with an interest in a particular issue or issues will
be producing material like this for campaigns. Again—find what you
need and use it.

VOTER ACTIVISTS

Given that organizations promoting civic activism and neighborhood
revitalization generally stay out of electoral politics, no one is producing voter education materials related to community concerns
such as economic development and affordable housing. Local groups
will have to come up with their own approaches here, based on the
issues of greatest concerns to them.

Nonetheless, community organizations could make a real contribution in this area by focusing on the groups that are generally hardest to reach—young people and adults with limited education. Here,
there *are* projects than can help us. The first, Rock the Vote, aims at
young people in their teens and early 20s. . The other—the Easy
Reader Voter Guides—concentrates on participants in adult literacy
programs. Persuading people in these groups to vote would make a
significant difference in the community as a whole.

Rock the Vote

You may already have heard about Rock the Vote. It was conceived in
1990 by members of the recording industry to fight what they now
describe on their Web site as "a wave of political attacks on freedom
of speech and artistic expression." In 1991, however, Rock the Vote
moved beyond rap to "advocate legislation that would have a positive
impact on 18 to 24 year-olds."

Their performance has been impressive by any standard. Rock the
Vote generated 250,000 postcards on behalf of the Motor Voter Bill.
They fought for Americorps, President Clinton's National Service

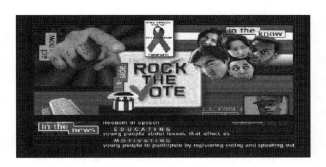

FIGURE 6-7
Rock the Vote's Web site targets online youth

Program. They even took part in the national debate over health care reform, concentrating on health issues affecting young people. And along the way—in 1992—Rock the Vote made a major effort to increase youth participation in the Presidential campaign.

Today, Rock the Vote is a serious presence on the Internet as well. There's an attractive Web site (shown in Figure 6-7).

The Rock the Vote Guide to Health Care Reform (Figure 6-8) is online.

Most importantly, Rock the Vote is now conducting its voter registration campaign through the Internet as well. They, too, post downloadable messages that are targeted directly to their audience.

```
Common misconceptions about voting:

1. But I'll get called for jury duty.

Ha! Try again! These days most states assign jury duty
from state driver's license and social service lists.
What are you going to do, give up driving?

Besides, if you do live in a state where the voter
list is used for jury duty and there was this young
person up on trial, don't you think you could get down
to the bottom of things better than some geezer?

2. The IRS will track me down.
```

FIGURE 6-8
Health care is not usually on young people's, but Rock the Vote tells them why it should be

A Guide To Health Care Reform
For Young Americans

introduction	overview
substance abuse	mental health
pregnancy	hiv/aids
violence	
legislation	survey

Nope. They don't have access to you this way.

3. I 'm not into joining some wacko political party.

So don't. But that doesn't mean you don't have a voice. Especially if yours is so unique, you better get yourself heard and vote!

Please note: In many states, to vote in the often important primary election you must be registered with either the Democratic or Republican party. But you can still vote in the general election for the candidate of your choice, whether you're registered with a party or not.

4. I'm a convicted felon. We can't vote.

It depends on the state. If you have served out your parole like a good boy or girl, in many states you can vote.

P.S. The vote you cast will be worth just as much as the judge's who put you away!

This is a "rap" generation version of the personal becoming political.

Easy Reader Voters Guide

The Easy Reader Voter Guide project is less visible, but no less important. In 1994, the Center for Civic Literacy (CCL) in San Francisco brought together a group of adult learners from the Bay Area to produce a voter guide that would help people reading at the 8th grade level—many of whom were simply intimidated by politics—gain both the understanding and the confidence needed to register to vote.

The Easy Reader Voter Guide did a fine job of translating complex information into language that "easy readers" could understand—as these portraits of the Democratic and Republican Parties suggest:

Democratic Party

The Democratic Party wants to "Put People First" on issues that matter to most Americans — economic growth, crime prevention, affordable health care and quality schools. We want to reform welfare and protect the environment. We believe in making people's lives better.

Top Priorities:

▪ Bring businesses back to California and expand job opportunities

- Make education a #1 priority again

- Make our neighborhoods free from violence, crime and drugs

Republican Party

The Republican Party believes in less government in our lives. Good government is based on the individual. Each person's ability, dignity, freedom and responsibility must be honored and recognized. Americans should preserve their feelings of national strength and pride.

Top Priorities:

- Stop illegal immigration

- Control crime with tougher penalties

- Improve the economy with pro-growth policies for business and reduce excessive regulation

The Easy Reader Voter Guide appeared initially as a printed guide, for use in the Bay Area programs that had helped develop it. Subsequently, however, the California Voter Foundation—whose overall Online Voter Guide I mentioned at the outset of this discussion—saw to it that an Internet version of the Easy Reader Voter Guide was added to the Web site so that adult literacy groups throughout the state could use it.

All of this led to the development of an Easy Reader Voter Guide for the 1996 California primary—this time with the express purpose of serving the entire state. The Center for Civic Literacy made more than 800,000 printed copies available to various groups. A number of newspapers reprinted the Guide, including the *Los Angeles Times*. And the 1996 Easy Reader Voter Guide has a Web site of its own (Figure 6-9)—also linked to the California Voter Foundation Web site.

The Director of the Center for Civic Literacy, Susan Clark, eventually hopes to produce a version of the Easy Reader Voter Guide for the entire country. With the Internet at her disposal, I have no doubt that she will.

Obviously, neither of these projects relies entirely on the Internet to reach its audience. Rock the Vote pops up on MTV with some frequency. The Easy Reader Voter Guides are available as booklets and in local newspapers all over California.

Yet it is precisely the hard-to-reach voters who require personal attention if they're going to respond. Rock the Vote and the Easy

FIGURE 6-9
Voter's guides and other tools are offered from CCL site

Reader Voter Guides are producing terrific materials, but somebody's got to use them. Local civic associations and human service agencies with ongoing programs for these groups would be ideal. And you can point out that by voting, they help not only themselves, but the entire neighborhood. In the process, you'll be strengthening the community as a whole.

Each of these projects, then, demonstrates how easy it is to use the Internet to find materials for grassroots organizing around political campaigns. If your own favorite organizations aren't represented in this discussion, use an Alta Vista or Lycos search to find them. If they're doing anything at all in voter education, it'll probably be online.

BROADCASTING TO THE POLITICIANS

How can you let politicians know what you're doing? As important, if you're working with a group of grassroots organizers, how can *they* let the politicians know what you're doing? Within a formal party organization, one of the privileges of being a committeeperson—if your party runs the government, at least— is having direct access to the people in power. Then, when you call party headquarters, you get special treatment. Every candidate speaks to you. For many party workers, this is enough to make it all worthwhile.

Advocacy organizations and community groups involved in voter education can insist on similar treatment from campaigns. Capitalizing on your proven technological sophistication, insist either that a candidate maintain an email list specifically for people working with you or, perhaps, for all volunteers—including yours. If you're work-ing on registration and turnout on a non-partisan basis, you can in-sist upon some form of access to all campaigns. And they'll give it to you: no candidate wants any group that's registering voters to say that he or she has been uncooperative in a get-out-the-vote effort. Even a simple arrangement like this can generate enthusiasm among your own workers and remind the candidates of what you're doing for them.

In Minneapolis-St. Paul, there's a project underway that is demon-strating how to build an entire Internet support system for grassroots electoral organizing—a Neighborhoods Online for activists in poli-tics, if you will. It's called E-Democracy, and it's managed and main-tained entirely by volunteers working with the Twin Cities FreeNet. It began in 1994 on a modest scale—focusing on the governor's and Senate races. In 1996, it is broadening its scope of activities and ex-panding its target area to include the entire state of Minnesota. This is a model well worth examining, especially if you're working with a community network like LibertyNet or a local Internet Service Pro-vider that can handle major projects.

CONTACT

Minnesota E-Democracy
http://www.freenet.map.mn
.us/govt/e-democracy/

At first glance, E-Democracy appears primarily to be an election information center, similar to the Online Voter Guide produced by the California Voter Foundation. The home page (Figure 6-10) points to a wide range of resources associated with the campaigns, neatly organized in one place for easy access.

Need to register at a new address, but unsure of the procedures? The League of Women Voters provides them on the Election and Voter Registration Information menu (Figure 6-11).

Trying to get information about a particular candidate or political party? It's all here (Figure 6-12).

Of course, there are national campaign Web sites like Politics USA that provide an overview of Congressional and gubernatorial contests on a state-by-state basis. Yet none of them is in a position to assemble all the information about procedures, parties, candidates, and issues for a city that E-Democracy brings together in one place. Local peo-ple are needed to deal with local issues and that's where this project excels.

Yet the "heartbeat" of E-Democracy—as its founder, Steven Clift puts it—is not the information center, but a series of email lists and electronic forums that make it easy for people involved in politics at all levels to connect with one another.

The most important of these is a list called MN-Politics. Launched in 1994 as part of E-Democracy, it's now taken on a life of its own. It

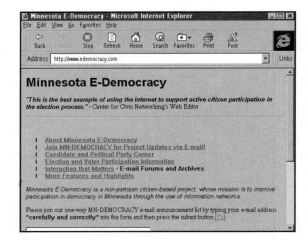

FIGURE **6-10**
*Minnesota's
E-Democracy is
a model of
Net Activism*

is scrupulously non-partisan. Among its more than 400 subscribers, you'll find Democrats and Republicans of varying ideological persuasions, an outspoken Libertarian or two, labor leaders, neighborhood activists, and reporters from the local press. Participants argue about the political parties, issues, candidates, campaigns, even political philosophy—all without tearing one another apart. A self-proclaimed neo-Nazi did try to insinuate himself into the discussion for a time, until it was clear that he wasn't getting anywhere with anyone and unsubscribed. In effect, MN-Politics is creating a virtual political community within a real political community that has developed an integrity and a power all its own.

As a result, when E-Democracy speaks, the politicians listen. In 1994, project organizers persuaded the major and minor party candidates for governor and the Senate candidates in Minnesota to

FIGURE **6-11**
*The League of
Women Voters
national home page*

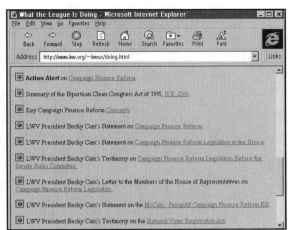

FIGURE 6-12
Sites like the LWV's can focus like a laser on issue important to their members

CONTACT

Scott Aikens
Creator and Director of the E-Debates

gsa1001@cus.cam.ac.uk

http://www2.dar.cam.ac.uk/www/gsa1001.htm

Minnesota Electronic Democracy

participate in what amounted to the first election debates via email in the history of American politics. They were moderated by a Scott Aikens (an active participant in the civic-values list, currently pursuing graduate studies at Oxford University), who posed questions related to crime, taxes, and government itself, to which the candidates responded online. Only a few thousand people were able to read the answers directly—this was 1994, mind you. But the press covered the debates and reprinted what they said. A similar debate via email is planned for Minnesota Senate candidates in 1996, and all of them are expected to participate. At this point, it would be embarrassing to refuse.

Think about what all this means to political organizers in Minneapolis-St. Paul. Now, anytime they want to recruit people for a campaign, or speak out on an issue, or relay a message to the press, they can log onto MN-Politics or a special issues forum and get it done. The actual number of participants remains tiny, when measured against the 800,000 residents of the Twin Cities who are eligible to vote. But the 1,000 people online know how to *reach* the 800,000 residents of the Twin Cities who are eligible to vote— through the media, through public events, and through canvassing within neighborhoods. E-Democracy is where they gather among themselves—to strategize, debate, and tell the candidates what they think. Political email lists are commonplace at the national level—as we have seen. E-Democracy is concentrating at the local level, where people live and vote.

Right now, E-Democracy exists only in Minnesota. It is, however, a powerful model for the future. Everywhere else in America, the candidates broadcast to us. In Minneapolis-St. Paul, active citizens can broadcast back—unimpeded by a belligerent "host" at the other end of the line. Now what might happen to American politics over the next ten years—when even more of us will be going online—if we developed an E-Democracy in every city in the country?

FROM VOLUNTEERS TO VOTERS—MAKING THE CONNECTION

What, however, can we do right now? We don't have an E-Democracy in every city in the country. Many of us don't even have a grass-roots party organization or strong non-partisan civic groups. Is there anything we can do on our own?

The answer, again, is yes.

Let me tell you about two friends of mine in the Philadelphia area who are taking the initiative.

Bill Davidon and Maxine Libros have been involved in liberal politics for a number of years. Neither of them makes a living at it or holds a position in the Democratic Party. They serve on the local board of Americans for Democratic Action, and they work on individual campaigns. That's it. They are among the millions of people in America of varying ideological persuasions who participate in politics out of a sense of obligation and, frankly, because they enjoy it.

In 1995, they decided to tackle a somewhat larger assignment. They were appalled at the Republican Contract with America. They were outraged that a local representative— Jon D. Fox, from the 13th Congressional District in Montgomery County—was part of the celebrated Republican "Class of 1994" that was making it happen. Fox had won his seat primarily because his opponent—Congresswoman Marjorie Margolies-Mezvinsky—cast the deciding vote for Clinton's 1993 budget, after first announcing that she would oppose it. That vote cost her the election. But as Davidon and Libros saw it, Jon Fox was now marching lock-step in the Gingrich parade, and this was equally unacceptable to the people of his district.

So, entirely on their own, they put together a network of 80 volunteers, all prepared to register voters, conduct house meetings, and distribute literature in an effort unseat Jon Fox. Now it even has a name: Fair Legislation Action Group (FLAG). When they started, they didn't even know who the Democratic nominee was going to be. Since then, they have met with him—a Montgomery county commissioner named Joe Hoeffel—and have started coordinating their

CONTACT

William C. Davidon
Fair Legislation Action
Group (FLAG)
wdavidon@haverford.edu

Maxine Libros
Fair Legislation Action
Group (FLAG)
mlibros@haverford.edu

efforts with his campaign. Yet even before they met with the candidate, FLAG was ready to go.

What's making much of this possible is the Internet.

Bill Davidon spends an hour a day on the Net, monitoring email from the ADA and exploring a wide range of political Web sites. He's especially pleased to be able circulate the electronic edition of the ADA Bulletin to 10 members of his group who already have Internet accounts and he's urging the others—many of whom at least have computers in their homes—to go online as well.

The Net also makes it possible for them to keep careful track of Jon Fox' votes in Congress. Here, the legislative monitoring provided by Project VoteSmart—which I mentioned in the discussion of the World Wide Web in Chapter 4—has proven to be an invaluable resource. It permits FLAG to focus on the votes of particular interest to Montgomery County and target their appeals accordingly.

Soon FLAG will be using the Internet to keep pace with the Hoeffel campaign itself. They'll be downloading his position papers and speeches from the candidate's Web site and sending feedback via email. They'll be able to broaden their own distribution list to include other Hoeffel volunteers with online accounts. All of this will create the kind of enthusiasm and solidarity during a campaign that money will never buy.

I have no idea at this writing whether Joe Hoeffel will defeat Jon Fox in November 1996. I do know that Bill Davidon, Maxine Libros, and FLAG are already an important part of the process. Not only do they bring a small army of workers to the campaign, but an email network and an activist bookmark list with links to every major political Web site in the country. In fact, their greatest frustration is that more people aren't yet on the Internet to join their network and ac-

FIGURE 6-13

The Americans for Democratic Action home page (http://kogod-b9. battelle1.american. edu/ada.htm)

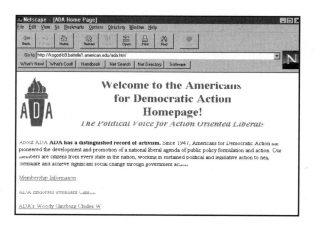

cess the World Wide Web for themselves. But this, they believe, will come in time.

A volunteer group like FLAG used to need an office and staff and a pile of money to put out mailings. Now they can use the Internet. The more people who join them online, the more powerful the group. These are the cyberspace committeepeople of the future.

The major parties lost interest in grassroots voter education years ago, however much they still pay lip service to it. As another political adage goes, however, "nobody cares about us *but* us." We either do it ourselves or it doesn't happen. People have been complaining about politicians for years. Bill Davidon and Maxine Libros have decided to fight back. Now they have the tools to do it.

7 We, the People

What, then, needs to happen to make the Internet an instrument of political empowerment?

The Net itself is just a bunch of list managers, Gophers, and Web servers transmitting to our computers through the phone lines. Some tell us that it's bound to create a new era of freedom and opportunity for everyone and that we should just sit back and enjoy it. Others warn that we shouldn't let technology run our lives, no matter emancipating it may appear to be.

▶ The Crossroads Ahead

▶ Partnerships

▶ The Internet/Activist Partnership B. Partnerships

▶ The Government Contribution

▶ Net Activism: A Final Checklist

▶ We, the People

THE CROSSROADS AHEAD

It's all so exciting—or unnerving, depending on your perspective. Clearly, however, technology is not neutral. Radio and television by their nature give a small group of people enormous power to determine what gets broadcast to the rest of us. Telephones and fax machines help us communicate with one another.

Mainframe computers gave rise to the centralized bureaucracies that dominated America in the post-war era. Desktop computers have fostered decentralization at every level of society.

And now we have the Internet—which can go either way.

It can continue to develop as a complex global communications system that transforms the way in which we relate to one another.

Or it can *devolve* into just another broadcasting system, where a new group of people gets to determine what passes from their transmitters to our screens.

Of course, it may be possible to have the best of both worlds— email by day; hit movies by night. But there is an equal chance that these distinct lines of development preclude one another and that we may have to choose between them.

So let's be clear about what we need.

Using the Internet for political empowerment is not about watching television through a laptop or ordering groceries via email. It's not even about downloading a digitized reproduction of the Mona Lisa for a term paper on the Renaissance.

It's about building discussion lists of activists from all over the country who share the same goals and want to work together to achieve them. It's about being able to keep track of government programs and pending legislation even if they don't appear in the newspapers every day. It's about emailing a message to a Congressperson on a Tuesday and getting a response by Wednesday afternoon.

It's about creating networks among organizers in their own neighborhoods and communities who go online to maintain contact with each other even when they're not in a position to meet. I've suggested various ways in this book that we can do all of these things right now. I've pointed to individuals and groups that are leading the way.

There is certainly a great opportunity here, but we're the ones who have to take advantage of it. It's not clear that we will.

PARTNERSHIPS

We should think about the possibilities in terms of partnerships. Nothing meaningful happens in the absence of partnerships. My first Internet account established a partnership with Delphi—where I also hosted a custom forum on building community for several months.

The civic-values email list grew out of a partnership between the Institute for the Study of Civics and the Center for Civic Networking. Neighborhoods Online is a product of yet another partnership—this time between the Institute and LibertyNet in Philadelphia. This book involves a partnership between myself and O'Reilly & Associates and Songline Studios, Inc.

These projects all represent partnerships related to the Internet that would not have been possible *without* the Internet. Most of us live too far away from each other to do business any other way.

This suggests a basic principle about the Internet in relation to politics that could serve as a guiding principle for its overall future development as well:

The Internet empowers us when it expands the range of partnerships available to us and enables us to work together on behalf of common goals.

No other technology fulfills this mission quite so well. We watch television. We listen to the radio. We talk on the telephone. Yet, on the Internet, we can meet, get to know one another, and start to collaborate—several hundred of us at a time. This is a precondition to success in organizing—and some might say, in life itself. So if we want to use the Net in politics, preserving it as a means of communications should be our number one priority.

There are specific steps we need to take, however, to bring about what I've been describing here. The resources of the Internet are available to activists right now, but only a relatively small number are in a position to use them. Everyone needs to be brought into the process.

To reach this point, we need to build a partnership between those with a stake in the Internet, people in government and politics, and the rest of us. Each of these broad groups needs to make specific contributions to this partnership in order to make it work. Let me spell out what I think they are.

THE INTERNET/ACTIVIST PARTNERSHIP

Support for an Internet/activist partnership from service providers, software developers, and policy advocates who are the *de facto* proprietors of the Net is crucial. They will determine whether the Net remains user-friendly or out of reach. They need to commit themselves to certain goals for Net access and development. Some of these are obvious; others may not be. All of them are important.

UNIVERSAL ACCESS

Offering universal access to the Internet has got to be the overriding goal. A great many people agree to this in principle, but getting there is another matter. To be sure, if the price of computers and software continues to drop, more people will be able to afford them. If an inexpensive "Internet computer" catches on, so much the better—unless (and this is a big "unless") there is no good way to manage email with it. Then it's just a cheap way to surf the Web and useless as a means of communications—which, as I've tried to suggest, is the priority here.

Even with less expensive equipment, however, it will be a long time before most people will have computers in their homes, let alone modems and phone lines. This makes it essential to help libraries and community centers provide public access to the Net, as LibertyNet is trying to do in Philadelphia. Moreover, we ought to ensure that every *organization* working within a community—and especially within a low-income community—has access to the Internet. They too can offer access to people who can't afford it, as well as share information obtained through the Internet with their members via newsletters and conventional mailings. If we can't guarantee universal access to the Internet itself right away, at least we can enlarge the group of people who benefit from it.

TRAINING

Providing Internet accounts without training is often useless. Most people need help in getting started, and activists are no exception. Everyone involved with the Internet should be assuming part of this responsibility—service providers, software manufacturers (where's the manual?), local community networks, colleges and universities, and even public schools. You may wonder how connecting schools to the Internet also contributes to community empowerment. Well, a reasonable number of activists in Philadelphia and elsewhere are learning how to access the Net from their kids.

MANAGEABLE EMAIL

The public discussion of the Internet now revolves almost entirely around the World Wide Web, with "ooohh—-aaahh" Web sites even appearing on the evening news. That's fine, but what activists—in fact, most people—want from the Internet is email. A significant contribution software developers can make is to ensure that every email management system on every service permits us to sort out messages by sender, category, and address—and send attached files to one another without difficulty. Many services meet this test already, but this should be the standard for everyone.

We also need substantial improvement in the software now used to manage email lists—listserv, listproc, and majordomo. As an example: each of these packages produces what are known as list "archives"—a file or files with every message reproduced in chronological order. This is crucial to anyone who wants to find out what transpired on a list in their absence.

Unfortunately, many of these packages make it impossible to retrieve only those messages related to a particular topic such as welfare reform—equivalent to the "find" function in database management and word processing programs. You have to wade through hundreds of messages chronologically to find the one or two you need. This seriously undermines the usefulness of list archives to anyone who needs them. E-Democracy has solved this problem in Minneapolis for its list archives. Everyone else should solve it as well.

This is just one example of the limits of listserv software.

It would also be nice if every email list package included:

- An option to hold up messages while you're away without having them flood the list manager's email box.

- A built-in function to permit members of a list to vote on something. There's been a lot of discussion of electronic voting mechanisms for the Internet. Here, I'm thinking about just a simple, "yes," "no," or "1,2,3,4,5" function that might be set up on a list and tabulated automatically for the list manager.

- A list manager command to temporarily block someone who is causing a problem on the list, without dumping him or her altogether. This would be a useful mechanism for preserving civility.

These are just a few steps that would make the world of online communications a lot easier for everyone involved.

ACCESSIBLE WEB PAGES

The fourth contribution entails a commitment from Internet software developers to continue to make it easy for most of us to develop Web pages of our own. There are those who merely surf the Web, but activists need to be able to write Web pages as well as read them. Right now, anyone with a word processing program can do it, but this may not last for long.

I'll use myself as an example. As I indicated earlier in the book, I've built two Web sites—Neighborhoods Online and civic-values. Even though I knew nothing at all about HTML prior to July of 1995, all it took was a two-hour seminar with Nate Gasser at LibertyNet on the subject—and a few mass-market "how to write Web pages in your spare time" books—and I was on my way.

There are no complex graphics at either of my sites—only clip-art. I've been able to incorporate scripts for forms and public conferencing into one or two of these pages because LibertyNet has made them accessible to information providers throughout its service. All we have to do is point to the scripts from our sites, and they do the rest. Without this help—as an example—people accessing our Neighborhood Empowerment menu could not send email back to us directly from the site requesting further information. This would be a serious limitation.

Despite my limits as a programmer, however, Neighborhoods Online and civic-values are now accessed by thousands of community activists, public officials, journalists, faculty and students every week. It doesn't matter to them that a little ticker tape banner doesn't thread across the bottom of the screen saying, "Welcome to Neighborhoods Online." They want the content.

Will this still be possible in 1999, however, when Java or some even flashier programming language rules the Internet? Will those of us who don't know how to design full-blown software applications for use online be driven from the Web altogether? There need be no formal policy here; only a new *de facto* standard for what a decent Web page requires. How many amateur painters think they belong in the Museum of Modern Art? This is where shaping the Web as a broadcasting system and preserving it as a means of mass communications run at cross-purposes.

I have no doubt that as the Web browser sweepstakes of the 1990s between Netscape, Microsoft, and other software manufacturers unfold, they'll make sure that eventually we can all read every Web page—even though there will be glitches between one browser and the next. The more serious risk lies in making Web pages so complicated that only programmers will be able to write them.

For those of us who believe that the Internet should be an instrument of citizen empowerment, the goal should be to keep Web page development as simple as possible. I raise this issue now—in 1996—before it's too late.

INTERNET ACTIVIST SUPPORT CENTERS

The most important contribution Internet activists could make to community activists on the Internet would be to help us develop Internet Activist Support Centers. Without a support system like this, in fact, nothing else I've described here is likely to happen.

An Internet Activist Support Center would be a place where any citizen group in a community could turn to get help in accessing the Internet—including securing an Internet account, learning how to use the software, training in Web page development—whatever they require on a one-stop-shopping basis. If a Center also maintained a relationship with an Internet Service Provider, they could even help organizations set up their own email lists. This is the sort of help that the Institute has received from both the Center for Civic Networking as far away as Massachusetts and from LibertyNet itself. Without it, I wouldn't have been able to do what I'm doing.

Is this unrealistic? Here's a sample of the services that International Global Communications (IGC) offers to its subscribers as of April 1996:

CONTACT

Institute for Global Communication

http://www.igc.apc.org
Phone: 415.561.6100
Fax: 415.561.6101

```
Internet and Electronic Publishing Services

* World Wide Web

If you're reading this, you know what World Wide Web
is. In addition to the Progressive Directory that IGC
maintains, IGC can make custom WWW "pages" for putting
your organization's information out on the Internet.

Costs to set up your own WWW space:

$50 per quarter (up to 5 HTML documents);

$150 per quarter (5-15 documents);

$300 per quarter (unlimited number of HTML documents).
```

Includes five megabyte of storage; additional storage is $2 per megabyte per quarter.

Also included: weekly "hit" reports (upon request);

support of CGI scripts, secure transactions, password access, full-text searching. Setup charges may apply.

*Internet Mailing Lists (Majordomo)

In addition to being able to subscribe to any of the existing Internet-wide mailing lists available (for no charge), IGC members may set up their own Internet mailing lists.

Cost to setup your own Majordomo List:

$50 setup fee.

No monthly fee for lists with less than 500 names.

IGC demonstrates how an Internet Service Provider can function as a support center as well. There are other models worth examining:

CONTACT

Mario Marino
Chairman
Morino Institute
mmorino@morino.org

info@morino.org

http://www.morino.org

- The **Morino Institute**, based in Virginia, is exploring a variety of ways to assist in the development local community networks around the country.
- **Handsnet** is setting up an Internet training center in Washington, D.C., for the staffs of human service agencies.
- **The Community Technology Centers' Network** (CTCNet), which grew out of **Playing to Win**, has established a terrific network of centers around the country, with a goal of helping people of all ages learn how to go online.

CONTACT

Center for Civic Networking
http://civic.net/ccn.html

- The **Center for Civic Networking** is now helping not only groups like the Institute for the Study of Civic Values and the Cambridge Civic Forum, but local governments associated with the "Innovations Group" and small businesses in rural communities that want to market their products to the world.
- In Philadelphia, a group called **Nonprofit Technology Resources**—founded more than ten years ago by a young man named Stan Pokras whose goal even then was to help community organizations learn how to network via computer—is now the major training center for the LibertyNet Bridge Project in the city's Empowerment Zone.

CONTACT

Stanley R. Pokras
President
Nonprofit Technology Resources
pokras@libertynet.org

http://www.libertynet.org/spokras/ntr.html

Of course, support services like this are readily available to corporations. Why not for community groups as well? This is what providing "universal access" to the Internet ought to mean.

So when the gurus of those multibillion dollar information super-highway conglomerates start considering how to help all the people who might benefit from the Internet—corporate executives, investors, consumers, teachers, students, hackers, hobbyists, housewives—they should add citizen groups to the list.

That would be a first step in building the Internet/activist partnership we need.

THE GOVERNMENT CONTRIBUTION

An Internet/activist partnership depends upon government as well. We can't send email to elected officials if they don't have Internet accounts. We can't use the World Wide Web to access information about city departments and pending legislation if it's not online. Since one of our goals is to help citizens communicate with government, government has to be able to communicate back.

The federal government has made real progress here and should be a considered model for the rest.

What do we need from state and local governments around the country? Here's a checklist that you can use in negotiating with them:

- **Email addresses** for all officials, public agencies, and departments, along with staff to handle replies.

- **A Web site for the entire government**, with at least one page for each department detailing its mission, ongoing programs and services, and sources of financial support.

- **A Web page for each elected official**, describing his or her background, priorities, and positions on important issues. The email address should be included on this Web page to facilitate contact with citizens.

- **A school district Web page**, listing the educational philosophy guiding the schools, academic standards, a calendar, and Web pages for each school.

- **A government calendar**, listing all pending sessions of the city council or legislature, hearings conducted by public agencies and departments, and opportunities for citizens to testify.

- **Pending legislation**, preferably summarized so that citizens can understand it. Online summaries should include the purpose of the legislation, its status, and a link to the entire bill for those who want to read it. Every online legislative reference service should provide s section highlighting "Hot Bills this Week" as well. This is one of the great features of "Thomas" (based in Washington) that ought to be imitated everywhere.

- **The city (or state) budget online** in various formats, so that it can be either read on the screen or downloaded for more careful scrutiny.

- **A Web page of all programs conducted in partnership with community groups,** such as recycling, block cleanups, or town watch, including program procedures and forms that can be downloaded by organizations that want to participate.

- **A Web page with links to all city or state agencies funded by the federal government**, including online summaries of plans submitted to Washington for approval and links to the relevant federal departments.

- **Voter registration and election returns**, covering at least the last election. Where possible, these figures should be provided by each legislative district, along with an estimate of the entire voting page population in each one as an incentive for registration drives.

It's an ambitious list, I know, but nothing here is impossible or even unreasonable. The federal government already provides much of this information online about itself.

Figure 7-1 shows how the city of Philadelphia is beginning to put its own Web site together. A growing number of state and local governments are moving in this direction as well The rest need to join them.

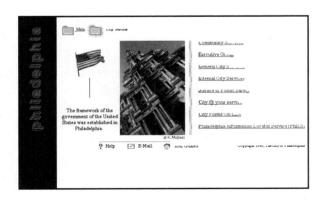

FIGURE 7-1
The City of Philadelphia struts its stuff on its own Web site

NETACTIVISM: A FINAL CHECKLIST

What, finally, do those of us who are community activists have to do to fulfill our end of this partnership? After all, it makes no sense for Internet Service Providers, software developers, and government agencies and politicians to bend over backward to accommodate us if we're not going to take advantage of what they have to offer. So what does each of us need to do?

The short answer is to simply follow the suggestions I make in this book:

- Establish an Internet account.
- Join one or more email lists that reflect your concerns.
- Build an activist bookmark list of Web pages that give you quick access to the organizations and government programs most closely related to your interests. Be sure to include your own elected representatives, especially if they already have email addresses.
- Encourage every organization within your own community to establish an Internet account and create Web page of its own.
- Agree to assist an Internet Activist Support Center if someone offers to create one.
- Fight so that every resident can gain access to the Internet and become part of the online community of citizens.
- Help your neighborhood association establish an email list for area residents so that you all can communicate with one another simultaneously.
- Pressure elected officials at every level of government to post information to the World Wide Web and maintain email accounts of their own.
- Share the legislative alerts that you receive via email with every individual and group that you think needs to act on them.
- Above all, use the Internet to support voter registration and voter education, especially aimed at people who are now shut out of the political process, so the Internet becomes a major force in building citizen power at the polls.

These are the steps that *we* need to take to promote activism online. We're the major partners in this process. If we don't act, no one else will act in our behalf. But if we do take these steps—everywhere—nothing will stand in our way.

WE, THE PEOPLE

March 1996 has been a busy month for me, as I struggle to finish this book. There's been an ongoing fight in Philadelphia around funding for the schools in which many of us are now involved. One night, I got so angry at an editorial in the *Philadelphia Daily News* that I drafted a letter to the editor on the spot and sent it via email to the paper. It appeared a few days later in a little box of its own, along with a few other letters on the issue. It's nice to be able do this even when you don't have a stamp.

Almost as soon as my letter appeared, I received an email message from a member of Senator Rick Santorum's staff, who said she agreed with it. I shot back a thank-you note, but expressed my concerns about the Senator's position on welfare reform and other issues affecting the poor. She emailed back that I ought to meet with the Senator directly.

I posted various items to neighbors-online related to school funding and the Medicaid cuts that were pending in the Pennsylvania legislature. It was also nice to hear from the Energy Coordinating Agency that an announcement about one of their programs drew quite a few replies.

Bruce Spector—an active participant on civic-values—brought a group of his students at Trinity College in Vermont to Philadelphia for a few days. I spent a couple of hours with them talking about urban problems. They seemed to like it, and now I can attach a face to the name 'Bruce Spector" when it appears on my monitor.

One of my own posts to civic-values discussing the Pat Buchanan phenomenon ended up on the Democratic-Farmer-Labor Party Web site in Minnesota.

Linda Ridihalgh—whom I hadn't seen in 15 years—stumbled on our Web site and invited me to speak at a symposium sponsored by the University District Organization in Columbus, Ohio, in April. It'll be good to start working with the University District Organization again—this time, via the Internet.

I spent an evening with Hugh McGuire from Hartford, Connecticut—another civic-values subscriber. Hugh was speaking at a conference in Philadelphia. At the time, we were in the midst of a rip-roaring exchange on the list on the role of class in America that had gone on for several weeks. This meeting had become a list event unto itself, inviting speculation as to what each of us would eat and drink. In the end, it was a great evening. He learned more about how we organize in Philadelphia and I learned more about how he helps dislocated workers reposition themselves in the labor market in

Hartford. We weren't so far apart after all—as we both told civic-values the next day.

LibertyNet cleared accounts for 17 groups working with Neighborhoods Online—the biggest batch yet. I added them to the email list.

I helped Caroline Ferguson from the Computing Resource Center at the University of Pennsylvania run a training for ten more non-profit staff members on the intricacies of Eudora, Netscape, and Neighborhoods Online itself, bringing to over 100 the number of community activists in Philadelphia she's trained over the course of the year.

I even managed to put a Rutgers graduate student from Palestine in touch with a woman living in Palestine who works for an institute trying to promote democracy there. The woman had visited our office as part of an international program on civic education and subscribed to civic-values when she returned home. I met the graduate student at a Rutgers symposium and set him her email address when *I* got home. Now there's an improbable bit of match-making for you.

Friends of mine in Philadelphia are still a bit bemused at all the time I'm spending on the Internet after so many years of working in the trenches here. But at this point I get two or three calls a week from groups asking how they can sign up for LibertyNet and participate in our training.

The people I meet through civic-values ask about what we do in Philadelphia. What are our issues? How do we organize? How, in fact, do we use the Preamble to the Constitution to help people in an individual neighborhood come together around common goals? For now, I refer them to the Social Contract Project on our Web site, but soon we'll be setting up the buildcom list to help groups all over the country apply this approach to their own communities.

There was a long period when I felt like I was building a hotel on Venus. There weren't many people on Venus yet, I'd say, but I wanted to be sure that when they arrived, there would be something more than dust and canals for them to see.

Now they've started to arrive—at our Web sites, on our email lists—from all over the country and beyond. They come filled with a great deal of anxiety and even anger over what's happening in America, but that's part of what's bringing us together. The hope is that, perhaps, through the Internet, we can talk with one another, come to grips with one another, and unite with one another as a people.

We, the people.

That's what it's all about, isn't it?

Useful Internet Sites

AFL-CIO
http://www.aflcio.org/
Labor site

Alta Vista
http://altavista.digital.com/
Internet search engine

American Prospect Magazine
http://epn.org/prospect.html

Brookings Institute
http://www.brook.edu/
Public policy think tank

Charlotte's Web
http://www.charweb.org/
Charlotte NC's community Web site

Children Now!
http://www.childrennow.org/
Children's rights activist site

Christain Coalition
http://www.cc.org/

Community Connections Information Center
http://www.comcon.org/
Federal housing program news and directory

Community Development Society
http://www.infoanalytic.com/cds/

Communiuty Techology Center's
http://www.ctcnet.org

Computer Professsionals for Social Responsibility
http://www.cpsr.org/dox/home.html

Democratic National Committee
http://www.democrats.org/

Digital Democrats
http://www.digitals.org/digitals/

Evirolink
http://envirolink.org/envirohome.html
Environmental activism online

Excite
http://www.excite.com
Internet search engine

FedWorld
http://www.fedworld.gov
Federal agency Web site directory

FrontPage
http://www.microsoft.com
Microsoft's HTML coder

Global Network Navigator
Web directory: http://www.gnn.com/

Handsnet
http://www.handsnet.org/
Non-partisan online networking site

Heritage Foundation
http://www.heritage.org/
Conservative think tank

Hoover Institute
http://www-hoover.Stanford.edu/index.html
Conservative think tank

House of Representative
http://www.house.gov
Republican and Democratic House Web sites

Internet Sleuth
http://intbc.com/sleuth/
Web search engine

Libertarian Party
http://www.libertarian.org

Liszt
http://www.liszt.com/
Listserv directory

Lycos
http://lycos.cs.cmu.edu/
Web search engine and directory

Mother Jones Magazine
http://www.mogones.com/

National Review Magazine
http://www.townhall.com/nationalreview/

NaviPress
http://intercom.com/NAVIPRES/download.htm
HTML coder

Neighborhoods Online
http://libertynet.org/community/phila/natl.html
The author's own activist Web site

New Party
http://www.newparty.org

Non-profit technology resources on line
http://www.libertynet.org/~pokras/ntr.html

Nonprofits on the Net
http://www.eskimo.com/~pbarber

Progress Directory
http://www.igc.apc.org/
Directory of progressive sites on the Net

Project Vote Smart
http://www.vote-smart.org/
Voter education and information site

Reform Party
http://www.reformparty.org

Republican National Committee
http://www.rnc.org/

Rock The Vote
http://www.rockthevote.org/and/RockVote/startup.html

Sausage Software
http://www.sausage.com
HTML coder HotDog

Seattle Community Network
http://www.scn.org/

Songline Studios

http://www.songline.com/

Internet book publisher

Thomas

http://thomas.loc.gov/home/thomas.html

Congressional online legislative service

US House of Representatives Web site

http://www.house.gov/

US Senate Web site

http://www.senate.gov/

Voter's Telecommunications Watch

http://www.vtw.org/

Online civil liberities activism

Webcrawler

http://webcrawler.com/

Web search engine and directory

White House

http://www.whitehouse.gov

The White House

Whole Internet Catalog

http://gnn.com/wic/

Web directory

Yahoo

http://www.yahoo.com

search engine & Web directory

Glossary

anonymous FTP

A site that lets you log on without a secret password and lets you move files between that computer and yours.

application

(a) Software that performs a particular useful function for you. ("Do you have an electronic mail application installed on your computer?")

(b) The useful function itself (e.g., transferring files is a useful application of the Internet).

ARPAnet

An experimental network established in the 1970s where the theories and software on which the Internet is based were tested. No longer in existence.

bandwidth

The size of a network and its ability to carry data. The more bandwidth or larger the network, the more data that can go through the network at once.

baud

When transmitting data, the number of times the medium's "state" changes per second. For example: a 2400-baud modem changes the signal it sends on the phone line 2400 times per second. Since each change in state can correspond to multiple bits of data, the actual bit rate of data transfer may exceed the baud rate. Also see "bits per second."

BBS (Bulletin Board System)

Used in networking to refer to a system for providing online announcements, with or without provisions for user input. Internet hosts often provide them in addition to Usenet conferences.

beta

A test version of a software application.

bits per second

The speed at which bits are transmitted over a communications medium.

bridge

Hardware used to expand the capability of a LAN by selectively forwarding information to another part of the LAN.

BTW

Common abbreviation in mail and news, meaning "by the way."

Chat (Internet Relay Chat or IRC)

A service that allows large group conversations over the Internet.

client

A software application (q.v.) that works on your behalf to extract a service from a server somewhere on the network. Think of your telephone as a client and the telephone company as a server to get the idea.

CMA

Comparative Market Analysis

commercial networks or service providers

Companies such as America Online, Prodigy, and CompuServe support private networks. Many of these networks now provide access to the Internet in addition to their own content. Because of their additional content and ease of use, they are often more expensive than going to an ISP.

CRS

Certified Residential Specialist

dial-up access

A type of connection to the Internet that allows you to call a computer directly on the Internet, staying connected only during the time you are online. Dial-up access is cheaper, but slower than direct access.

direct access

A permanent connection to the Internet that continues even if you are away from your computer. Direct access is faster and more expensive than dial-up access.

distribution list

A mailing list that sends out a newsletter or bulletin to its subscribers. This may be the list's sole purpose.

DNS (Domain Name System)

A distributed database system for translating computer names (like *ruby.ora.com*) into numeric Internet addresses (like 194.56.78.2), and vice versa. DNS allows you to use the Internet without remembering long lists of numbers.

download

To move a file from a remote computer or server onto yours.

email

One of the most popular tools on the Internet. With email software, you can send messages, documents, and graphics to other people connected to the Internet.

Ethernet

A kind of local area network. There are several different kinds of wiring, which support different communication speeds, ranging from 2 to 10 million bits per second. What makes an Ethernet an Ethernet is the way the computers on the network decide whose turn it is to talk. Computers using TCP/IP are frequently connected to the Internet over an Ethernet.

FAQ (Frequently Asked Questions)

Either a frequently asked question, or a list of frequently asked questions and their answers. Many Usenet newsgroups, and some non-Usenet mailing lists, maintain FAQ lists (FAQs) so that participants don't spend time answering the same set of questions. (Pronounced "fack" or spelled out F-A-Q.)

firewall

A software program on a host computer that blocks access to unauthorized entry.

flame

A virulent and (often) largely personal attack against the author of a Usenet posting. Flames are unfortunately common. People who frequently write flames are known as "flamers."

frame relay

A data communication technology which is sometimes used to provide higher speed (above 56 Kb and less than 1.5 Mb) for Internet connections. Its usual application is in connecting work groups rather than individuals.

Freenet

An organization providing free Internet access to people in a certain area, usually through public libraries.

FSBO

For Sale By Owner

FTP

(a) The File Transfer Protocol; a protocol that defines how to transfer files from one computer to another.

(b) An application program that moves files using the File Transfer Protocol.

FYI

A common abbreviation in mail and news, meaning "for your information."

gateway

A computer system that transfers data between normally incompatible applications or networks. It reformats the data so that it is acceptable for the new network (or application) before passing it on. A gateway might connect two dissimilar networks, like DECnet and the Internet, or it might allow two incompatible applications to communicate over the same network (like mail systems with different message formats). The term is often used interchangeably with router (q.v.), but this usage is incorrect.

GIF (Graphical Interchange Format)

Developed by CompuServe online services, this graphic file format allows images to transfer over telephone lines more quickly than other graphic formats.

Gopher

A menu-based system for exploring Internet resources.

GRI

Graduate Realtors Institute

hit

The number of times someone accesses a Web site.

home page

The introductory page to a Web site. You may start with this page or you may start elsewhere on the Web site depending on how you entered.

hostname

That portion of a URL that defines who the host is, i.e., *ibm.com* or *apple.com*.

hotlink

A color-coded portion of text displayed on a Web site that, if clicked on, takes you to another site or document.

HTML (HyperText Markup Language)

The language in which World Wide Web documents are written.

HTTP (HyperText Transfer Protocol)

The language computers speak to each other to transfer World Wide Web data.

hypermedia

A combination of hypertext (q.v.) and multimedia (q.v.).

hypertext

Documents that contain links to other documents; selecting a link automatically displays the second document.

IAB (Internet Architecture Board)

The "ruling council" that makes decisions about standards and other important issues.

IETF (Internet Engineering Task Force)

A volunteer group that investigates and solves technical problems and makes recommendations to the IAB (q.v.).

image
A picture or graphic that appears on a Web page.

IMHO
Common abbreviation in mail and news, meaning "in my humble opinion."

Internet (or Net)
(a) Generally (not capitalized), any collection of distinct networks working together as one.

(b) Specifically (capitalized), the worldwide "network of networks" that are connected to each other, using IP and other similar protocols. The Internet provides file transfer, remote login, electronic mail, news, and other services.

intranet
Private portions of the Internet set up mostly by companies that want to use the powerful networking features of the Net for their own company networking purposes.

IP (Internet Protocol)
The most important of the protocols on which the Internet is based. It allows a packet to traverse multiple networks on the way to its final destination.

IRC
(See Chat)

ISDN (Integrated Services Digital Network)
A digital telephone service. With ISDN service, phone lines carry digital signals, rather than analog signals. If you have the appropriate hardware and software, if your local central office provides ISDN service, and if your service provider supports it, ISDN allows high-speed home or office access to the Internet (56 Kb).

ISOC (Internet Society)
An organization whose members support a worldwide information network. It is also the governing body to which the IAB (q.v.) reports.

ISP (Internet Service Provider)
An organization that supplies users with access to the Internet.

Java
A program produced by Sun Microsystems that allows for a higher degree of interactivity, motion, and sound on Web pages.

jpeg/jpg
A graphic (pictures) format that compresses an image and makes it easier to transmit.

keyword search

An electronic search that allows you to find more information than a subject search because the computer looks at words in the titles and content of a source as well as the subjects. It also allows you to find more specific information, because each source yields many more keywords than subjects. The challenge in using keyword searching is to refine your topic so that the search yields an adequate number of useful citations.

kill file

A list of newsgroup users whose postings you do not want to read. You can create a kill file and include email addresses of people whose messages you don't wish to read.

LAN (local area network)

A network that connects computers and other peripherals in a small area, such as a building or classroom.

leased line

A permanently connected private telephone line between two locations. Leased lines are typically used to connect a moderate-sized local network to an Internet Service Provider.

link

The text or graphic you click on to make a hypertext jump to another page.

listserv

(See mailing list)

mailing list

A conference/discussion group on a specific topic where all messages are sent to one email address and then redistributed to the email boxes of the list's subscribers. If the list is moderated, someone will review the messages before redistributing them.

MLS

Multiple Listing Service

modem

A piece of equipment that connects a computer to a data transmission line (typically a telephone line of some sort). Most people use modems that transfer data at speeds ranging from 1200 bits per second (bps) to 19.2 Kbps. There are also modems providing higher speeds and supporting other media. These are used for special purposes, for example, to connect a large local network to its network provider over a leased line.

moderated

A newsgroup or mailing list that has a person screening the messages coming in before he or she posts them to subscribers.

Mosaic

One particular browser for the World Wide Web; supports hypermedia. Mosaic is often used (incorrectly) as a synonym for the World Wide Web.

multimedia

Documents that include different kinds of data; for example, plain text and audio, text in several different languages, or plain text and a spreadsheet.

Netscape

The most well-known and commonly used browser; many people use "Netscape" as a generic term to refer to the Web or to browsers in general.

newbie

A newcomer to the Internet.

newsgroup

A conference/discussion group where people post and read messages at the newsgroup site rather than in a mailbox. Reading the messages requires your ISP to subscribe to the newsgroup and for you to use a newsreader. Newsgroups are organized by subject area (i.e., alt.politics.clinton)

newsreader

A software program that allows you to read and post messages to newsgroups.

PAC

Political Action Committee.

packet

A bundle of data. On the Internet, data is broken up into small chunks, called packets; each packet traverses the network independently. Packet sizes can vary from roughly 40 to 32,000 bytes, depending on network hardware and media, but packets are normally less than 1500 bytes long.

port

(a) A number that identifies a particular Internet application. When your computer sends a packet to another computer, that packet contains information about what protocol it's using (e.g., TCP or UDP), and what application it's trying to communicate with. The port number identifies the application.

(b) One of a computer's physical input/output channels (i.e., a plug on the back of the computer).

Unfortunately, these two meanings are completely unrelated. The first is more common when you're talking about the Internet (as in "Telnet to port 1000"); the second is more common when you're talking about hardware ("connect your modem to the serial port on the back of your computer").

post
> An individual article sent to a Usenet (q.v.) newsgroup, or the act of sending an article to a Usenet newsgroup.

PPP (Point-to-Point Protocol)
> A protocol that allows a computer to use the TCP/IP (Internet) protocols (and become a full-fledged Internet member) with a standard telephone line and a high-speed modem. PPP is a new standard, which replaces SLIP (q.v.). Although PPP is less common than SLIP, it's quickly increasing in popularity.

protocol
> A definition of how computers will act when talking to each other. Protocol definitions range from how bits are placed on a wire to the format of an electronic mail message. Standard protocols allow computers from different manufacturers to communicate; the computers can use completely different software, providing that the programs running on both ends agree on what the data means.

real time
> Synchronous communication. For example, talking to someone on the phone is in real time, whereas listening to a message someone left on your answering machine is not (asynchronous communication).

router
> A system that transfers data between two or more networks using the same protocols. The networks may differ in physical characteristics (e.g., a router may transfer data between an Ethernet and a leased telephone line).

scanner
> A piece of computer equipment that converts photos and other hardcopy into graphic computer files.

search engine
> A Web-based tool that finds Web pages based on terms and criteria specified.

server
> (a) Software that allows a computer to offer a service to another computer. Other computers contact the server program by means of matching client (q.v.) software.
>
> (b) The computer on which the server software runs.

service provider
> An organization that provides connections to a part of the Internet. If you want to connect your company's network or your personal computer to the Internet, you have to talk to a service provider.

shareware

Software made available, usually over the Internet, for free on a trial basis. The developer asks those who keep and use it to pay a nominal fee.

shell

On a UNIX system, software that accepts and processes command lines from your terminal. UNIX has multiple shells available (e.g., C shell, Bourne shell, Korn shell), each with slightly different command formats and facilities.

signature

A file, typically about five lines long, that people often insert at the end of electronic mail messages or Usenet news articles. A signature contains, minimally, a name and an email address. Signatures usually also contain postal addresses, and often contain silly quotes, pictures, and other things. Some are elaborate, though signatures more than five or six lines long are in questionable taste.

SLIP (Serial Line Internet Protocol)

A protocol that allows a computer to use the Internet protocols (and become a full-fledged Internet member) with a standard telephone line and a high-speed modem. SLIP is being superseded by PPP (q.v.), but is still in common use.

smiley

Smiling faces used in mail and news to indicate humor and irony. The most common smiley is :-). You'll also see :-(meaning disappointment, and lots of other variations.

snail mail

Mail sent via the post office or express delivery service.

spamming

The frowned-upon practice of sending large amounts of junk email to people who have not requested it.

subject search

An electronic search based on the traditional method of categorizing books and other materials by subject. These subjects are usually fairly broad general topics established by an authority such as the Library of Congress.

subscribe

Joining a mailing list or newsgroup to read and send message to the group.

surf

To mindlessly click from link to link on the Internet looking for something interesting.

TCP (Transmission Control Protocol)

One of the protocols on which the Internet is based. TCP is a connection-oriented reliable protocol.

telecommuting

Working from home using a computer over an on-line network.

Telnet

(a) A terminal emulation protocol that allows you to log in to other computer systems on the Internet.

(b) An application program that allows you to log in to another computer system using the protocol.

tiff file

Another graphic format for pictures.

timeout

What happens when two computers are talking and one computer, for any reason, fails to respond. The other computer will keep on trying for a certain amount of time, but will eventually give up.

UNIX

A popular operating system that was very important in the development of the Internet. Contrary to rumor, though, you do *not* have to use UNIX to use the Internet. There are various flavors of UNIX. Two common ones are BSD and System V.

upload

To move a file from your computer to another computer or server.

URL (Universal Resource Locator)

The combination of letters and numbers that uniquely identifies a Web resource.

Usenet

An informal, rather anarchic, group of systems that exchange news. News is essentially similar to bulletin boards on other networks. Usenet actually predates the Internet, but these days, the Internet is used to transfer much of the Usenet's traffic.

username

The name you receive from your service provider to identify your account on the host computer. Generally, your user name is created from your real name, such as your first name and last initial. Your user name is to the left of the @ symbol in your email address.

value-added network (VAN)

A computer network that groups related businesses so they can provide their customers with a one-stop service. For example, a real estate VAN would include real estate offices, title and insurance companies, pest control firms, and lenders.

WAIS (Wide Area Information Service)

A powerful system for looking up information in databases or libraries across the Internet.

Web

(See World Wide Web)

Web browser

A software program that allows you to view, search, and download items from the Web. Common browsers are Netscape and Mosaic.

Web page

A file accessible by a Web browser. Web pages can contain text, sounds, pictures, movies, and hypertext links to other Web pages.

Web server

A computer directly connected to the Internet that responds to requests from browsers to send Web pages.

Web site

A set of Web pages for a person or organization.

Webmaster

A person who maintains a Web site.

World Wide Web

A hypertext-based system for finding and accessing Internet resources. Also known as WWW or the Web.

WWW

(See World Wide Web)

Index

AAUW (American Association of
   University Women), 163-64
action plans, 102
activists
   action plans, 102
   benefits of Internet, 12-17, 106,
      127, 186-87
   communication among groups,
      14-15
   going online, 149-51, 178, 185
   importance of information to, 5-
      10
   influence on national politics, 15-
      16
   Internet tools, 127, 181-82, 185
   mailing lists, 130, 144-45
   partnerships, 177-78
   party, 159-62
   in Philadelphia, 131-35
   political involvement, 154-56,
      172-74
   power of, 122
   training in organizing, 106-7
   voter, 164-68
   See also advocates
ADA (Americans for Democratic
   Action), 172, 173
addresses
   email, 38, 39-40
   of Web pages (*see* URLs)
advertising, political, 3
advocates, 101, 162-64
   Children's Defense Fund, 113-18,
      119
   for homeless, 11
   restrictions proposed on
      federally-funded organizations,
      119-22
   use of Internet, 10-12, 118-22
   See also Christian Coalition
AFL-CIO, 16
Aikens, Scott, 171
Almanac of American Politics, 158
Alta Vista, 10, 77-78, 90-92

American Association of University
   Women (AAUW), 163-64
The American Prospect, 8
Americans for Democratic Action
   (ADA), 172, 173
America Online, 23, 25, 28, 30
   See also online services
Armey, Richard, 103
attachments, to email, 41
audio files, 73

bandwidth, 26
Barber, Putnam, 45-46
block associations, 144
Bonchek, Mark S., 10, 11
Bonham, George, 131
bookmarks, 94-96
Boss, Al, 53-54
Boulder (Colorado), neighborhood
   handbook, 149
Boulder Community Network, 149
Bran, Eric, 43
Bridge Project, 143, 182
Brookings Institution, 8
Brown, Jerry, 66
browsers. *See* Web browsers
Bryant, Anne, 163
Bui, Jim, 160
buildcom mailing list, 145

California
   advocates for homeless, 11
   state laws available on Internet,
      11-12
   voter education, 166-68
California Voter Foundation, 157,
   167
campaigns
   contributions, 88-89
   email debates, 171
   use of Internet, 66, 173-74
Cappabiannca, Italo, 147-48
Capweb, 71

CCL (Center for Civic Literacy), 166-68
CCN (Center for Civic Networking), 136, 182
cd4urban mailing list, 53-56
CDA. *See* Telecommunications Reform Act of 1995
CDBG (Community Development Block Grants), 82, 133
CD-ROMs, 22
censorship of Internet, protests, 97-101, 122-23
Center for Civic Literacy (CCL), 166-68
Center for Civic Networking (CCN), 136, 182
chats, 6
Children Now, 15-16
Children's Defense Fund, 113-18, 119
Chinese students, 10-11
Christian American, 80, 103
Christian Coalition, 9, 102-7, 108, 123
    Congressional scorecard, 104-5
    position on Goals 2000, 80
    sound files, 73
    training provided by, 106-7
    Voter Guides, 162
    Web site, 12
Cisler, Steve, 46-47
city governments, Internet use, 183-84
civic groups
    political impotence, 134
    use of Internet, 127-31
    See also activists
civic values, 13-14, 187
    See also Institute for the Study of Civic Values
civic-values mailing list, 56-63, 64, 118, 121, 136, 145, 186
civic-values Web site, 35, 180
Civille, Richard, 136
Clark, Susan, 168
Clift, Steven, 170
Clinton, Bill
    Goals 2000, 80, 93-94
    Telecommunications Reform Act of 1995, 97
    welfare reform and, 83, 114
Coleman, Joseph E., 155-56
Colorado, Boulder, 149

commercial online services. *See* online services
Communet, 43-49, 65-66
communications software, 29-32
Community Decency Act (CDA). *See* Telecommunications Reform Act of 1995
community development, mailing lists, 53-56
Community Development Block Grants (CDBG), 82, 133
community networks, 65, 150
    Boulder, 149
    Communet, 43-49, 65-66
    Minneapolis Freenet, 130
    Twin Cities FreeNet, 169
community organizing
    mailing lists, 145
    See also activists
CompuServe, 23, 28
    See also online services
computers
    choosing, 27, 28, 34
    donated, 28
    laptop, 27
    in libraries, 143, 150
    old, 25
    requirements for Internet use, 22, 28
    technical support, 29
Congress
    Capweb, 71
    Christian Coalition scorecard, 104-5
    elections of 1994, 102-3
    Environmental Legislative Scorecard, 112
    lobbying, 12
    Thomas Web site, 4-5, 8, 73-75, 92-93
    Web sites of members, 8
    See also elected officials
Congressional Record, 5, 8, 92-93
Contract with America, 172
contributions, campaign, 88-89
C-Span, 88

Davidon, Bill, 172-74
dedicated connections, 26
Delphi, 38
Democratic National Committee, Web site, 9, 159
Democratic Party
    Digital Democrats, 160-62
    mailing lists, 50-51

in Philadelphia, 155-56
dialogue mailing lists, 56-64
dial-up connections, 23-26
Digital Democrats, 160-62
direct connections, 26
directories
    files in, 71
    See also search engines
DMRA (Downtown Minneapolis Residents Association), 127-31, 149
documents
    attaching to email, 41
    finding on Web, 77-78
    Web addresses, 75-76
domain names, 39-40, 75, 76
Downtown Minneapolis Residents Association (DMRA), 127-31, 149

Easy Reader Voters Guide, 166-68
Edelman, Marian Wright, 113, 114-16
E-Democracy, 169-72, 179
education
    Christian Coalition and, 103
    Goals 2000, 80-82, 87-88, 90-94
    Internet access in schools, 178-79
    school district Web sites, 183
    of voters, 164, 166-68
EFF (Electronic Frontier Foundation), 98, 122-23
elected officials
    communicating with, 10-12, 146-48, 168-72
    monitoring, 84-89, 140, 173
    ratings of, 9, 86-87, 104-5, 112, 162, 163
    relationship with voters, 126
    voting records, 85-86, 87-88
    See also politicians
elections
    1994 Congressional, 102-3
    campaign contributions, 88-89
    See also voting
Electronic Frontier Foundation (EFF), 98, 122-23
electronic mail. *See* email
electronic voting, on mailing lists, 179
Elementary and Secondary Education Act, 103
email
    addresses, 38, 39-40

advantages, 6, 39
advocacy using, 118-22
attachments, 41
candidate debates, 171
information exchanged on,
11-12, 35
managing volume of, 67
message parts, 40-41
programs, 31, 41-42, 179
signatures, 40
uses, 6-7, 34-35
See also mailing lists
empowerment, 7, 122-23, 177
of neighborhoods, 125, 140,
148-51
Envirolink, 108-13
environmental issues, 108-13, 140
Environmental Protection Agency
(EPA), 140
EPA Citizens' Guide to
Environmental Protection, 140
Eudora, 31
Excite, 78

Fair Legislation Action Group
(FLAG), 173-74
Family Research Council, 93-94
favorite places, 94-96
Ferguson, Caroline, 143, 187
Fidelman, Miles, 56, 57, 136
files
email attachments, 41
Internet addresses, 71
sound, 73
text, 71-72
FLAG (Fair Legislation Action
Group), 173-74
flames, 67
Foley, Thomas, 156
Follow the Money, 88-89
Fox, Jon D., 172-73
freedom of speech issues
advocacy by federally-funded
organizations, 119-22
Telecommunications Reform Act
of 1995, 97-101, 122-23
Free Library of Philadelphia, 143
FrontPage, 72

Gallie, Charles, 160
Gasser, Nate, 137
Global Network Navigator. *See*
GNN
GNN (Global Network Navigator),
24

Goals 2000, 80-82, 87-88, 90-94
Goode, W. Wilson, 132
Gopher, 71-72, 75
government
accountability, 14
Internet use, 183-84
state, 11-12, 83, 183-84
See also elected officials; U.S.
government
Gramm, Phil, 105
graphical user interface (GUI), 25
grassroots activists. *See* activists
Green, Bill, 132
GUI (graphical user interface), 25
Guthery, Scott, 58-59

Handsnet, 14-15, 182
hardware. *See* computers
hazardous wastes, 110
headers, message, 40-41
health care reform, 165
Health and Human Services (HHS),
Department of, 83
Helms, Jesse, 105
Heritage Foundation, 8
HHS (Department of Health and
Human Services), 83
Higgins, Chris, 64-65, 136
Hoeffel, Joe, 173-74
homeless, advocates for, 11
home pages, 36
See also Web pages
Homuth, Don, 61
Hoover Institute, 8
hostnames, 40, 75
HotDog, 72
hotlists, 94-96
House of Representatives. *See*
Congress
housing, Community Development
Block Grants, 82
Housing and Urban Development
(HUD), Department of, 82, 133
HTML (HyperText Markup
Language), 36, 72, 73
HTTP (HyperText Transfer
Protocol), 75
HUD (Department of Housing and
Urban Development), 82, 133
hypertext, 36, 73
HyperText Markup Language. *See*
HTML
HyperText Transfer Protocol
(HTTP), 75

Idelkope, Julie, 131
ignorance, 126-27
images, on Web pages, 36
impotence, political, 127, 134
Independent Federation of Chinese
Students and Scholars, 10-11
Industrial Areas Foundation, 134
inet-news, 53
information
available on Internet, 4-5, 35,
78-79
exchanged on mailing lists, 35,
116-18, 120-22, 146-48
finding on Internet, 71, 75-76,
77-78
on government programs, 15,
79-80, 84
importance to activists, 5-10
lack of organization, 9-10
on legislation, 11-12, 73-75, 92-
93, 183-84
on Web sites, 35, 93-94, 122
See also search engines
Institute for the Study of Civic
Values, 5-6, 131-33, 134, 141,
142-44, 150
Web sites, 35, 100, 121, 135,
180
See also Neighborhoods Online
International Global
Communications (IGC), 181-82
Internet
access for non-profit groups,
141-44
benefits to activists, 12-17, 106,
127, 186-87
daily use, 34-36
description, 22-23
dial-up connections, 23-26
direct connections, 26
information available, 4-5, 35,
78-79
lack of organization, 9-10
potential, 134, 176, 177
universal access, 65, 113, 143,
178, 182
Internet Activist Support Centers,
181-82, 185
Internet Directory, 43
Internet Service Providers (ISPs),
23, 24-26
local, 24
neighborhood organizations
and, 149-50, 181-82
servers, 71

services, 181-82
    Web sites at, 28
Internet Sleuth, 77
ISDN lines, 26
isolation, 126, 133
ISPs. *See* Internet Service Providers
issues
    tracking on Internet, 89-94
    See also advocates
Istook amendment, 119-22
Istook, Ernest, 119-22

journalists, mailing lists, 53

Knauer, Josh, 112

laptop computers, 27
LCV. *See* League of Conservation
    Voters
League of Conservation Voters
    (LCV), 9, 112, 163
League of Women Voters, 169
legislation
    California, 11-12
    information on Internet, 4-5, 8,
        11-12, 73-75, 92-93, 183-84
    Thomas Web site, 4-5, 8, 73-75,
        92-93
Libertarian Party, 9
LibertyNet, 65, 135, 137, 141-44,
    150, 180, 182
libraries
    Philadelphia, 143
    Seattle, 150
Libros, Maxine, 172-74
links, in Web pages, 36, 73
listproc, 51
    See also mailing lists
listserv, 51
    See also mailing lists
Liszt Discussion Group Directory,
    49, 67
lobbying. *See* advocates
local governments, Internet use,
    183-84
Lycos, 10, 78

Macintosh computers, 27
    See also computers
magazines, online, 8
mailing lists
    approved, 52
    archives, 179
    benefits, 42
    choosing, 66-68
    dialogue, 56-64

directories of, 49-51
electronic voting, 179
finding, 49-51, 67
informational, 52-56
information exchanged on, 35,
    116-18, 120-22, 146-48
moderated, 52
as online community, 64, 65-66
open, 52
operation of, 51-52
of organizations, 6-7, 68
participating in, 44-49, 67
project, 64-66
software, 51-52, 179
staying on topic, 53, 65, 67
subscribing, 43-44, 51, 67
types, 43
unsubscribing, 67
used by activists, 6, 11-12,
    42, 68
    See also email
majordomo, 51
    See also mailing lists
Margolies-Mezvinsky, Marjorie,
    172-73
Mazur, Tim, 57-59
McGuire, Hugh, 186-87
McWilliams, Wilson Carey, 131
Medicaid, 114-15
message body, 40, 41
message headers, 40-41
Microsoft Explorer, 31
Million Man March, organizing
    committees, 151
Minneapolis, 127-31, 149, 169-72
Minneapolis Freenet, 130
Minnesota
    Downtown Minneapolis
        Residents Association, 127-31,
        149
    E-Democracy, 169-72
    email debates, 171
    political mailing lists, 170-71
MN-Politics mailing list, 170-71
modems, 23
Morino Institute, 182
Mother Jones, 8

names
    domain, 39-40, 75, 76
    email, 38
    host, 40, 75
    server, 76
National Association of
    Neighborhoods, 134

National Civic League, 141
National Endowment for the Arts
    (NEA), 12, 105
National Endowment for the
    Humanities, 145
National Peoples' Action, 134
The National Review, 8
National Rifle Association (NRA),
    9, 88-89
National Telecommunications
    Information Agency (NTIA),
    65, 143, 149
NaviPress, 72
NEA (National Endowment for the
    Arts), 12, 105
neighborhood activists. *See* activists
neighborhoods
    empowerment of, 125, 140,
        148-51
    Internet use, 149-50, 181-82
    organizing, 131-35
Neighborhoods Online, 15, 35,
    100, 135-44, 180
    local, 137, 138-40
    mailing lists, 135, 144-45
    national, 137-38
Nethercutt, George, 156, 163
Netscape, 31, 72, 73, 97, 99
*New Community Networks:
    Wired for Change* (Schuler), 150
New Party, 9
newsgroups, 6, 11, 35
newsletters
    mailing lists as, 52-56
    on Web sites, 129-30
New York Times, 12
Nie, Norman, 3
non-profit groups
    Internet access, 141-44
    See also activists
Non-Profit Technology Resources,
    182
NRA. *See* National Rifle Association
NTIA. *See* National
    Telecommunications Information
    Agency

Office of Education, 80-82
OMB Watch, 119-22
O'Neill, Thomas P. (Tip), 125
online services, 23, 32-33
    costs, 32
    objectives, 5
    political information on, 4
    software, 30

tools, 38
Web sites on, 28

Packard, Ed, 59-61
PACs (political action committees), 88-89
parties. *See* political parties
partnerships, 177-78
party activists, 159-62
pathnames, 75
PCs, 27
 See also computers
PEN (Public Electronic Network), 11
Pennsylvania
 mailing lists, 135, 144-45
 See also Philadelphia
Perot, Ross, 9
Philadelphia
 block associations, 144
 city Web site, 184
 Democratic Party organization, 155-56
 Internet access, 65, 141-44
 LibertyNet, 65, 135, 137, 141-44, 150, 180, 182
 libraries, 143
 mailing lists, 135, 144-45
 neighborhood organizing, 131-35
 politics, 132, 155-56
 Southwest Germantown, 155-56
 Web sites, 137
Philadelphia Council of Neighborhood Organizations, 132, 133
Playing to Win, 182
Point-to-Point Protocol (PPP), 25-26
Pokras, Stan, 182
policy journals, online, 8
political action, training, 106-7
political action committees (PACs), 88-89
Politically Incorrect (Reed), 103
political participation, 14
 See also voting
political parties
 activists, 159-62
 Democratic, 9, 50-51, 155-56, 159, 160-62
 Libertarian, 9
 New, 9
 Reform, 9

Republican, 9, 49-50, 102, 103, 159-60, 172
politicians
 attitudes of activists toward, 154
 See also campaigns; elected officials
politics, 154
 effects of mass media, 1-2, 3
 in Minnesota, 170-71
 national, 15-16
 in Philadelphia, 132, 155-56
 in Washington state, 156
 See also campaigns
PPP (Point-to-Point Protocol), 25-26
Precinct Worker, 161
Prodigy, 23, 28
 See also online services
programs. *See* software
project mailing lists, 64-66
Project VoteSmart, 9, 86-88, 173
protocol identifiers, 75
Public Electronic Network (PEN), 11

radio, 3, 7
Real Audio, 73
Reed, Ralph, 73, 103, 108, 123
Reform Party, 9
Republican National Committee, Web site, 9, 159-60
Republican Party
 Christian Coalition and, 102, 103
 Contract with America, 172
 mailing lists, 49-50
research, using Internet, 35, 71, 90-92
Ridihalgh, Linda, 186
Rizzo, Frank, 132
Robertson, Pat, 102, 108
robots, 77-78
Rock the Vote, 164-66, 168
Rowe, Terrie, 62, 63

Santa Monica (California), advocates for homeless, 11
Santorum, Rick, 88-89, 186
Schaar, John, 131
schools. *See* education
Schuler, Doug, 150
search directories. *See* search engines
search engines, 10, 35, 36, 77-78, 90

Seattle, public library, 150
Senate. *See* Congress
Serial Line Internet Protocol (SLIP), 25-26
servers, 26, 71
 domain names, 39-40, 75, 76
 maintaining, 28
 names, 76
 unavailable, 76
shell accounts, 24-25
signatures, email, 40
sites. *See* Web sites
Skivington, Kristen, 54
SLIP (Serial Line Internet Protocol), 25-26
Smolen, Rick, 101
Snow, Stephen, 47-48
software
 choosing, 29-32, 34
 communications, 29-32
 email programs, 31, 41-42, 179
 Internet, 30-31
 mailing list management, 51-52, 179
 needed by activists, 22
 voter registration, 161
 Web browsers, 31, 36, 72-75
 Web page editing, 72
 word processing, 72
sound files, 73
Specter, Arlen, 85-88, 104-5
Spector, Bruce, 186
Stand for Children March, 115-16
state governments
 Internet use, 11-12, 183-84
 welfare reform, 83
Sternberg, Sam, 53
St. Paul (Minnesota), 169-72
subscribing, to mailing lists, 43-44, 51, 67
Surdna Foundation, 145
surfing, 71, 73-75

T1 lines, 26
T3 lines, 26
TCP/IP (Transmission Control Protocol/Internet Protocol), 25-26
TCP Man, 30-31
technical support
 for computers, 29
 for neighborhood groups, 150
telecommunications
 as political tool, 5
 See also Internet

Telecommunications Reform Act of
1995, 98
protests, 97-101, 122-23
telephones
ISDN lines, 26
separate lines for Internet use,
29
system, 22-23
television
advertising, 3
control of, 7
effect on politics, 1-2, 3
Thomas Web site, 4-5, 8, 73-75,
92-93
Time Warner, 85
toxic wastes, 110
training
in Internet tools, 142-44, 150,
151, 178-79, 182, 187
political action, 106-7
24 hours in cyberspace, 101
Twin Cities FreeNet, 169

U.S. Commerce Department,
National Telecommunications
Information Agency (NTIA),
65, 143, 149
U.S. Department of Health and
Human Services (HHS), 83
U.S. Department of Housing and
Urban Development (HUD),
82, 133
U.S. government
Community Development Block
Grants (CDBG), 82, 133
Environmental Protection
Agency (EPA), 140
Goals 2000, 80-82, 87-88,
90-94
information on programs,
15, 79-80, 84
Web sites, 8-9, 183

welfare reform proposals,
83, 114
White House Web site, 4, 8
See also Congress
United States National Student
Association, 131
universal access, to Internet,
65, 113, 143, 178, 182
Universal Resource Locators.
See URLs
UNIX, 27
unsubscribing, from mailing lists,
67
URLs (Universal Resource
Locators), 36, 71
error messages, 76
parts, 75-76
Usenet. See newsgroups

Verba, Sidney, 3
voter registration, 155, 164-68, 169
software for, 161
VoteSmart, 9, 86-88, 173
voting
education, 164, 166-68
electronic, 179
encouraging, 3-4, 157-59,
163-64
power of, 154-56
rates, 2-4, 158
records of elected officials,
85-86, 87-88
See also political participation

Warren, Jim, 11
Washington (state)
politics, 156
Seattle, 150
Web
importance, 75
navigating, 70-71, 73-75
See also search engines

Web browsers, 31, 36, 72-75
Webcrawler, 78
Web pages, 72
black in protest, 97-101
creating, 72, 180-81
editing, 72
error messages, 76
home, 36
images, 36
links, 36, 73
sound files, 73
See also HTML
Web robots, 77-78
Web sites, 36
bookmarks, 94-96
costs, 28
establishing, 28, 35-36, 180-81
exchanging information on, 93-
94, 122
information available on, 35,
78-79
online newsletters, 129-30
retaining ease of development,
180-81
time needed, 151
welfare reform proposals, 83, 114
White House, Web site, 4, 8
Whole Internet Catalog, 77
William Penn Foundation, 136,
142, 143
Witt, Loretta, 155
women's organizations, 163-64
Woodstock Institute, 55-56
word processing software, 72
World Wide Web. See Web
WWW. See Web

Yahoo, 74, 77, 99-100
Yoakam, Cy, 54-55

Informed

MAKE AN

CHOICE

With PBS ONLINE®

The success of a democracy relies upon its citizens being informed and involved. *The PBS Democracy Project* is a multimedia campaign that looks at American politics and policy from the citizen's point of view and offers the kind of information that engages people in the democratic process.

The PBS Democracy Project Web site **(http://www.pbs.org/democracy)** is a special initiative designed to connect citizens with the democratic process online. Visitors to the PBS Democracy Project Web site can find links to PBS programs like *CHARACTER ABOVE ALL* and *THE ONLINE NEWSHOUR,* voter registration information, classroom activities, inspiring messages from other visitors, the Constitution and much more!

The PBS Democracy Project also provides viewers with innovative news and public affairs television programming built upon traditional PBS programming strengths–depth, dialogue, diversity of viewpoints and duration.

PBS ONLINE® (http://www.pbs.org) is the premier choice for unique and compelling interactive content developed specifically for the Internet.

You're looking for ease of use, security and power...

Meet Your New Partners

Begin publishing quickly on your intranet or to the whole Web. Distribute critical information to empower key people, and draw users to your site with our interactive Web tools. You'll find the software you're looking for from O'Reilly, the Internet experts.

PEOPLE ARE TALKING—ON YOUR WEB!

Get people talking on your Web site with WebBoard™, the conferencing system that lets people use their Web browsers to participate in online discussions.

List Price: $149

CREATE A DYNAMIC SITE. PolyForm™ is a forms tool for Windows 95 and NT that will help make your Web pages interactive. PolyForm™ enables you to create Web pages with forms, so you can generate and manage reliable informa-

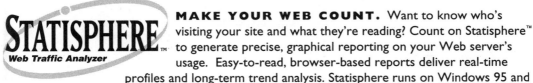

WEB FORMS CONSTRUCTION KIT

tion from your Web visitors. No complex programming is required. Order PolyForm™ today, and make your Web server an interactive experience that keeps users coming back!

List Price: $149

MAKE YOUR WEB COUNT.

Want to know who's visiting your site and what they're reading? Count on Statisphere™ to generate precise, graphical reporting on your Web server's usage. Easy-to-read, browser-based reports deliver real-time profiles and long-term trend analysis. Statisphere runs on Windows 95 and Windows NT, and can analyze ASCII Web server log files on any platform. So you can monitor Web traffic on Windows-, UNIX-, and Mac-based Web servers—all from a single Windows work station. Order now and win the Web numbers game with Statisphere.

Available: Fall '96

O'REILLY™
SOFTWARE

WebSite, WebSite Professional, WebBoard, PolyForm, and Statisphere are trademarks of O'Reilly & Associates, Inc. All other names are registered trademarks or trademarks of their respective companies.

TO ORDER: **800-889-8969** (CREDIT CARD ORDERS ONLY); **order@ora.com**; http://www.ora.com
OUR PRODUCTS ARE AVAILABLE AT BOOKSTORES OR SOFTWARE STORES NEAR YOU.

Stay in touch with O'REILLY™

Visit Our Award-Winning World Wide Web Site

http://www.ora.com/

VOTED

> "Top 100 Sites on the Web" —*PC Magazine*
> "Top 5% Websites" —*Point Communications*
> "3-Star site" —*The McKinley Group*

Our Web site contains a library of comprehensive product information (including book excerpts and tables of contents), downloadable software, background articles, interviews with technology leaders, links to relevant sites, book cover art, and more. File us in your Bookmarks or Hotlist!

Join Our Two Email Mailing Lists

LIST #1   NEW PRODUCT RELEASES: To receive automatic email with brief descriptions of all new O'Reilly products as they are released, send email to: listproc@online.ora.com and put the following information in the first line of your message (NOT in the Subject: field, which is ignored): **subscribe ora-news "Your Name" of "Your Organization"** (for example: **subscribe ora-news Kris Webber of Fine Enterprises)**

List #2   O'REILLY EVENTS: If you'd also like us to send information about trade show events, special promotions, and other O'Reilly events, send email to: **listproc@online.ora.com** and put the following information in the first line of your message (NOT in the Subject: field, which is ignored): **subscribe ora-events "Your Name" of "Your Organization"**

Visit Our Gopher Site

- Connect your Gopher to **gopher.ora.com**, or
- Point your Web browser to **gopher://gopher.ora.com/**, or
- telnet to **gopher.ora.com** (login: **gopher**)

Get Example Files from Our Books Via FTP

There are two ways to access an archive of example files from our books:

REGULAR FTP — ftp to: **ftp.ora.com** (login: **anonymous**—use your email address as the password) or point your Web browser to: **ftp://ftp.ora.com/**

FTPMAIL — Send an email message to: **ftpmail@online.ora.com** (write "help" in the message body)

Contact Us Via Email

order@ora.com — To place a book or software order online. Good for North American and international customers.

subscriptions@ora.com — To place an order for any of our newsletters or periodicals.

software@ora.com — For general questions and product information about our software.
   • Check out O'Reilly Software Online at **http://software.ora.com/** for software and technical support information.
   • Registered O'Reilly software users send your questions to **website-support@ora.com**

books@ora.com — General questions about any of our books.

cs@ora.com — For answers to problems regarding your order or our products.

booktech@ora.com — For book content technical questions or corrections.

proposals@ora.com — To submit new book or software proposals to our editors and product managers.

international@ora.com — For information about our international distributors or translation queries.
   • For a list of our distributors outside of North America check out:
   http://www.ora.com/www/order/country.html

O'REILLY™

101 Morris Street, Sebastopol, CA 95472 USA
TEL 707-829-0515 or 800-998-9938 (6 A.M. to 5 P.M. PST)
FAX 707-829-0104

TO ORDER: **800-889-8969** (CREDIT CARD ORDERS ONLY); **order@ora.com**; **http://www.ora.com/**
OUR PRODUCTS ARE AVAILABLE AT A BOOKSTORE OR SOFTWARE STORE NEAR YOU.

Listing of Titles from O'REILLY™

INTERNET PROGRAMMING

CGI Programming on the
World Wide Web
Designing for the Web
Exploring Java
HTML: The Definitive Guide
Web Client Programming with Perl
Learning Perl
Programming Perl, 2nd.Edition
(Fall '96)
JavaScript: The Definitive Guide, Beta
Edition (Summer '96)
Webmaster in a Nutshell
The World Wide Web Journal

USING THE INTERNET

Smileys
The Whole Internet User's Guide
and Catalog
The Whole Internet for Windows 95
What You Need to Know:
Using Email Effectively
Marketing on the Internet (Fall 96)
What You Need to Know: Bandits on the
Information Superhighway

JAVA SERIES

Exploring Java
Java in a Nutshell
Java Language Reference
(Fall '96 est.)
Java Virtual Machine

WINDOWS

Inside the Windows '95 Registry

SOFTWARE

WebSite™ 1.1
WebSite Professional™
WebBoard™
PolyForm™

SONGLINE GUIDES

NetLearning
NetSuccess for Realtors
NetActivism (Fall '96)

SYSTEM ADMINISTRATION

Building Internet Firewalls
Computer Crime:
A Crimefighter's Handbook
Computer Security Basics
DNS and BIND
Essential System Administration,
2nd ed.
Getting Connected:
The Internet at 56K and Up
Linux Network Administrator's Guide
Managing Internet Information Services
Managing Usenet (Fall '96)
Managing NFS and NIS
Networking Personal Computers
with TCP/IP
Practical UNIX & Internet Security
PGP: Pretty Good Privacy
sendmail
System Performance Tuning
TCP/IP Network Administration
termcap & terminfo
Using & Managing UUCP (Fall '96)
Volume 8: X Window System
Administrator's Guide

UNIX

Exploring Expect
Learning GNU Emacs, 2nd Edition
(Fall '96 est.)
Learning the bash Shell
Learning the Korn Shell
Learning the UNIX Operating System
Learning the vi Editor
Linux in a Nutshell (Fall '96 est.)
Making TeX Work
Linux Multimedia Guide (Fall '96)
Running Linux, 2nd Edition
Running Linux Companion
CD-ROM, 2nd Edition
SCO UNIX in a Nutshell
sed & awk
Unix in a Nutshell: System V Edition
UNIX Power Tools
UNIX Systems Programming
Using csh and tsch
What You Need to Know:
When You Can't Find Your
UNIX System Administrator

PROGRAMMING

Applying RCS and SCCS
C++: The Core Language
Checking C Programs with lint
DCE Security Programming
Distributing Applications Across
DCE and Windows NT
Encyclopedia of Graphics File
Formats, 2nd ed.
Guide to Writing DCE Applications
lex & yacc
Managing Projects with make
ORACLE Performance Tuning
ORACLE PL/SQL Programming
Porting UNIX Software
POSIX Programmer's Guide
POSIX.4: Programming for
the Real World
Power Programming with RPC
Practical C Programming
Practical C++ Programming
Programming Python (Fall '96)
Programming with curses
Programming with GNU Software
(Fall '96 est.)
Pthreads Programming
(Fall '96)
Software Portability with imake
Understanding DCE
Understanding Japanese Information
Processing
UNIX Systems Programming for SVR4

BERKELEY 4.4 SOFTWARE DISTRIBUTION

4.4BSD System Manager's Manual
4.4BSD User's Reference Manual
4.4BSD User's Supplementary Docs.
4.4BSD Programmer's Reference Man.
4.4BSD Programmer's Supp. Docs.

X PROGRAMMING
THE X WINDOW SYSTEM

Volume 0: X Protocol Reference Manual
Volume 1: Xlib Programming Manual
Volume 2: Xlib Reference Manual
Volume. 3M: X Window System
User's Guide, Motif Ed.
Volume. 4: X Toolkit Intrinsics
Programming Manual
Volume 4M: X Toolkit Intrinsics
Programming Manual, Motif Ed.
Volume 5: X Toolkit Intrinsics
Reference Manual
Volume 6A: Motif Programming Man.
Volume 6B: Motif Reference Manual
Volume 6C: Motif Tools
Volume 8 : X Window System
Administrator's Guide
Programmer's Supplement for Release 6
X User Tools (with CD-ROM)
The X Window System in a Nutshell

HEALTH, CAREER, & BUSINESS

Building a Successful Software Business
The Computer User's Survival Guide
Dictionary of Computer Terms
The Future Does Not Compute
Love Your Job!
Publishing with CD-ROM

TRAVEL

Travelers' Tales: Brazil (Summer '96 est.)
Travelers' Tales: Food (Summer '96)
Travelers' Tales: France
Travelers' Tales: Hong Kong
Travelers' Tales: India
Travelers' Tales: Mexico
Travelers' Tales: San Francisco
Travelers' Tales: Spain
Travelers' Tales: Thailand
Travelers' Tales: A Woman's World

International Distributors

Customers outside North America can now order O'Reilly & Associates books through the following distributors. They offer our international customers faster order processing, more bookstores, increased representation at tradeshows worldwide, and the high-quality, responsive service our customers have come to expect.

EUROPE, MIDDLE EAST AND NORTHERN AFRICA (except Germany, Switzerland, and Austria)
INQUIRIES
International Thomson Publishing Europe
Berkshire House
168-173 High Holborn
London WC1V 7AA, United Kingdom
Telephone: 44-171-497-1422
Fax: 44-171-497-1426
Email: **itpint@itps.co.uk**

ORDERS
International Thomson Publishing Services, Ltd.
Cheriton House, North Way
Andover, Hampshire SP10 5BE,
United Kingdom
Telephone: 44-264-342-832 (UK orders)
Telephone: 44-264-342-806 (outside UK)
Fax: 44-264-364418 (UK orders)
Fax: 44-264-342761 (outside UK)
UK & Eire orders: **itpuk@itps.co.uk**
International orders: **itpint@itps.co.uk**

GERMANY, SWITZERLAND, AND AUSTRIA
International Thomson Publishing GmbH
O'Reilly International Thomson Verlag
Königswinterer Straße 418
53227 Bonn, Germany
Telephone: 49-228-97024 0
Fax: 49-228-441342
Email: **anfragen@arade.ora.de**

AUSTRALIA
WoodsLane Pty. Ltd.
7/5 Vuko Place, Warriewood NSW 2102
P.O. Box 935, Mona Vale NSW 2103
Australia
Telephone: 61-2-9970-5111
Fax: 61-2-9970-5002
Email: **info@woodslane.com.au**

NEW ZEALAND
WoodsLane New Zealand Ltd.
21 Cooks Street (P.O. Box 575)
Wanganui, New Zealand
Telephone: 64-6-347-6543
Fax: 64-6-345-4840
Email: **info@woodslane.com.au**

ASIA (except Japan & India)
INQUIRIES
International Thomson Publishing Asia
60 Albert Street #15-01
Albert Complex
Singapore 189969
Telephone: 65-336-6411
Fax: 65-336-7411

ORDERS
Telephone: 65-336-6411
Fax: 65-334-1617

JAPAN
O'Reilly Japan, Inc.
Kiyoshige Building 2F
12-Banchi, Sanei-cho
Shinjuku-ku
Tokyo 160 Japan
Telephone: 81-3-3356-5227
Fax: 81-3-3356-5261
Email: **kenji@ora.com**

INDIA
Computer Bookshop (India) PVT. LTD.
190 Dr. D.N. Road, Fort
Bombay 400 001
India
Telephone: 91-22-207-0989
Fax: 91-22-262-3551
Email: **cbsbom@giasbm01.vsnl.net.in**

THE AMERICAS
O'Reilly & Associates, Inc.
101 Morris Street
Sebastopol, CA 95472 U.S.A.
Telephone: 707-829-0515
Telephone: 800-998-9938 (U.S. & Canada)
Fax: 707-829-0104
Email: **order@ora.com**

SOUTHERN AFRICA
International Thomson Publishing Southern Africa
Building 18, Constantia Park
240 Old Pretoria Road
P.O. Box 2459
Halfway House, 1685 South Africa
Telephone: 27-11-805-4819
Fax: 27-11-805-3648

O'REILLY™

TO ORDER: **800-889-8969** (CREDIT CARD ORDERS ONLY); **order@ora.com**; **http://www.ora.com**
OUR PRODUCTS ARE AVAILABLE AT A BOOKSTORE OR SOFTWARE STORE NEAR YOU.

 *NetActivism: How Citizens Use the Internet* includes the GNN Internet service and GNNpress for Windows 95 on the enclosed CD-ROM. The GNN Internet service gives you full Internet connectivity plus GNN content. GNNpress is a Web authoring tool that allows GNN members to create their own Web sites quickly and easily.

GNN does provide its own Web browser, but you can use others, such as Netscape, if you prefer. You can download the Netscape browser by pointing the GNN Web browser to *http://home.netscape.com/comprod/mirror/client_download.html*

A Macintosh version of the GNN service and GNNpress with a customized Netscape browser will be available at a later time. Contact 1-800-819-6112 for more information.

Here's a page we encourage readers to tear out...

O'REILLY WOULD LIKE TO HEAR FROM YOU

Which book did this card come from?

_____

Where did you buy this book?
- ❏ Bookstore   ❏ Computer Store
- ❏ Direct from O'Reilly   ❏ Class/seminar
- ❏ Bundled with hardware/software
- ❏ Other _____

What operating system do you use?
- ❏ UNIX   ❏ Macintosh
- ❏ Windows NT   ❏ PC(Windows/DOS)
- ❏ Other _____

What is your job description?
- ❏ System Administrator   ❏ Programmer
- ❏ Network Administrator   ❏ Educator/Teacher
- ❏ Web Developer
- ❏ Other _____

❏ Please send me *ora.com,* O'Reilly's catalog, containing a complete listing of O'Reilly books and software.

Name	Company/Organization

Address	

City	State	Zip/Postal Code	Country

Telephone	Internet or other email address (specify network)

Songline Studios specializes in
developing innovative, interactive
content for online audiences. Visit
the many online and print properties created by Songline Studios
through their Website located at
http://www.songline.com

POST CARD

Songline Inc., 101 Morris Street, Sebastopol, CA 95472-9902

BUSINESS REPLY MAIL
FIRST CLASS MAIL   PERMIT NO. 80   SEBASTOPOL, CA

Postage will be paid by addressee

O'Reilly & Associates, Inc.
101 Morris Street
Sebastopol, CA 95472-9902